THE AUSTRALIAN
FRONTIER WARS

John Connor is a PhD student in the School of History, University of New South Wales at the Australian Defence Force Academy, Canberra. A graduate of the Australian National University, the University of Canberra and the University of New South Wales, he has written on many aspects of Australian military history.

THE AUSTRALIAN
FRONTIER WARS
1788–1838

1901-2001
Centenary of Federation

John Connor

UNSW
PRESS

To Eric Andrews (1933–2001)

A UNSW Press book

Published by
University of New South Wales Press Ltd
University of New South Wales
UNSW Sydney NSW 2052
AUSTRALIA
www.unswpress.com.au

© John Connor 2002
First published 2002

National Library of Australia
Cataloguing-in-Publication entry:

Connor, John, 1966– .
The Australian frontier wars, 1788–1838.

Bibliography.
Includes index.
ISBN 0 86840 756 9.

1. Australia — History, Military — 1788–1851. 2. Australia —
Colonization — History. 3. Great Britain. Army — History — 18th century.
4. Great Britain. Army — History — 19th century. I. Title.

355.00994

Cover image From Godfrey Charles Mundy's *Our Antipodes, or, Residence and Rambles in the Australian Colonies, with a Glimpse of the Gold Fields,* Richard Bentley, London, 1852.

This project has been supported by the National Council for the Centenary of Federation and the Australian Historical Association.

A Centenary Library of Australian History

1901-2001
Centenary of Federation   *Printer* Griffin Press

CONTENTS

ACKNOWLEDGMENTS

This book could not have been written without the help of many people. At the University of New South Wales at the Australian Defence Force Academy (ADFA), Associate Professor Jeffrey Grey suggested the idea of writing a military history of the Australian frontier wars, Mr Gerry Walsh was the best supervisor a student of Australian history could hope for, Professor Peter Dennis and Associate Professor Robin Prior, successive heads of school, permitted me to take study leave and funded research trips to Sydney and Hobart; while everyone in the School of History was helpful and supportive, I especially wish to thank Lieutenant-General John Coates (rtd), Debbie Furphy, Bernadette McDermott, Dr David Blaazer, Dr Al Palazzo, Dr John Reeve, Jean Bou, Damien Fenton, and Lieutenant-Commander Jason Sears, RAN.

Further afield, the thesis examiners and manuscript readers all made many useful comments. Mr Clem Sargent let me draw on his vast knowledge of the nineteenth century British Army, and I had many useful discussions with Brad Manera about the Bathurst frontier. Professor Johan de Villers of the University of Zululand, Associate Professor David Philips of the University of Melbourne and Simon Chaplin, Senior Curator, Museums, of The Royal College of Surgeons in England, generously answered queries from a complete stranger.

The staffs of the Australian Institute of Aboriginal and Torres Strait Islander Studies Library, the National Library of Australia, the State Library of New South Wales and the Archives Office of Tasmania were all most helpful to me during my research. Special thanks must go to the always friendly staff of the ADFA Library, especially Christopher Dawkins, Anna Papoulis, Wilgha Edwards, and Madeliene Keay.

Peter Browne and Nicola Young, at UNSW Press, and Roderic Campbell treated a first-time author with patience and professionalism; Keith Mitchell of the Australian National University produced the maps with his usual calm yet exact manner. Of course, all errors, omissions and interpretations are my own.

Finally, and most importantly, I must thank my family for their constant support, especially my wife and *mo chara*, Karen.

INTRODUCTION

The European colonial expansion between the sixteenth and twentieth centuries led to frontier wars on every continent. There is a rich literature of military history covering frontier conflicts almost everywhere from Angola to Alaska.[1] As part of this worldwide European expansion, the British invaded and settled Australia. Since the 1970s there has been a large number of books and articles published about frontier conflict in Australia. However, unlike the overseas literature, very little of this work can be classed as military history.[2] Richard Broome, Jeffrey Grey and, most recently, John Coates have written excellent pieces of military history on the Australian frontier,[3] and this book attempts to build on their pioneering work to provide the first book-length military history of the Australian frontier wars.

Some Australian readers may be surprised at the idea of wars being fought on the Australian frontier, as these wars are not part of the Australian history they know. Before the 1970s Australian historians ignored frontier conflict, and Aborigines more generally, as part of what the anthropologist WEH Stanner termed in 1968 'the Great Australian Silence'. Stanner pointed out that in 'the archives of all the States there is ample material to prove that the aborigines fought a very vigorous if unavailing battle'; this silence was broken by historians using these archives, especially by Henry Reynolds in books such as *The Other Side of the Frontier*. While his work is not above criticism, Reynolds is the most important historian of the Australian frontier because of the volume of his work and the fact that he writes for both general and academic audiences.[4]

The main issue for historians studying the Australian frontier has been to shed light on what Beverley Nance describes as 'the level of violence'. The so-called 'Black-Armband' historians argue that the frontier was universally violent and massacres of Aborigines were common, while Keith Windschuttle counters that settlers could not have killed many Aborigines because it was against their Christian religion and against the law. Between these two extremes are historians such as Richard Broome and Heather Goodall, who suggest that relations between Aborigines and settlers included both conflict and collaboration and who stress regional variation over frontier uniformity.[5]

Related to this debate is the controversy over whether the treatment of indigenous Australians should be defined as 'genocide'. The 1948 United Nations Genocide Convention defines 'genocide' as, not just the physical extermination of a group, but also the attempt to destroy a group by the forcible transfer of children. This latter definition was used in the 1997 report of the Human Rights Commission to argue that the government policy of separating Aboriginal and Torres Strait Islander children from their families was 'genocidal'. Nineteenth century Tasmania (then called Van Diemen's Land) is often cited as an example of genocide, but, as Reynolds points out, these claims are made out of ignorance by writers with little actual knowledge of Tasmanian history. The British sociologist Alison Palmer contends that genocide was committed against Aborigines in Queensland in the 1800s, but she concedes that this genocide was 'piecemeal and occurred in many small and relatively isolated incidents', was carried out 'over a long period of time' and without 'an overtly defined policy'. As Reynolds suggests, when dealing with 'hundreds of individuals in many parts of a large colony over a period of fifty years', it is impossible to show that all settlers acted with intent to commit genocide.[6] Dispute over the appropriate use of such emotionally charged words is not confined to Australia. When Tariana Turia, the New Zealand associate minister for Maori Affairs, used the term 'holocaust' in 2000 to describe the Maori colonial experience, there was such an uproar that the Labour prime minister, Helen Clark, told all her ministers that the word 'must never be used again in a New Zealand context'.[7]

This book is an examination of the weapons, tactics and conduct of warfare on the Australian frontier during the first fifty years of British colonisation. It argues that Aborigines developed tactics for frontier warfare that differed from the tactics used in their traditional warfare. This new form of warfare, which I term 'Australian frontier warfare', concentrated on raiding crops, animals and farmhouses. Aborigines took goods and foodstuffs when they were useful and destroyed them when they were not. When the terrain assisted them, they were able temporarily to stop settlers occupying their land. On the British side, fighting was carried out by both settlers and soldiers. The British Army arrived with experience of frontier warfare in other parts of the empire, but at first found it difficult to operate on the Australian frontier. Aboriginal tactics overcame British muskets, and Aboriginal warriors evaded pursuing British soldiers. The situation changed in 1825, when soldiers were provided with horses. This extra mobility enabled them to track and attack Aboriginal groups.

This book proposes that the Australian frontier was not universally violent and that certain frontiers, such as the early period at Sydney, were relatively peaceful. At certain times, however, in certain places there was sustained conflict that can only be defined as 'war'. The *Australian National Review* asserted in 1996 that frontier conflict was not 'war' because there had been no declarations of war or peace treaties, but to extend this logic to Australia's post-1945 conflicts, likewise bereft of declarations of war or peace treaties, would mean that the conflicts in Korea or Vietnam were not 'wars' either. Historians suggesting that 'war' occurred in Australia have used definitions of 'war' from people as diverse as the British general Bernard Law Montgomery and the American anthropologist Margaret Mead to support their case. In his *Military History of Australia*, Jeffrey Grey shows how the Prussian military thinker Carl von Clausewitz's classic definition of war — 'an act of force to compel our enemy to do our will' — applies to the Australian frontier.[8]

This book does not use terms such as 'Koori', used by Aborigines in southeast Australia, or 'Pallawah', used by Tasmanian Aborigines, because in the period under discussion these regional Aboriginal identities did not yet exist.[9] The *Encyclopaedia of Aboriginal Australia* has been generally used as the reference for spelling the names of Aboriginal peoples, except when I was aware of an alternative spelling used by that Aboriginal community.[10]

The term 'British', rather than 'Whites' or 'Europeans', has been used to refer to non-indigenous people because the United Kingdom was the only colonising power in Australia, and the army and methods of warfare used on the frontier were specifically British.[11] Readers should be aware that the term also includes non-indigenous Australian-born people, who, as Craig Wilcox suggests, can be accurately described as 'British Australians' at least until the 1950s.[12] I use both 'invasion' and 'settlement' to describe the dual aspects of the British arrival in Australia. 'Invasion' conveys the fact that the British arrived on Aboriginal land uninvited and then took it for their own use, while the term 'settlement' is needed, as Reynolds writes, to convey the fact that once the land had been taken, the British settled the land with their farms and towns.[13]

Although settlers did most of the fighting on the British side of the frontier,[14] this book concentrates on the British Army's part in the frontier wars. This is because when fighting rose above a certain level, settlers lacked the weapons and horses to respond and British and colonial governments were willing to deploy troops against Aborigines. In fact, a good indication of the effectiveness of Aboriginal tactics is when it forced settlers to call for military assistance. The frontier wars in Australia were fought on a much smaller scale than, for example, those of New Zealand, but they still should be put into the context of military operations in other parts of the British Empire.

In writing a book an author is forced, for reasons of space, to pursue one strand of investigation to the exclusion of other, equally valid perspectives. For this reason, this book does not attempt to describe the 'face of battle' as popularised by the British historian John Keegan, and does not add to Broome's use of this genre in writing about the Australian frontier.[15] This book does not discuss the attitudes of Aborigines and the British to the fighting and to each other, nor have I entered the debate between Windschuttle and Reynolds on how many people were killed on the Australian frontier.[16] Debates like this are common in military history. As Micheal Clodfelter wrote in his book on casualty statistics, in the 'chaos and confusion' of war, 'an absolute count of the consequences is highly improbable'. There are disputes over the numbers of casualties even in well-documented conflicts such as the American Civil War, while estimates of Soviet casualties in the Second World War are just as likely to be subject to arguments about bias and methodology as those of the Australian frontier wars.[17] A study of how casualty estimates have been constructed for other wars may provide models that can be applied to Australia.

Frontier conflict continued in Australia until at least 1928, but this book finishes in 1838. This date has been chosen, not because it defines a neat fifty-year period of British colonisation, but because this year saw a major change in the fighting. The last major British Army deployment to the frontier took place in 1838. While some troops had killed Aborigines indiscriminately, the army had generally been a moderating force preventing excessive violence. When soldiers left the fighting to settlers and civilian police after 1838, the Australian frontier became more violent.

Joan Beaumont wrote recently of the need for 'a wider-ranging debate about Australian military history'.[18] By attempting to bring the Australian frontier wars into the mainstream of military history, I hope this book can be a useful addition to this debate, and to the general understanding of Australian history.

WARRIORS AND SOLDIERS

Warfare was common in pre-contact Aboriginal societies, but many historians minimise the level of traditional Aboriginal warfare, or suggest that it cannot be defined as 'war'. In Peter Turbet's *The Aborigines of the Sydney District Before 1788* weapons make up almost half the section on Aboriginal artefacts but Turbet makes no mention of warfare. Michael Martin, in *On Darug Land: An Aboriginal Perspective*, asserts that 'traditional Aboriginal society was not an internally hostile one' and brings the reader's attention to the belt and head-band worn by a Darug man in an illustration, but not to the club, spear and shield he is carrying.[1] Goodall says that traditional Aboriginal warfare was 'highly ritualised', Reynolds describes it as 'intermittent', while Broome argues that conflict between Aborigines should not be defined as war because it was 'triggered by violations of the sacred, disputes over women, and homicides rather than questions of land or property'.[2]

Historians should be able to chronicle the achievements of traditional Aboriginal societies and the survival of Aboriginal culture without denying the existence of traditional Aboriginal warfare. Traditional societies did fight wars[3], and modern Western European definitions of war should not be imposed on societies where it does not apply. The idea that 'the natural pattern of human affairs consists of prolonged periods of peace interspersed with brief, intensive wars', does not apply to Ireland in the 700s, where there was continual fighting without the modern distinction between war and peace; nor does the idea that wars are fought for 'the seizure of territory ... or economic advantage' apply to the Ottoman Empire in the 1400s, where the concept of war was based on the Islamic *jihad*. The Western idea that only states can fight wars does not apply to native Americans in northeast North America in the 1700s, where small groups or even individuals could fight wars.[4]

Traditional Aboriginal warfare must be understood in its own terms and not by definitions of 'war' imposed from other cultures. Aborigines did not have separate concepts of war and peace, and traditional warfare took place between groups on a continual basis. Aboriginal groups carried on great rivalries. As Aleksey Rossiysky, a Russian naval officer who visited Sydney in 1814, wrote of the Eora:

> And each man considers his own community to be the best. When he chances to meet a fellow-countryman from another community, and if someone speaks well of the other man, he will invariably start to abuse him, saying that he is reputed to be a cannibal, robber, great coward, and so forth.[5]

The aims and methods of traditional Aboriginal warfare came out of Aboriginal social structures; therefore, definitions of warfare based on the economic and political structures of modern Western Europe are clearly inappropriate. Whereas warfare in modern Western Europe was carried out by states for defined political or economic goals, Aboriginal warfare was carried out by small autonomous groups. To fight a war of territorial conquest like a Western European army was beyond the resources of one of these small Aboriginal groups. In addition, Aboriginal culture was based on a connection to a particular piece of land, and there may have been little advantage in capturing territory over which one did not have any spiritual connection. The aim of traditional Aboriginal warfare was therefore to continually assert the superiority of one's groups over neighbouring groups, rather than to conquer, destroy or displace those groups.

It is impossible to know the level of pre-contact Aboriginal warfare using post-contact written evidence. However, warfare must have been common because it often appears in Aboriginal oral traditions, and the British, when they first arrived in Sydney in 1788, found Aborigines with wounds that could only have caused by fighting with other Aborigines.[6] Each Aboriginal tribe, and indeed each of the autonomous groups within a tribe, was unique with its own economy, culture and artefacts. However, as Edward John Eyre wrote in 1845, Aboriginal culture, though 'so varied in detail', was 'similar in general outline and character'[7], and there are sufficient similarities in the weapons and warfare of these groups to allow generalisations about traditional Aboriginal warfare to be made.

Traditional Aboriginal warfare was at the same time both limited and universal. It was limited in the number of combatants because the groups involved were small, and the non-hierarchical nature of Aboriginal society made the combination of several groups difficult to negotiate. It was also limited in the duration of the fighting because warriors always had to stop campaigning to resume food gathering. Traditional Aboriginal warfare was universal in that the entire community participated in it. Boys learnt to fight by playing with toy spears, clubs and boomerangs, and every initiated male became a warrior.[8] Women were participants in warfare — sometimes, as we shall see, as combatants, but more often as victims.

The structures and beliefs of Aboriginal societies determined the forms which traditional Aboriginal warfare took. In 1840 Horatio Hale, a visiting American scientist, identified four types of Aboriginal warfare: formal battles, ritual trials, raids for women, and revenge attacks.[9]

Formal battles, in which two groups of Aborigines fought each other and ended hostilities after a few participants had been killed or wounded, have often been described as rituals rather than true warfare. However, Lawrence Keeley points out that ending formal battles after a few casualties was not simply a quaint cultural practice. In a group of, say, a hundred members, losing one or two casualties in every raid or battle would add up to a sizeable percentage loss if warfare was constant. Casualties in conditions of continual conflict needed to be controlled to ensure the survival of the groups involved. While it was impossible to control casualties in impromptu raids and ambushes, it was possible to limit losses in formal battles to the benefit of both sides.[10] One settler wrote that if Eora formal battles had resulted in casualties as high as those in 'the Battles of those Nations who are stiled *Civilized* and *Christian* the race would soon be extirpated from the country'.[11] Formal battles were usually fought to settle grievances between Aboriginal bands, and sometimes required days of preparation while the protagonists assembled. The Eora limited the duration of their formal battles by beginning them late in the afternoon and ending them soon after dusk. Eora women did not take part in the actual fighting of formal battles, but they took part in ceremonies commencing the battle and shouted on the sidelines so loudly that they could be heard over 'the Clashing of Spears and the strokes of lances'.[12]

Ritual trials, related to formal battles, were a form of trial in which men were punished, usually for an assault or murder but possibly for other crimes as well. Some may quibble with Hale's description of this as warfare, but if 'war' is defined as any 'organized and socially sanctioned violence'[13], then trials carried out under Aboriginal customary law can certainly be included. The weapons used in ritual trials varied between Aboriginal nations: the Waka Waka north of Brisbane used spears[14], the Wiradjuri of the Macquarie River used clubs[15], while the Kurnai of Gippsland threw boomerangs at the man being punished.[16] In all cases, the man was expected to stand his ground and accept any wounds he might receive.

Broome argues that 'disputes over women' cannot be considered warfare as they are different to 'questions of land or property'. However, the economic historian Noel Butlin points out that in traditional Aboriginal societies, women's food-gathering and childbearing abilities were economic resources which were fundamental to the group's survival. Some Aboriginal men held property rights over women, and Butlin argues that these property rights were at least 'very important', and were probably 'basic to Aboriginal order'.[17] Aboriginal raids for women were, therefore, raids to transfer property from one group to another and must be considered warfare in the same way that fighting for land would be considered warfare in agricultural societies. Sometimes women were 'abducted' only after they had given prior consent and her group's resistance 'was only simulated', but other raids were violent and in earnest. During Captain Nicolas Baudin's visit to Van Diemen's Land in 1802, some Oyster Bay men thought a French teenage apprentice carpenter was a woman and carried out a raid to abduct him. They roared with laughter once they realised their mistake and released him.[18]

The final form of traditional Aboriginal warfare was the revenge attack. According to the beliefs of many Aboriginal peoples, most deaths were the result of some other person's action, carried out by direct violence or by sorcery. The Eora funeral ceremony included a ritual in which the corpse would be 'asked' who had caused the death and a person, or perhaps a group, would be named as responsible. That person, or someone from that person's group, would then be killed in revenge. Eora women took part in revenge killings. In 1792 a young Eora woman, with the assistance of two other women, avenged the murder of her husband by capturing a small girl from the murderer's group and beating her to death. On the Murray River revenge attacks involved two or three men stealing silently into campsites at night and strangling their victim, sometimes with such stealth that the camp did not know about the killing until they discovered it in the morning. These war parties were grimly referred to as 'the ones who take you by the throat'.[19]

The main traditional Aboriginal weapons were the spear — often used with the woomera (or spear-thrower) — and the club, while boomerangs, stones and shields were also used. In close combat short, thrusting spears were used, those of the Tasmanian Aborigines being about 1 metre long. The Tasmanian Aborigines' throwing spears measured up to 4 metres in length and were made from ti-tree branches straightened in fire with one end sharpened into a point. The Gandangara people in the Blue Mountains and the Yuggera people on the Brisbane River also made spears like this, but solid wood spears were heavy to throw.[20] For this reason, where they were able to, Aborigines made their spears lighter by using a composite construction consisting of a light hollow reed or grass-tree stalk for the spear body, which was attached by gum to a short spear-head of solid wood with a spear-point of shell, stone or bone.[21] The designs of war spears varied widely. For example, the Iwaidja people of the Cobourg Peninsula in Arnhem Land used a light spear pointed with saw-like serrations, while their neighbours, the Tiwi people of Melville Island, made heavier spears with barbs like fish-hooks.[22] Serrated or barbed spear-points were used because they inflicted a lacerating wound more deadly than that caused by a straight point. In Eora and Darug society men were rarely seen without spears because each group was identified by its own individual spear design. By contrast, Wiradjuri men did not carry their spears constantly because their groups were identifiable from the totem marking worn on their cloaks.[23]

'Woomera' is the Eora word for 'spear-thrower', and has passed into Australian English as the generic term for all Aboriginal spear-throwers. Using a woomera increased the spear's velocity and accurate range. Broome calculates that a spear thrown with a woomera could reach a speed of 160 kilometres per hour and could be thrown accurately to a range of 50 metres.[24] The woomera excited great interest in Sydney among both British and non-British observers. In 1793 the visiting Spanish botanist Luis Née described the woomera as the *disparador* (trigger) for the spear; in 1805 the Maori Te Pahi praised the woomera for the 'much additional velocity' it gave to the spear.[25]

Tasmanian Aborigines used neither the woomera nor the boomerang. This latter word comes from the Darawal people south of Sydney. Bungaree of the Eora used one in a ritual fight in 1804 and the *Sydney Gazette* breathlessly wrote that the boomerang, when 'thrown at 20 or 30 yards distance, twirled round in the air with astonishing velocity, and alighted on the right arm of one of his opponents, actually rebounded to a distance of not less than 70 or 80 yards, leaving a horrible contusion behind, and exciting universal admiration'.[26]

Like spears, clubs were made in a wide variety of designs by all Aboriginal peoples. The Tiwi used a club about half-a-metre in length and a kilogram in weight, with a grooved handle to provide a better grip; the Eora made clubs with stone heads, some with wooden heads the shape of mushrooms and others with oyster shells attached to the club head, which, as Née wrote, 'conquer in the end by opening up dangerous wounds'.[27]

As the Tasmanian Aborigines' solid wood spears could not be thrown long distances, their main projectile weapons were stones. While seemingly primitive, stones were easy to collect and could be thrown accurately over a fair distance. Baudin was badly bruised by one 'thrown from a distance of the range of a musket'. Tasmanian Aborigines may even have chipped stones on one side to form a sharp edge to increase injuries. When thrown from high ground onto an enemy below, stones could be surprisingly effective.[28]

Shields were used by most Aboriginal peoples, except the Tasmanian Aborigines, and were mostly used in formal battles. The Yuggera people made two types of shields, both from the corkwood tree. The first was light and large and used for deflecting spears, while the second was small, circular and 15 centimetres thick and used when fighting with clubs. The face of both types was covered with beeswax, but only the larger shield was painted with red and white ochres, probably because any decoration on the smaller shield would soon have been defaced in hand-to-hand combat.[29]

The structure and beliefs of Aboriginal societies determined the forms their warfare took, but tactics were developed to make the most effective use of their weapons. The weapons of the Eora and Darug determined the course of their formal battles. The first phase of the battle consisted of an exchange of spears with the light bark *eleemong* shield being used to parry them away. In the second phase the protagonists charged and fought at close quarters with clubs and boomerangs, using the solid wood *arragong* shield for protection.[30]

The limitations of spears and clubs determined the tactics used in raids for women and revenge attacks. While a spear could be thrown accurately and could be lethal, an Eora spear thrown from a distance of 50 metres took about two seconds to reach its target. As Bradley wrote, 'the spears may be easily avoided if you see the Man, who is going to throw it'. In the same way, while a club could be an effective weapon, the intended victim was unlikely to stay still and allow a death blow to be struck. The solution was to use surprise to ensure the target could not see the spear or club coming. Even though Captain David Collins unfairly refers to the Eora tactic of spearing unsuspecting enemies in the back as 'treachery', surprise is surely a legitimate tactic of war.[31]

Surprise could be effected in a number of ways, but especially by ambush tactics. The most effective way to kill a person was to attack them while asleep, and night attacks were common. Raiding parties, often painted in ochres, chose their route carefully and moved stealthily to avoid being detected. These ambush and raiding tactics naturally led to the development of counter-measures. Tasmanian Aborigines built their camp-fires so they could be extinguished in a few moments in case a raiding party approached, while Aborigines on the Murray regularly changed campsites to deceive attackers. Further tactics were developed to ensure the safe withdrawal of raiding parties under hot pursuit. Baudin noted at Bruny Island that when a man of the Nuenonne group of the South East Tribe tried to take a French officer's sword, three men armed with spears were positioned on a nearby hill to cover his escape.[32]

The British in the late eighteenth century and early nineteenth century also had an established military system, but, because British society was very different from that of the Aborigines, its military system also differed greatly. In contrast to the Aborigines' small groups with subsistence economies and part-time warriors, the British state in the early 1800s had a population over 10 million and an industrialising economy which employed professional soldiers and sailors to fight its enemies. The invasion and settlement of Aboriginal Australia has to be understood in the context of British imperial expansion worldwide. By the time the British reached Australia in 1788 the moral justifications for taking land from indigenous peoples had been developed on earlier frontiers, and the Royal Navy and British Army were well-experienced in colonial service and frontier warfare. The argument of *terra nullius,* first cited by John Locke in his *Second Treatise of Government* (1689–90) to justify the British dispossession of the native Americans, was used to ignore native sovereignty in the Andaman Islands in 1789 as well as to claim that Australian Aborigines had no title to their land.[33] Most Europeans accepted these colonial claims as legitimate, but there were a few dissenters. Baudin, the visiting French naval captain, told Governor Philip Gidley King in Sydney in 1802 that the British action of taking Aboriginal land was against 'justice and equity', while as long ago as 1776 the English writer Richard Price pointed out the hollowness of the *terra nullius* argument when he wrote: 'If sailing along a coast can give a right to a country, then might the people of Japan become, as soon as they please, the proprietors of Britain?'.[34]

During the eighteenth century, Britain developed the bureaucratic framework and the transport and logistical resources to deploy forces worldwide, and British soldiers served during the period 1788–1838 on every continent (see table 1.1 and map 1.1).[35]

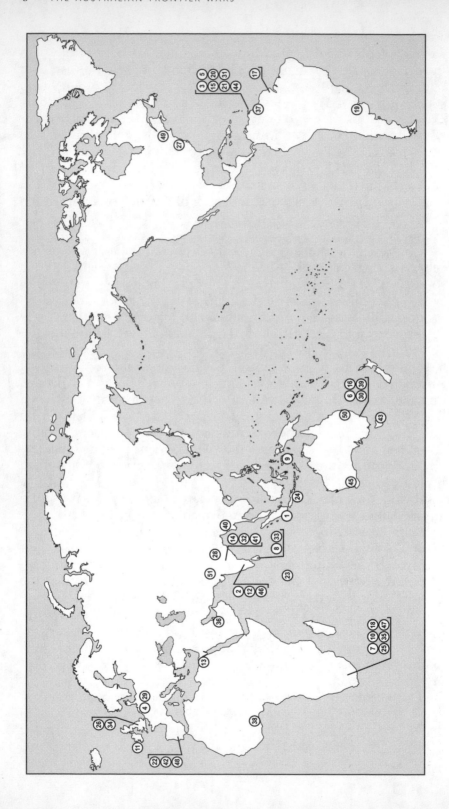

MAP 1.1
British Army operations, 1788–1838

SOURCES Michael Barthorp, *The British Army on Campaign 1816–1902*, Vol 1, Osprey Publishing, London, 1987; PJ Marshall (ed.), *The Oxford History of the British Empire*, II, Oxford University Press, Oxford, 1998; Roger Norman Buckley, *The British Army in the West Indies: Society and the Military in the Revolutionary Age*, University of Florida Press, Gainesville, Florida, 1998.

TABLE 1.1
British Army operations, 1788–1838[36]

Map key	Date	Conflict
1	1789	Revolt in Bencoolen, Sumatra
2	1790–92	Third Mysore War
	1793–1802	War with France
3	1793, 1795	Expeditions against French West Indies
4	1794–95	Low Countries expedition
5	1795	Spanish Trinidad captured
6	1795	Hawkesbury River punitive expedition
7	1796	Dutch Cape captured
8	1796	Dutch Ceylon captured
9	1796	Dutch Moluccas captured
10	1796–1802	Third Cape Frontier War
11	1798	Irish rebellion
12	1799	Mysore captured
13	1799–1801	French defeated in Egypt
	1803–15	War with France
11	1803	United Irish uprising, Ireland
14	1803	Second Maratha War
15	1803–09	French Leeward Islands captured
16	1804	New South Wales convict revolt
17	1804	Dutch Guiana captured
18	1806	Dutch Cape captured
19	1806–07	River Plate expedition
20	1807	Danish West Indies captured
21	1808–09	Martinique & Guadeloupe captured
22	1808–14	Peninsular campaign
23	1810	French Mauritius captured
24	1811	Dutch Java captured
25	1811	Fourth Cape Frontier War
26	1811–18	Luddite riots, England
27	1812–15	War with the United States
28	1814–16	Nepal War
29	1815	Battle of Waterloo
30	1816	Hawkesbury-Nepean punitive expedition
31	1816	Barbados slave rebellion
32	1817–19	Third Maratha War
33	1817–19	Ceylon rebellion
34	1819	'Peterloo Massacre', England
35	1819	Fifth Cape Frontier War

Map key	Date	Conflict
36	1819, 1821	Persian Gulf punitive expeditions
37	1823	Demerara slave rebellion
38	1824	Ashanti campaign
39	1824	Bathurst martial law & punitive expedition
40	1824–26	First Burma War
41	1825–26	Siege of Bharatpur
42	1827–28	Portuguese expedition
43	1828–31	Van Diemen's Land martial law & 'Black Line'
44	1831	Jamaica slave rebellion
45	1834	Pinjarra encounter
46	1834	Coorg campaign
47	1835	Sixth Cape Frontier War
48	1836–38	Carlist War, Spain
49	1837–38	Canadian rebellion
50	1838	Liverpool Plains punitive expedition
51	1838–42	First Afghan War

The first colonial garrison in New South Wales was a detachment of four companies of Marines numbering 212 men, who sailed with the First Fleet and served from 1788 to 1791 at Sydney, Parramatta and Norfolk Island. The Marines (from 1802, Royal Marines) normally did not carry out garrison duties, and were probably chosen because they were experienced in serving at sea on Royal Navy warships and so were the best troops to guard the convict transports on the long voyage.[37]

With the departure of the First Fleet Marines, the British Army took responsibility for garrison duties and, until their withdrawal in 1870, British infantry regiments remained the main military force in all the Australian colonies.[38] In the Australian context, a regiment consisted of one battalion of about 800 men at full strength (actual strength was generally much lower), divided into ten companies. A colonel commanded the battalion and each company was commanded by a captain with two junior commissioned officers, either lieutenants or ensigns, and about eight non-commissioned officers consisting of a colour sergeant, a pay sergeant, sergeants and corporals. The men considered to be the best soldiers were placed in the grenadier and light infantry companies, which were collectively known as the 'flank companies'. From 1825 regiments embarking for colonial duty took between six and eight companies with them as 'service companies' and left between two and four 'depot companies' behind in Britain to recruit and train replacements for the service companies. A British regiment included, not only adult male soldiers, but also drummer boys — such as William Jameson who enlisted in the New South Wales Corps at the age of five — and soldiers' wives, whom the army shipped to colonial garrisons at a ratio of twelve women per hundred men. These women cooked and cleaned for the soldiers and served from Van Diemen's Land in the south to Melville Island, off the northern coast of Australia. The wife of Corporal Delmage was wounded when Nyungar warriors raided the 21st Regiment's outpost on the upper Swan River in Western Australia in May 1834. The Australian colonies with their strange plants and animals were a new experience for the regiments, but in other ways garrison life had similarities to other parts of the empire. The heat, for example, reminded Caribbean veterans of their service in the West Indies.[39]

The first regiment to serve in Australia was the New South Wales Corps, which, as its name suggests, was specially formed in 1790 for service in that colony.[40] Infantry regiments were normally referred to as 'regiments of the line' and were numbered in order of seniority, but, because the New South Wales Corps was a garrison unit raised for permanent duty in a particular colony, it was not counted as a regiment of the line. The New South Wales Corps has become notorious in Australian history for the supposedly high number of convicts in its ranks, the commercial activities of its officers, and for its role in deposing Governor William Bligh in 1808. However, historians have unfairly maligned the New South Wales Corps in a belief that its composition and behaviour was somehow different from the rest of the British Army. In fact, all regiments contained some ex-convicts, and officers stationed in India, just as their New South Wales counterparts did, engaged in trade. Furthermore, conflict between governors and regiments was a common symptom of a British colonial system which gave most governors little control over the regiments stationed in their colony. The arrest of Bligh by the Corps was not so much a *coup d'état* as an example of insubordination towards a superior officer, similar to incidents during the British campaigns in the Low Countries in 1794–95 and in the Peninsula in 1808–09.[41] The New South Wales Corps carried out its military duties effectively and played a major role in the development of the colony. Following the so-called 'Rum Rebellion' of 1808, the New South Wales Corps was added to the regiments of the line as the 102nd Regiment in preparation for its removal from the colony. The regiment took part in the British-American War (1812–15), occupying Eastport, Massachusetts (now in the State of Maine), in 1814; it was finally disbanded in 1818.[42]

The New South Wales Corps was replaced by the 73rd Regiment in 1809. From now on, the Australian colonies were garrisoned by line regiments serving in Australia as part of a cycle which saw them sail from the United Kingdom to Australia, then to India and finally back to the United Kingdom. This rotation system was considered successful because it prevented regiments spending too long in unhealthy areas and the system was adopted for British colonial garrisons in other parts of the world in the late 1830s. In 1838 elements of the 21st, 28th, 50th, 51st and 80th Regiments were serving in the Australian colonies.[43]

The duties carried out by the garrisons in the Australian colonies were the same as for garrisons in the rest of the empire: administration, exploration and survey, developing infrastructure, and protecting British interests from external enemies and internal revolt.[44]

The main war fought by the British during this period was against France and her Dutch and Spanish allies (1793–1802, 1803–15). General Orders in Sydney stated in 1803 that a French attack on 'this remote part of the Globe' was 'improbable', but the French did take a military interest in Australia. Baudin's ostensibly scientific expedition, which visited New South Wales during the brief peace of 1802, carefully mapped Sydney's defences and stole a nominal roll of the New South Wales Corps. In 1810 Napoleon ordered the governor of Mauritius, the closest French colony to New South Wales, to prepare an expedition to capture Sydney, but by this stage of the war, Mauritius lacked the resources to mount such an attack, and the British captured Mauritius soon afterwards.[45] Plans to use elements of the New South Wales Corps in expeditions against the Spanish colonies in South America came to nothing, but Sydney was used as a base for British privateers (merchant ships authorised in wartime to attack enemy shipping and ports). The first of several Spanish ships to be captured was escorted into Port Jackson in 1799. A Vice-Admiralty Court was convened and declared the ship a legal prize, whereupon part of her cargo was auctioned.[46]

Like the British garrison's other duties in Australia, the deployment of troops to fight Aborigines on the frontier must be seen in the context of frontier warfare in the rest of the empire. Through wars with other indigenous peoples, the British had developed a repertoire of strategies and tactics which they applied as appropriate to Australian conditions. The British regularly made alliances with indigenous groups and recruited local forces for colonial garrisons, such as the Khoi ('Hottentots'), who served in the Cape Mounted Rifles in South Africa. These forces were cheaper to sustain and were less susceptible to local diseases than British troops. The British made effective use of these colonial troops during the war against France. Following the costly debacles of sending British troops to the West Indies in the 1790s, the British found it more effective and more successful to use Indian troops to capture Mauritius and Java and to use the former slaves who formed the West Indies Regiment to capture Caribbean islands and later to garrison African colonies.[47] In Australia the British Army used Aboriginal guides to accompany punitive expeditions and, following calls to recruit Aborigines 'like the sepoys in India, the Black Troops in Western Africa, and the

Hottentots on the Caffre Frontier', a short-lived unit of Native Police was formed in the Port Phillip District of New South Wales (now Victoria) in 1837, followed by a more permanent force in 1842.[48]

Logistics and transport played an important part in British frontier warfare. The British professional soldier, fed and supplied out of the extensive resources of the British Empire, had a great potential advantage over an indigenous warrior who could only fight for short periods before having to return to food gathering or farming. However, this theoretical advantage did not always exist in the frontier reality of roadless tracts and rugged terrain. As the American historian Francis Parkman wrote of the Canadian frontier in the Seven Years War (1756–63): 'The question was less how to fight an enemy than how to get at him'.[49] Studies of the British Army in the Ohio Valley in the 1750s and the English East India Company's Madras Army in Burma in the 1830s show that campaigns failed if supplies became unreliable.[50] In Australia Aborigines often evaded British troops, and even the enormous resources expended on the 'Black Line' in Van Diemen's Land in 1830 did not guarantee success.[51]

British troops fighting indigenous peoples generally deployed as light infantry — that is, as skirmishers who moved and fired individually. This differed from conventional European warfare, in which troops fought as line infantry, standing in formation and firing in volleys. The light infantry concept arose out of tactics used by the Austrian Army in central Europe and the British Army in Scotland in the 1740s, which were developed by the British in North America during the Seven Years War. The first regular regiment of light infantry was formed in 1756 by the Earl of Loudon, commander-in-chief of His Majesty's forces in North America, and in 1759 Sir Jeffrey Amherst, Loudon's successor, ordered that one-tenth of each regiment under his command be converted to light infantry. Amherst's reform spread to the rest of the army, with a company of light infantry being formed in each regiment.[52] The British Army's punitive expeditions in Australia were light infantry operations, in which patrols in extended order 'scoured' the bush, often searching for Aboriginal camp-fires at night. When four men of the 63rd Regiment joined Captain Theophilus Tighe Ellis and some civilians in Western Australia on 16 May 1833 to arrest the Wajuk man Midgigooroo, they searched in a line with each man about 10 metres apart. When Ellis, who was on the extreme left of the line, saw movement in front of him, he ordered 'right shoulders forward', and the party came in and surrounded and captured Midgigooroo. British troops were sometimes faced with uniquely Australian difficulties during their patrols. On 11 May 1833 another patrol of the 63rd Regiment were about to strike at a Wajuk group at Lake

Monger, in North Perth, when 'a flight of cockatoos crossing at the time, with their deafening cry, … warned them of the approach of an enemy' and enabled the Wajuk to escape.[53]

There were no large-scale police forces in the British Empire in this period, so the main peacetime role of the British Army was maintaining public order and quashing dissent both at home and in the colonies. These duties ranged from putting down Luddite riots in English mill-towns to crushing slave revolts in the West Indies.[54] In the Australian colonies the army had mundane duties such as guarding convict work-gangs; but it also had to defeat a convict revolt in New South Wales on 5 March 1804 and capture bushrangers in Van Diemen's Land during the 1810s and 1820s by constant, exhausting and dangerous patrols, which sometimes required troops to dress in disguise.[55]

The British Army's constant employment during peacetime in keeping public order (now termed 'Aid to the Civil Power') meant that regiments were almost always split into small detachments spread throughout the countryside. This made it almost impossible to give troops training. Reynolds in *Fate of a Free People* points out that the British garrison in Van Diemen's Land was not trained for frontier warfare, but then goes on to suggest that the troops were trained for European warfare, giving the wonderful example of the 40th Regiment's drill in Hobart in 1826, and Governor Arthur's satisfaction at the men's formation of a square — a manoeuvre used when facing hostile cavalry! However, as Houlding suggests, it is more correct to say that British peacetime garrisons were not properly trained for *any* kind of warfare.[56] While regimental drills of the kind described by Reynolds did take place, they were quite rare. The 80th Regiment was constantly dispersed to keep public order in the United Kingdom following the Napoleonic wars (see map 1.2) and for the first three years after its return to Britain had no regimental training at all.[57] When the 80th arrived in New South Wales, it was again split into small detachments (see map 1.3). As Governor Sir Richard Bourke wrote of the Sydney garrison in 1833:

> tho' I form this garrison from one Regiment only, with a view of keeping that Regiment as much as possible together, the Commanding officer has but little opportunity of exercising his Men in Field Movements, the Guards and Escorts constantly requiring a large proportion for Duty.[58]

The first British drill-book after the end of the Napoleonic wars, Sir Henry Torrens's *Field Exercise* of 1824, accepted that regiments would have to fight as light infantry in frontier warfare and expected all line infantry to be able to act as light infantry[59], but few regiments ever had the opportunity to practise this drill.

Disposition of Companies
- ◼ 1831 West Midlands, England
- ▼ 1832 Ulster, Ireland
- ★ 1832 Leinster, Ireland

MAP 1.2
Deployment of the 80th Regiment, United Kingdom, 1831–32

SOURCE 80th (South Staffordshire) Regiment Digest, I, National Library of Australia, Australian Joint Copying Project, Reel M815.

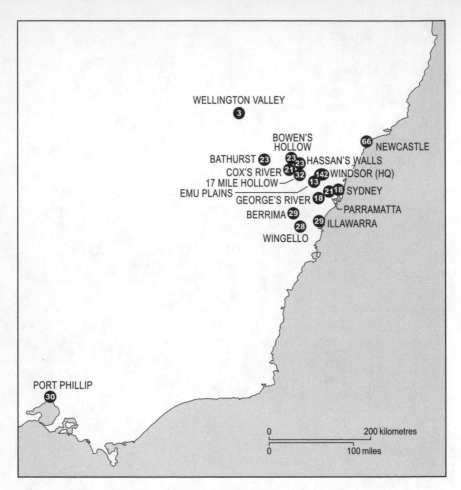

Map 1.3 Deployment of the 80th Regiment, New South Wales, 1838

SOURCE After Alan Atkinson & Marian Aveling (eds), *Australians 1838*, Fairfax, Syme & Weldon Associates, Sydney, 1987, p 381.

While the fact that a '"*Guerilla*" war' was fought on the Australian frontier cannot be forgotten, it must be remembered that the fighting was on a much smaller scale than that of comparable conflicts, such as the New Zealand wars.[60] The non-hierarchical organisation of Aboriginal society meant they were unable to unite against the invaders, and each Aboriginal group fought the British on its own. On the British side, the Australian frontier before 1838 was less violent than it became later for two reasons. First, the settlers lacked organisation and weapons. Despite a request by Port Phillip District settlers in 1838, civilians in Australia were never organised into militia units to fight on the frontier.[61] Civilian gun-ownership on the frontier in this early period of settlement was not as common as it became later. Colonial governors sometimes issued muskets to settlers considered in danger of Aboriginal attack, but Sir Thomas Brisbane, the New South Wales governor, wrote in 1825 that 'it would not be expedient to thrust Arms generally into the hands of the people'.[62] Prior to 1838 settlers, when they faced strong Aboriginal resistance, generally expected the colonial garrison to be deployed to the frontier. In 1837 settlers west of Geelong told Governor Bourke that 'without assistance' they would be 'unable to check' Wathaurong attacks; even as late as 1850 farmers at Moreton Bay expected troops to protect their crops from Yuggera raids.[63] The second reason for the relatively limited level of violence on the Australian frontier before 1838 was that professional soldiers were more likely to be controlled in their use of violence than untrained settlers. There were exceptions to this, such as Captain Nathaniel Lowe in the Hunter Valley and Major James Nunn on the Liverpool Plains. These men who killed Aborigines indiscriminately are balanced, however, by officers such as Captain Peter Bishop, who in 1826 negotiated an end to conflict between settlers and Ngunnawal around Lake George 'without shedding a drop of human blood', or Captain William Lonsdale, who in 1838 refused a soldier's request to shoot an Aboriginal man rather than arrest him. Just as some British officers fighting the French during the Peninsular War were appalled by the atrocities committed by armed Spanish civilians (the original *guerrillas*) fighting alongside them, so soldiers like Colonel George Arthur complained of the conduct of armed British settlers on the Australian frontier.[64]

With few exceptions, Aborigines did not possess or use firearms on the frontier. The two reasons put forward by historians to explain why Aborigines did not adopt firearms are that Aborigines 'preferred traditional weaponry over the unreliable pre-1850 firearms', and that warfare was such a central part of Aboriginal culture that a 'spear tradition' required that traditional weapons be used.[65] The importance of the 'spear tradition' should not be discounted too lightly. As we have seen, spears played an important symbolic role in the lives of Eora men, and it is possible that the Eora thought it inconceivable to carry out warfare with muskets rather than spears. If this was the case, the situation can be compared to the West African kingdom of Dahomey, where the traditional arc-shaped fighting formation was retained in frontier warfare, not for its efficacy, but because the position of each group of warriors in the arc reflected the relative importance of their chief. To change the tactic would have required a radical change to Dahomey society.[66]

The argument that Aborigines *preferred* not to use pre-1850 firearms needs, however, to be considered carefully. First, the argument suggests that, once firearms became more efficient — as they did after 1850 when rifles replaced muskets — Aborigines perceived the technological advantage of the new weapon and adopted it. However, even after 1850, the Aboriginal use of firearms in frontier warfare remained limited.[67] Second, the argument presupposes that there was little advantage in using muskets over spears. When Aborigines held the advantage in frontier warfare, it was through superior bushcraft and tactics and not from superior weaponry. The main firearm used on the Australian frontier, and indeed the main infantry weapon used by British soldiers and marines from the 1730s to the 1830s, was the 'Brown Bess' flintlock musket — a name probably derived from its colour and *büche*, the German word for 'gun'. The Brown Bess was heavy and cumbersome and weighed 12 pounds (5.4 kg) unloaded. It had a 0.753 inch (19.1 mm) calibre, which made it the largest bore infantry musket in service with any European army of the period. By comparison, an unloaded 0.303 inch (7.6 mm) calibre Lee-Enfield rifle — as used by the Australian Army from 1913 to 1959 — weighed only 8 pounds 15 ounces (4.1 kilograms). A fully trained soldier in the best possible conditions could fire a Brown Bess no more than three times a minute. The Brown Bess was designed for use by line infantry on European battlefields, where massed ranks of soldiers fired in volleys at each other over a short distance. It could be easily loaded in battle because the barrel was substantially wider in diameter than the bullet, which meant that the musket ball could be easily and quickly rammed down the barrel. However, this difference in diameter, known as 'windage', meant that the weapon was inaccurate at any other than short distances. Accuracy of individual weapons was not vital in European warfare of the eighteenth century and early nineteenth century because soldiers fired in volleys, and it is significant that the British Army never bothered to systematically test the accuracy of the Brown Bess until it was about to be replaced. Trials held in 1825–26 found that the Brown Bess fired with a 66–70 per cent accuracy at 100 yards (90 m), but that accuracy was reduced to 25–30 per cent at 200 yards (180 m). The misfire rate of the flintlock mechanism in dry conditions was calculated in 1834 to be 5 per cent.[68] In humid conditions the misfire rate increased markedly because, if the gunpowder loaded in the musket became damp, it would not properly ignite. When the Eora man Wileemarin speared Governor Arthur Phillip on the beach at Manly on 7 September 1790, four British sailors pulled the triggers on their muskets, but in the humid conditions only one musket fired properly.[69]

The inaccuracy of the Brown Bess due to windage and humidity was accentuated by the soldier's method of firing and by lack of practice. As a British Army officer noted in 1834:

In nine cases out of ten the difficulty of pulling the trigger makes the soldier open the whole of the right hand in order to aid the action of the forefinger; this gives full scope to the recoil: the prospect of the blow makes him throw back his head and body at the very moment of giving fire; and as no aim is ever required he shuts his eyes, from the flash of the pan, at the same instant, so that the very direction of the shot becomes a matter of mere accident.[70]

The lack of peacetime training also meant soldiers had little opportunity to become proficient in the use of their weapon. Ward estimates that during the eighteenth century a British soldier was allocated on average only four musket balls per year for training, while one of the few examples of target practice in Australia allocated only three hours' firing time to an entire regiment! It is no wonder that Hughes asserts in his study of weapon effectiveness that the musket was 'a most inefficient weapon throughout the whole of its life'.[71]

But, despite all these shortcomings, the Brown Bess was still a devastating weapon when compared to a spear. While several spears could be thrown in the time it took to load and fire a musket (which in the hands of an inexperienced soldier in bush conditions probably declined to one shot per minute), each individual spear was potentially far less lethal than each musket ball. Dr Stephen Geury Wilks, who carried out autopsies on stockmen killed by Wiradjuri warriors near Bathurst in 1824, found that the Wiradjuri's spears caused a puncture wound half-an-inch (12 mm) long. While one spear entering the chest cavity and puncturing the lungs and heart was enough to cause death (and had been in the case of one of the stockmen), a spear could be deflected by a thick waistcoat. A musket ball, however, travelled about seven times faster, tore through clothing and skin, and could shatter a thigh bone or several ribs. Because the 19 mm diameter ball spread out in flight, it inflicted a much larger wound than a spear did.[72] The contrast in lethality can shown by comparing Governor Arthur Phillip, who was speared in the shoulder and survived, with the Eora man Bangai, who was shot in the shoulder and died because the large wound made by the ball severed an artery. While historians have claimed the contest between spear and musket was even, the fact that Aborigines preferred not to seek combat with armed settlers and soldiers suggests they thought otherwise.[73]

However, even if Aborigines wanted to make more use of firearms, they found it difficult to gain access to them. Trade between Europeans and indigenous peoples in other parts of the world led to the wide-scale adoption of firearms: in New Zealand Maori traded foodstuffs, greenstone, timber and flax for muskets; West Africans traded slaves, while native Americans traded wampum (shell money) and beaver pelts. Aborigines were unable to obtain a steady supply of muskets for two reasons. The first is that Britain was the only colonial power in Australia and was in a position to prevent firearms passing across the frontier. This was in contrast to New Zealand and West Africa, where the absence of colonial governments and competition between individual sealers, whalers and slavers led to a flourishing arms trade, and to North America, where the presence of rival European colonies enabled native Americans, particularly the Iroquois, to ensure a continued arms supply by playing the English off against the Dutch and the French. The second reason Aborigines had difficulties obtaining muskets was that the traditional Aboriginal economy did not produce any commodities in sufficient quantities to enable the growth of large-scale trade. Barter between settlers and Aborigines took place, but Aborigines, unlike the Maori, lacked the bargaining power to force the British into trading for firearms.[74]

It is accepted that contact with Europeans led some indigenous groups to undergo a military revolution. James Belich argues in *The New Zealand Wars* that the Maori after 1845 created a new system of warfare unlike both traditional Maori warfare and contemporary British frontier warfare. Belich's claim that the Maori invented trench warfare must be rejected, but his main thesis that the Maori countered British artillery and infantry by developing fortifications with rifle trenches and anti-artillery bunkers is unquestioned.[75] Historians have accepted that Australian Aborigines did not undergo such a military revolution. In *The Oxford Companion to Australian Military History* Ewan Morris says that Aboriginal societies were capable of change, but they did not change their warfare because fighting was a ritualised activity, because they did not have the economic base to allow sustained warfare, and the non-hierarchical nature of Aboriginal societies meant that change could not be imposed from above.[76]

It is important to differentiate between a technological military revolution and tactical innovation. It is true that, apart from using steel tomahawks and tipping their spears with glass chips, Aborigines fought settlers on the frontier with largely the same weapons they had previously used to fight among themselves.[77] However, while a technological military revolution did not take place in Australia, tactical innovation did. The British were a new enemy and to fight them Aborigines required new tactics. The settlers had muskets and tactics had to be developed to minimise their danger. The British took land, which had not occurred in traditional Aboriginal warfare, and used it to grow crops and graze stock. The Aborigines found that these introduced crops and animals were the means by which settlers could be most effectively attacked. Previously Aborigines had stopped fighting when they had to gather food, but now food gathering became a form of warfare and the Aborigines developed effective tactics to raid farmhouses and farms. Though raids for women had an aspect of taking property about them, the economic warfare carried out against settlers on the frontier had no precedent in traditional Aboriginal warfare. These tactics deserve to be recognised as a new form of warfare: Australian frontier warfare.

The development of Australian frontier warfare was even more remarkable because it took place in the non-hierarchical Aboriginal societies. As Morris pointed out, it is easier to enact change in a hierarchical society, and Eid asserts that in North America only hierarchical societies developed new forms of warfare, while egalitarian groups were unable to change and did not survive.[78] Australian frontier warfare was not a uniform set of tactics applied by each Aboriginal group in exactly the same way. Instead, it was a variety of tactics developed by each individual group in response to the British invasion.

Aborigines used Australian frontier warfare tactics to retard settlement in certain areas, but they could not prevent British encroachments over the whole frontier. The tactics did not enable Aborigines to attack farms in open country, or defeat large numbers of soldiers and settlers. However, few indigenous peoples anywhere in the world were able to defeat the British and force them to retreat. The few exceptions include the Caribs, who defeated British planters on the Caribbean island of Saint Vincent in 1772, and the Dyaks, who destroyed the English East India Company trading post on Balambangan Island, off the northern tip of Borneo, in 1775. Even the Iroquois confederation of North America, a large nation with knowledge of agriculture, metal-working, and an arsenal of firearms, was eventually defeated by settlers.[79] The British government, through the Royal Navy and British Army, could project power to frontiers around the world; as Aboriginal numbers declined owing to disease and warfare, and settler numbers increased owing to emigration, the defeat of the Aborigines was inevitable. As Jeremy Black has written in general about colonial expansion: 'The demographic imbalance was such that the use of force, especially after the initial contact engagements, was a matter not so much of battle, but of what the invaders construed as "pacification"'.[80]

The Anzacs at Gallipoli are praised for their gallantry and resourcefulness despite their defeat by the Turks. The Aborigines' ability to create a new style of warfare and use it to fight the world's largest empire should likewise be seen as a remarkable achievement, regardless of their eventual defeat.

2

SYDNEY, 1788–1791

Some time in 1788 a British officer and two men, all carrying firearms and possibly marines, wandered through the bush near Sydney. Unknown to them, fourteen Eora warriors in Indian file, each armed with a spear in his right hand and a large stone in his left, strode quickly and quietly towards them. Suddenly the leader of the Eora party, covered in body paint, emerged from the bush. The British clung tightly to their muskets, expecting an attack. However, the Eora, while all armed and outnumbering the British five to one, ignored them, and continued on their way.[1] As this incident shows, encounters between groups of armed men on the Sydney frontier did not always end in violence. While the Eora resented the British occupation of some of their land, they found that it was possible to make some accommodation with the invaders. There was some fighting between convicts and Eora, but Governor Arthur Phillip and his garrison of Marines generally avoided conflict.

In 1788 an estimated 1500 people of the Eora language group lived in the area around Port Jackson and Botany Bay (see map 2.1). The Eora were bounded by the Kuring-gai people to the north, the Darug to the west, and the Darawal to the south.[2] While Eora speakers shared the same language, geographic location and economic activities, they identified themselves with the autonomous group in which they lived, rather than with the language group as a whole. These smaller autonomous groups, some of no more than fifty people, shared family relationship, or ownership of certain land, and, as Governor Phillip wrote, each group 'deemed its strength and security to consist wholly in its powers'.[3] The Eora ate bush fruits, vegetables, animals and the occasional beached whale, but fish caught in

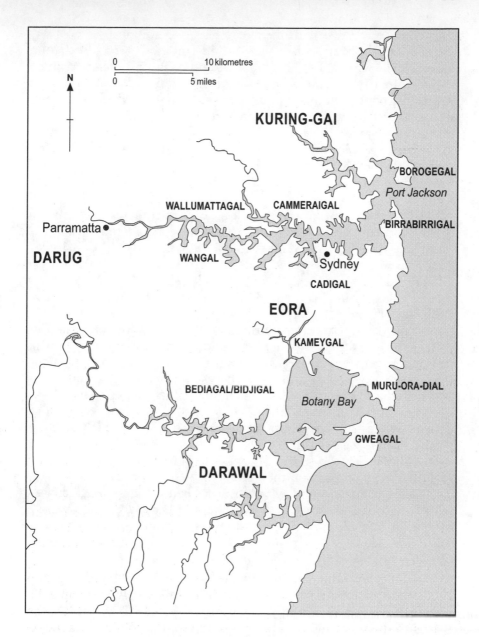

MAP 2.1
Eora lands, 1788

SOURCE After JL Kohen & Ronald Lampert, 'Hunters and Fishers in the Sydney Region', in DJ Mulvaney & J Peter White (eds), *Australians to 1788*, Fairfax, Syme & Weldon Associates, Sydney, 1987, p 345.

the coves and inlets of Broken Bay, Port Jackson and Botany Bay formed a major part of their diet. Fishing methods were divided on gender lines: women used fishing lines and men used spears. Women always fished from canoes, while men mostly fished from rocks. In winter fish stocks declined and the Eora were forced to bind their stomachs with cords in an attempt to prevent hunger pangs. To make the Eora's winter even harsher, their reliance on fish rather than marsupials meant they had few animal pelts to make cloaks. Their only protection from the cold was camp-fires and fish oil smeared on the skin, which left them with a 'remarkable strong Fishy scent'.[4]

Historians have advanced various explanations as to why the British government decided in 1786 to found a colony in Australia.[5] Following the loss of the American colonies, there was the desire for a new penal colony. There was an interest in developing trade with China and also the hope that Norfolk Island timber and New Zealand flax could be used for the Royal Navy's ships and sails. Probably all these factors contributed to the decision, but it is important to remember that Britain and France were at war almost continuously from 1690 to 1815[6] and, as Alan Frost has shown, strategic factors also played their part.[7] During the late 1780s the British expanded eastwards with the establishment of several out-posts: Diego Garcia in the Indian Ocean in 1786, Penang in Malaya in 1786, Port Cornwallis in the Andaman Islands in 1789 and, of course, Sydney in New South Wales in 1788.[8] The French reaction to the First Fleet's departure was to order two French warships in the Pacific, under the command of the Comte de La Perouse, to sail to Botany Bay and spy on their rival's newest colony.

While the colony of New South Wales had a military character — with Phillip, a naval officer, as governor, and David Collins, a marine officer, in charge of the legal system — the settlement at Sydney Cove did not look like a fortress. Phillip had originally envisioned using earthwork walls and the natural barriers of rivers to divide and defend the garrison from both convict uprising and native attack. On his arrival, however, Phillip built no fortifications and instead sited the marine camp so it would separate, and protect the storehouses from the convicts. An earth-walled redoubt was built at Parramatta when it was founded in July 1788, but Phillip later reduced the marine garrison there to that required to safeguard the stores from convict theft.[9]

La Perouse's expedition, by contrast, built a wooden stockade during their stay at Botany Bay. This was because in the previous month La Perouse had lost twelve men killed and twenty wounded in a battle in Samoa. Ironically, the first violent incident of the British invasion of Australia was initiated by the French. Some time during the first two weeks of their stay, French sailors or marines fired their muskets at the Bidjigal group of Botany Bay. The number of casualties is unknown, but Bradley was convinced that some had been killed.[10] On 10 March 1788 the French ships sailed from Botany Bay, and their voyage of violence would end in shipwreck and the death of both crews in fighting on Vanikoro Island, north of Vanuatu.

The news of the French shooting at Botany Bay and the devastating effect of firearms spread quickly among the Eora. Tench noted that the Eora at Sydney Cove suddenly became more wary towards the British. The Eora called muskets 'gooroobeera' or 'stick of fire' and learnt to divide the male settlers into two groups: unarmed men, who could be ambushed under the right conditions; and men carrying muskets, whom they normally refrained from attacking. For example, marines took part in fifteen exploration parties during their time in New South Wales, and were never attacked during any of these journeys.[11] One marine officer wrote that the Eora were 'treacherous' because 'they attack every person they meet unarmed, and appear civil to all those they meet armed'.[12] However, it might be more accurate to attribute this behaviour to good sense.

Unarmed British men were able to survive potentially deadly situations by pretending they had muskets. On 28 July 1788 several Eora chased a sailor through the bush until he picked up a stick and pointed it at them as if it was a musket. The pursuers stopped and the sailor escaped. On 18 December 1788 convicts working at Brickfield Hill similarly warded off an attack from a large number of warriors by 'pointing their spades and shovels at them, in the manner of guns'.[13]

The first fight between British convicts and Eora, in which the Eora wounded some convicts, took place on 10 March 1788 in the bush not far from the settlement. The first British man to be killed by the Eora was the convict Peter Burn, who was speared on 22 May 1788, probably at Woolloomooloo Bay; while the first Eora killed by the British was probably a person attacked the following day by convicts at Blackwattle Bay. British officers suspected that the convicts had murdered 'one of the Natives', but, in what would become a familiar refrain in Australian history, Bradley wrote, 'the proof could not be got, [and] they were dismissed without coming before a Criminal Court'.[14]

By the end of 1791 the Eora had killed only eight convicts and possibly killed an unarmed marine and a naval officer.[15] This statistic can be put into perspective by noting that during the same period, Governor Phillip hanged seventeen convicts and six marines.[16] The Eora also wounded at least twenty convicts, and one non-convict — Governor Phillip himself, who was speared by Wileemarin at

Manly on 7 September 1790.[17] Eora casualties are impossible to calculate from the written record. The only certain Eora death is that of Bangai, who was tracked and killed by pursuing marines on 28 December 1790 after he took potatoes from a garden, while Henry Hacking, the quartermaster of HMS *Sirius*, killed or wounded two from a group of about fifty men who attacked him at Middle Head on 26 September 1789.[18] It is impossible to know the number of casualties from the French shooting at Botany Bay. Moreover, as Phillip had ordered that there would be no fighting with the natives, no convict or marine would be likely to confess to incidents which would lead to punishment. For example, John McEntire, a convict who was employed to shoot animals in the bush for food made a deathbed confession that he had wounded or killed only one Eora man during his hunting trips. While Hunter believed his confession, Tench felt McEntire was lying and had killed more.[19] However, it is fair to say that the number of Eora killed between 1788 and 1791 could not have been large.

Relatively peaceful frontiers like Sydney can be termed 'beachhead frontiers'. In these frontiers British settlement was limited in size and numbers, and few civilians had access to firearms, while Aborigines remained in control of most of their land, and were able to share resources with the British. The term 'beachhead' has been chosen for two reasons: most frontiers of this type existed on the coast, and this type of frontier was generally the transition to increased settlement on pastoral and agricultural frontiers, where sharing land and resources was not possible and sustained frontier warfare resulted.

The British side of the frontier was peaceful during this period because naval and marine officers in New South Wales had a genuine desire to avoid conflict with the Eora. Phillip wrote in 1787 that he hoped to found the colony 'without having any dispute with the natives', and in Sydney ordered that the marines were not to fire on the Eora, except in self-defence. In the first British use of firearms in a threatening way against the Eora, on 22 February 1788, Midshipman Francis Hill ordered some marines to fire on Eora men who were taking tools at Woolloomooloo, but tried to minimise injury by telling the troops to load bird-shot — less dangerous than ball ammunition — and to aim at their legs.[20] Bradley described his part in the abduction of Bennelong and Colbee on 25 November 1789 as being 'by far the most unpleasant service I ever was order'd to Execute', even though the incident took place without any muskets being discharged or anyone being killed or wounded. Lieutenant Dawes refused to command the punitive expedition sent to Botany Bay in December 1790, and, while Tench obeyed Phillip's order and led the expedition, he described it as a 'painful pre-eminence' and, as we shall see, was able to lessen the severity of the orders for the conduct of the expedition.[21] The fact that almost all the victims of Eora attacks were convicts also decreased the chances of military retaliation. The officers looked down on the convicts, and were ready to blame them, and not the Eora, for the attacks. The ability of convicts to inflict casualties on the Eora was limited because few had access to firearms. For most of this time the only convicts allowed to carry muskets were McEntire and two other men designated hunters.[22]

Governor Phillip attempted to protect the Eora by punishing British subjects who committed crimes against them. In May 1791 a convict found guilty of stealing the fishing tackle of Daringa, Colbee's wife, received fifty lashes in punishment in the presence of many natives. In September 1791 a sailor who sank an Eora man's canoe in Sydney Cove was ordered to give the man a suit of clothing 'as a satisfaction for the injury he had done him, as well as to induce him to abandon any design of revenge which he might have formed'. The sailor was also confined to his ship while it was in port as a further punishment.[23]

The Eora showed some anger at losing control of their land, but they were able to continue most of their economic activities. In this period the British settlement was compact and little land had been alienated for farming. The Eora still had access to the harbour for fishing and to the land for food gathering. The two groups were able to coexist remarkably well. Collins wrote of the Eora that 'they must always consider us as enemies'[24], but it appears that the Eora viewed the British in the same way they viewed other indigenous groups: as enemies certainly, but enemies with whom accommodation was often possible. In what Goodall argues was the typical Aboriginal initial reaction to settlers, the Eora tried to integrate the British into their existing social system, even thinking for a while that the settlers were reincarnated relatives.[25] Exchange and trade had been important in traditional Aboriginal society, and the Eora attempted to develop social relations with the British by trading names and goods. Gnungagnunga, the husband of Bennelong's sister, took the name 'Collins' from the judge-advocate the first day he visited the settlement, while Dourrawan and Tirriwan organised a meeting with Lieutenant Ralph Clark of the Marines at Lane Cove on 15 February 1790 to trade a metal hatchet for two spears.[26] The Eora gained great benefits from trade. As early as 28 January 1788 Eora men and women assisted in bringing British fishing nets ashore in exchange for a share of the fish. They traded to gain blankets (a better way to keep warm than a layer of fish oil); glass, which they used to tip spears; and bread and salt-pork, which were more convenient than traditional foods. Most importantly, the Eora adopted British spaniels and terriers as watch-dogs against the traditional Aboriginal tactic attacking of campsites at night. As Collins wrote, soon 'not a family was without one or more of these little watch-dogs, which they considered as invaluable as guardians during the night'.[27]

It is possible that the Eora's attacks on convicts are another sign of this integration. Phillip and the First Fleet diarists claimed all attacks were caused by the convicts stealing Eora property[28], but this reflects the writers' general bias against convicts, rather than a knowledge of why the Eora committed each attack. While it is likely that many attacks were in retaliation for convict thieving, it is possible that some attacks were revenge killings for deaths 'blamed' on British sorcery and that, to this extent, the Eora considered the British as part of their society.

Eora groups in contact with the British tried to limit access of other Aborigines to them. An extreme example of this took place in December 1796, when a young Darug girl, orphaned by the frontier war on the Hawkesbury and brought to live at Government House, was killed by the Eora and her arms severed. As Collins wrote, because the girl 'belonged to a tribe of natives that was hostile to the Sydney people,' the Eora 'could not admit of her partaking in those pleasures and comforts which they derived from their residence among the colonists, and therefore inhumanly put her out of the way'.[29] Isabel McBryde points out that Bennelong in particular attempted to monopolise the 'new sources of social power' that came from contact with the British. Bennelong appears to have viewed the British as an ally to be used against other Aboriginal groups and asked Phillip on several occasions to use the Marines to 'exterminate' the Cammeraigal and Bidjigal groups. Phillip's gift in November 1790 to Bennelong of a brick house built on the eastern point of Sydney Cove (now Bennelong Point) and a shield 'double cased with tin, to ward off the spears of his enemies', may have been a factor in the Cammeraigals' invitation for Bennelong to take part in a male initiation ceremony the following month. In August 1791 Bennelong asked Phillip to allow his wife Barangaroo to give birth in Government House. According to Atkinson, Bennelong asked for this privilege to extend and increase the bond between himself and Phillip. However, Phillip did not realise this, and suggested that the most appropriate place to give birth was the hospital.[30]

As on frontiers in other parts of the world, disease had a devastating impact on Eora society. In 1789 an epidemic, which the First Fleet diarists referred to as 'smallpox', killed probably one-half of the Eora population.[31] David Day asserts in *Claiming a Continent* that there is 'considerable circumstantial evidence' that the Eora were deliberately infected with smallpox by either Major Robert Ross, the detachment commander of the Marines, by unknown marine privates or convicts, or a combination of all three. Day wrote that:

> Marine officers like Major Ross who were concerned at the possible threat posed by the Aborigines may well have felt impelled to take decisive action to end this uneasy stalemate in which the Aborigines were becoming increasingly assertive ... With Phillip disparaging the need for fortifications and refusing to arm the convicts who necessarily had to work at a distance from the protection the settlement afforded, it is possible that Ross may have seized upon the variolous material as the most effective way to deal with the Aborigines. He would have been conscious of the ravages that smallpox could wreak on a susceptible population that had not been exposed to it. He also would have been aware, from his previous service in North America, that smallpox had been used there by the British army to devastate a hostile Indian population.[32]

However, Day's claim that Ross or others used biological warfare against the Eora is unsustainable on four grounds. The United States historian Elizabeth Fenn points out that there was an understanding in eighteenth century North America of how one's enemies could be infected with smallpox and that the British did deliberately infect native Americans besieging Fort Pitt (now Pittsburgh, Pennsylvania) with smallpox in 1763. However, it is unlikely Ross would have learned about this incident from his service in North America because he was not there when it occurred. Ross served in Canada from 1757 to 1760, during the Seven Years War, and left three years before the smallpox incident occurred. Ross returned to the American colonies in 1775 and stayed about a year, fighting in the opening battles of the American Revolution in Massachusetts before returning to England. Fenn also refers to claims made by the rebel Americans that the British used smallpox against them at Boston in 1775. While Ross served around Boston at this time, Reynolds sensibly warns 'we should treat with caution claims made about enemies in the middle of a war'.[33]

The second difficulty is Day's claim that Ross was concerned about the lack of fortifications. It is true that Ross wrote on 10 July 1788 to Sir Philip Stephens, the Admiralty Secretary, complaining that no fortifications had been built in Sydney, but historians have generally seen this letter in the context of Ross's campaign to attack Phillip's reputation at the Admiralty. The strained relationship between Ross and Phillip is well known: Ross's entry in the *Australian Dictionary of Biography* states that he 'missed no opportunity of embarrassing and hindering Phillip', and Maurice Austin doubts the 'sincerity' of Ross's complaint about the lack of fortifications. It is unlikely that Ross really believed in 1788 and 1789 that fortifications should be built, because during this period he delayed construction of any kind by refusing to allow his marines to oversee convict labour gangs.[34]

The third difficulty with Day's assertion is that there is no direct evidence that the British deliberately infected the Eora with small-pox. The British decision to infect the Delaware warriors besieging Fort Pitt in 1763 is documented in several papers, ranging from an order from the British commander-in-chief, Major-General Sir Jeffrey Amherst, that the infection should take place, to a memo by the Fort Pitt commissary officer noting the withdrawal from stores of two blankets and two handkerchiefs, which were then infected and given to the Delaware chiefs as goodwill gifts during ceasefire negotiations.[35] No such direct evidence exists for a deliberate infec-tion of the Eora.

Butlin in *Our Original Aggression* took the First Fleet diarists' statement that the epidemic was smallpox at face value. Knowing that smallpox can only be spread by human contact, and that there was no record of smallpox during the First Fleet voyage or in the British settlement to 1789, Butlin hypothesised that the only way smallpox could have broken out among the Eora was for it to be transmitted, either accidentally or deliberately, from a bottle of smallpox scabs that had been brought out for medical reasons.[36] However, it is quite likely that the disease which devastat-ed the Eora was not smallpox. The medical historian James Watt suggests that the epidemic was probably 'some other viral infection with a heavily infected vesicular eruption [skin blisters]', which was mistaken for smallpox owing to 'the anomalous clinical features' caused by 'the first exposure of a non-immune population to a new infection'.[37] The British invasion exposed the Aboriginal population to a whole range of diseases which they had never been exposed to before including chicken pox, which spreads more easily than smallpox, covers the body in pustules like smallpox and would have caused many fatalities among a non-resistant population. The devastating effect of the epidemic among the Eora made the First Fleet diarists believe they were witnessing a smallpox epidemic.

Finally, Day's argument offers no proper motive why Ross or anyone else in the British settlement in 1789 wanted to exterminate the Eora. The British certainly were capable of using smallpox as a weapon against indigenous populations; in later Australian history individual settlers certainly attempted to exterminate Aboriginal groups. However, Sydney was not besieged by the Eora and, just as importantly, the British at this time viewed the colony as a port look-ing out to sea and had no desire to depopulate the land and occupy the continent. A British attempt to exterminate the Eora in 1789 is unlikely, simply because they had nothing to gain by doing so.

Conspiracy theories and circumstantial evidence are intriguing, but they lack that one essential ingredient: hard facts.

During the period 1788–91 Phillip sent armed parties against the Eora on seven occasions. They were sent for three reasons. First, to abduct Arabanoo on 31 December 1788 and Bennelong and Colbee on 25 November 1789 in attempts to open communication with the Eora. Second, to investigate the sites where convicts had been killed. These parties were sent on three occasions. Phillip made it clear, when he led the first of these parties to Cockle Bay (now Darling Harbour) on 31 May 1788, that he 'did not mean to punish any of the natives for killing these people' as he was sure it was self-defence, but that he wanted to track down the Eora involved in order to retrieve the rushcutters' tools, and for 'some explanation to take place'.[38] The third reason that parties were sent out was as punitive expeditions. Phillip did not order any retaliation following his own spearing, which apparently puzzled the Eora, who expected Wileemarin and anyone associated with him to become the target of British revenge attacks.[39] However, he did order two punitive expeditions in December 1790 against the Bidjigal of Botany Bay, following Pemulwuy's killing of John McEntire.

The punitive expeditions of December 1790 have become notorious because Phillip's original orders instructed the expedition to capture two Bidjigal men and kill ten. The dead were to be beheaded, and their heads bought back to Sydney 'for which purpose, hatchets and bags would be furnished'.[40] Reynolds refers to this original order when he states that Phillip advocated using terror against Aborigines. This is true, but the word 'terror' must be understood in the way Phillip would have defined it, as an integral part of the legal system. The British historian Douglas Hay has written that the eighteenth century British were 'a people schooled in the lessons of Justice, Terror and Mercy'. Inga Clendinnen adds that Phillip, in issuing this first order, was attempting to stage 'a histrionic performance of the terror of British law in accordance with the fine late-18th-century tradition of formal floggings, elaborate death rites, and breathless last-minute reprieves and repentances'.[41]

Reynolds neglects to mention that the expedition did not take place under the original order to behead ten Aborigines. As part of the legal 'theatre', Phillip decided to moderate his terror with mercy and asked Tench, the expedition's commander, if he wished to 'propose any alteration of the orders'. Tench suggested that the capture of two and killing of ten be reduced to the capture of six. Phillip 'instantly' agreed, though he insisted that if six were captured, two would be hanged as punishment for the deaths for which the Bidjigal were responsible; if six could not be captured, they were to be shot. Phillip further restrained the conduct of the punitive expedition by

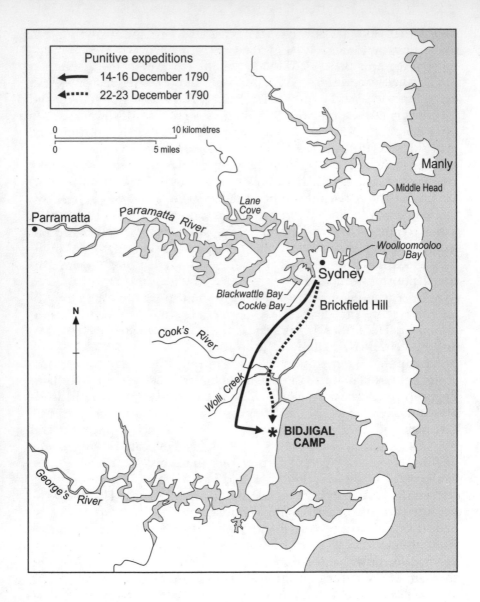

MAP 2.2
British punitive expeditions, 1790

SOURCE Watkin Tench (ed. LF Fitzhardinge), *Sydney's First Four Years: being a reprint of A Narrative of the Expedition to Botany Bay and A Complete Account of the Settlement at Port Jackson* [1788, 1793], Royal Australian Historical Society in association with Angus & Robertson, Sydney, 1961, pp 207–14.

stating that women and children were not be harmed, huts were not to be destroyed, and that no ruses were to be used to draw the Bidjigal towards the expedition.

The first expedition — consisting of Tench, Captain Hill of the newly arrived New South Wales Corps, Lieutenant Poulden and Lieutenant Dawes, the surgeons Worgan and Lowe, three sergeants, three corporals, and forty privates — left Sydney with three days' provisions at 4:00 AM on 14 December 1790 (see map 2.2). They halted for the night, probably between Cook's and George's rivers, and began marching at dawn the next day towards the mouth of the George's River with the aim of working down the coastline towards the Cook's River. However, the two convict guides, who had been with McEntire when he had been speared, and were perhaps anxious to avoid a similar fate themselves, turned towards the coast too early, with the result that the marines suddenly found themselves on the bay, halfway between the two rivers, near five Eora men. Tench wrote: 'We pursued; but a contest between heavy-armed Europeans, fettered by ligatures, and naked unencumbered Indians, was too unequal to last long'. The expedition then rushed to some nearby huts, but the people there escaped by canoe. Tench ordered a search of the huts for weapons, but they found only fishing gear.

The expedition having failed, the party returned to Sydney. Phillip then ordered Tench out for a second expedition. This time Tench used three tactics in an attempt to gain surprise. The first, in an attempt to lull the Bidjigal into a false sense of security, was an open announcement that the new expedition was aimed at the man who speared Phillip at Manly and not the Bidjigal at Botany Bay. The second, to save time and keep the element of surprise, was his attempt to cross the Wolli Creek estuary.[42] This decision backfired, because three men — including Tench — got stuck in the mud and had to be hauled out with ropes. The third attempt to surprise the Bidjigal occurred when the party came near the huts just before dawn. Tench divided the detachment into three groups and ordered them, under 'the most perfect silence … to take a different route, so as to meet at the village at the same moment'. Tench was pleased with the marines' execution of this order: he wrote 'nothing could succeed more exactly than the arrival of the several detachments'. However, the huts were empty and had probably been so since the first expedition. The party rested up in the heat of the day and returned to Sydney at 9:00 AM the next morning. Private John Easty took part in both expeditions and reckoned they were nothing but a 'Troublesome Teadious March'.[43]

Many of the British settlements founded around the Australian coastline between 1788 and 1838 can be defined as 'beachhead frontiers' with relatively little initial conflict. Like the early colony at

Sydney, most of these settlements occupied small areas of land because they were founded either as places of secondary punishment for incorrigible convicts (such as Newcastle, 1804; Port Macquarie, 1821; Moreton Bay, 1824), or as outposts to block French colonial ambitions — such as the northern and southern settlements in Van Diemen's Land (1803, 1804), the military garrison at King George Sound in Western Australia (1825) and the short-lived settlements at Port Phillip (1803), Westernport (1826–28), and Fort Dundas on Melville Island (1824–29).[44] It may seem curious that several Australian cities were founded for no better reason than to block a colonial rival, but this was a stated British policy. In 1806 the British Foreign Secretary justified the occupation of Egypt on the sole grounds that if the British were there, the French could not be.[45]

John Mulvaney and Neville Green use a similar phrase to 'beach-head frontier' when they describe the King George Sound outpost as 'a limpet-like garrison of soldiers of the King and crown prisoners, with no presence of free settlers intending to occupy the territory'. The contemporary observer James Backhouse noted that this settlement covered only a small area, which meant that 'the country of the Blacks has suffered but little, actual invasion'.[46]

Of course, there was some conflict on these 'beachhead frontiers'. On 3 May 1804 troops of the New South Wales Corps at Risdon Cove, across the Derwent from Hobart, panicked at the sight of a Moomairremener hunting party and fired on them killing an unknown, but probably substantial number of them; at Moreton Bay, on 17 October 1830, Yuggera warriors ambushed and killed Captain Patrick Logan of the 57th Regiment.[47] However, such incidents were the exception. In the early period of settlement at the Swan River, Adelaide and the Port Phillip District (now Victoria), there was little violence.[48] At Newcastle, Port Macquarie and King George Sound, the Awabakal, Dunghutti and Minang peoples helped troops capture escaped convicts.[49] The Hobart frontier was peaceful for many years following the Risdon massacre, and a number of Aborigines lived within the township.[50]

While British settlements occupied only small areas of land, Aborigines were able to continue their traditional food-gathering activities. Fels shows there was little competition between Aborigines and settlers for land on the early southern Vandemonian frontier. However, 'beachhead frontiers' soon began to expand onto large tracts of Aboriginal land through what Hobart General Orders in 1819 described as 'the extension of the grazing Grounds, and progressive occupation of the Country'.[51] With this expansion, frontier warfare began.

3

THE HAWKESBURY-NEPEAN RIVER, 1795–1816

In the clear and crisp autumn days of May 1795 farmers harvested the Indian corn on the outer limit of British settlement in New South Wales — the Hawkesbury River. Farms lined the riverbank: tiny fields, hacked out of the eucalypt forest and still studded with tree stumps; their farmhouses, small thatched-roofed, two-roomed huts. The road to Sydney, a 32-mile (53 km) track passing through forest and scrub, was too rough for carts to carry the corn, so it came to Sydney by boat after a 140-mile (235 km) voyage down the meandering river and into the open sea. That May, however, the settlers were not the only ones harvesting the corn. Out of the gum-trees' shadow came a large group of Darug men, women and children wearing animal-skin cloaks and a few European clothes. They picked the corn, and carried it away in blankets and fishing nets. When the settlers tried to stop them, the Darug men used their spears, killing Alex Wilson and his labourer William Thorp. On hearing news of the Darug raids, Captain David Collins in Sydney wrote that 'open war' had 'commenced between the natives and the settlers'. Collins had been in the colony since 1788, but this was the first time he had ever described any outbreak of violence between the British and Aborigines as 'war'.[1] There had been conflict between the Eora and the British in Sydney, but this had been limited. The British settlement there was concentrated on a small piece of land and the two sides were able to share the resources of the harbour. The Hawkesbury was different. Here the resource was land, and land, unlike the waters of Port Jackson, could not be shared. Either the Darug would control the land, or the settlers would; once the violence began, compromise became impossible. It was this conflict over land which made the Hawkesbury-Nepean River the location of the first frontier war in Australia.

The main river to the west of Sydney flowed through the traditional lands of the Darug people (see map 3.1). The Darug called the river Deerubbun, and gathered yams from its fertile river banks. The name 'Darug' probably comes from their word for 'yam', a food that was very important to their survival. The British, because their exploring parties reached Deerubbun in 1789 in two separate places without realising they were at the one watercourse, gave the river two different names. They called the river's lower reach (that is, nearest the sea) the Hawkesbury, and its upper reach the Nepean. The Darug were bounded to the north by the Darkinung people, who lived in the valley of the MacDonald River, which joins the Hawkesbury near Wiseman's Ferry; to the east, by the Eora; to the south, around what is now Campbelltown, by the Darawal people; and to the south and west, by the Gandangara people.[2]

The British exploring parties in 1789 had reported the rich alluvial soils of the Hawkesbury to Governor Arthur Phillip, who knew from his experience as a farmer that this land would be valuable agricultural country. However, Phillip also knew that to settle the Hawkesbury immediately would overstretch his young colony, so he limited agriculture to the districts with good soil around Parramatta.[3] Phillip's successor, Lieutenant-Governor Francis Grose, had no such qualms and in January 1794 granted land at Green Hills (now Windsor) on the Hawkesbury to twenty-two settlers. Phillip's fear that the colony would lack the resources to administer the Hawkesbury was proved correct: once the road was built from Sydney to the Hawkesbury, the British population there swelled to almost 400 people by March 1795, and the Hawkesbury became a frontier of the most lawless kind.

When Captain John Hunter arrived to take up the post of governor in September 1795, he tried to limit movement to the frontier by introducing a pass system, but by then it was too late. In the first eighteen months of British settlement, the mostly convict population committed crimes of every kind against the Darug. Their farms prevented the Darug gathering their yams. They kidnapped Darug children to work as unpaid labour and, despite pleading from the children's relatives, refused to release them. By September 1794, the settlers had killed at least six Darug. Then, in October 1794, settlers seized a Darug boy, bound him, tortured him by pulling him through a fire, threw him into the Hawkesbury, and shot him dead while he was trying to swim to safety. It is no wonder that Richard Atkins, the magistrate at Parramatta, wrote in his diary in May 1795: 'It would be impossible to describe the scenes of villiany & infamy that passes at the Hawkesbury'.[4]

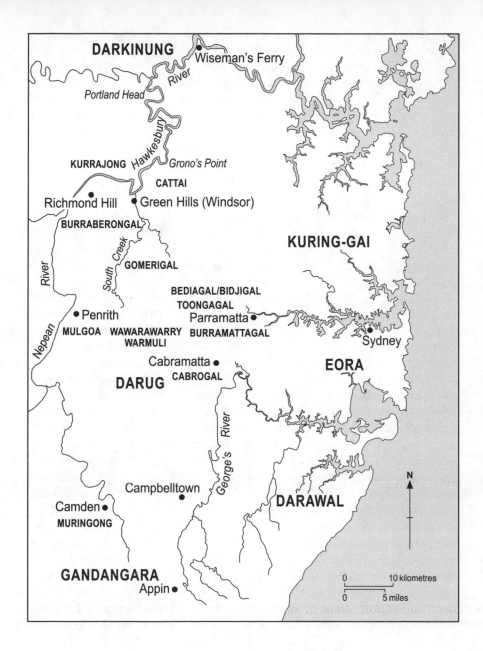

MAP 3.1
Darug lands, 1795

SOURCES After JL Kohen & Ronald Lampert, 'Hunters and Fishers in the Sydney Region', in DJ Mulvaney & J Peter White (eds), *Australians to 1788*, Fairfax, Syme & Weldon Associates, Sydney, 1987, p 345; James Kohen, *The Darug and their Neighbours: the traditional Aboriginal owners of the Sydney Region*, Daruglink in association with Blacktown & District Historical Society, Blacktown, NSW, 1993, p 21.

The Darug responded in kind to the settlers' violent invasion of their land. They killed five settlers on the Hawkesbury in the first half of 1795. One of these men was Thomas Webb, who had taken a farm at Grono's Point in late 1794. Webb had left Sydney after being sued by Colonel Grose for libel and (not surprisingly, considering the military's control of the legal system) having lost the case. Speared by Darug warriors on 28 March, Webb died of his wounds on 19 May. The epitaph on his tombstone was addressed to his brother Robert. The two of them had come to New South Wales together as sailors on HMS *Sirius*. It read:

> Forbear dear Brother
> Weep not [—] it's vain
> On Hawkesbury banks
> By Natives I was slain[5]

The Darug raiding during May 1795 was so intense that Grose's successor, Lieutenant-Governor William Paterson, feared that the Hawkesbury settlement would have to be abandoned. Unwilling to lose this fertile farmland, he ordered a detachment of the New South Wales Corps to go to the Hawkesbury and kill any Darug they found and hang their bodies from gibbets as a warning to the rest. While gruesome, this was a common British practice — the bodies of executed convicts were placed on gibbets at Pinchgut (now Fort Denison) in Sydney Harbour. On 7 June 1795 two officers, and sixty-six other ranks, with three drummer boys keeping the beat, marched from Parramatta along the rough track to the river. On their arrival, the detachment forced a boy to reveal the location of a Darug group, probably members of the Bediagal. That night the soldiers made contact with the Darug in the forest not far from the farms. The roar of muskets filled the night air, followed by the screams of the wounded and dying. The soldiers saw seven or eight Darug fall down in the undergrowth, but when they went out the next morning to find the bodies and string them up, they found the Darug had carried away their comrades' bodies during the night. The detachment captured a man, five women and some children. One of the captured women had a baby at her breast when she had been shot in the shoulder, wounding both her and the baby. The prisoners were taken to Sydney and held at a hut near the hospital in the Rocks. The wounded baby died, and the women and the other children were held for a short time before they were released. The Darug man had been one of the warriors taking part in the attacks, but by pretending to be a cripple he managed to put his captors off-guard. When the chance offered itself, he escaped by diving into the water and, swimming under where the Sydney

Harbour Bridge now spans, made it safely to the north shore.[6]

Once the New South Wales Corps detachment had withdrawn from the Hawkesbury, the Darug immediately took their revenge by attacking William Rowe's farm near Richmond Hill, killing Rowe and his child. Mrs Rowe was wounded and survived only by crawling to the river and hiding in the reeds. This attack forced Paterson to deploy a permanent garrison at the Hawkesbury; with two officers and ninety-three other ranks, this was second in size only to the Sydney garrison. In October 1795 Governor Hunter asked for an expansion of the New South Wales Corps because the need to send troops to the frontier had 'so considerably increased the duty of officers and soldiers'. The troops were divided among the farms, with the lieutenant in charge based at Green Hills, and — according to William Goodall, the detachment's stores sergeant from 1795 to 1797 — 'Parties of Soldiers were frequently sent out to kill the Natives'.[7] The garrison was soon reduced in size from its high point of 1795, but remained at a strength of around forty men until 1800. In that year men captured during the 1798 Irish rebellion began arriving as convicts in New South Wales and, when a rumour started that they were planning to rebel again in the colony, the officer at the Hawkesbury, and then most of the men were withdrawn to Sydney.[8] (The Irish convicts did revolt at Castle Hill in 1804.) Following this withdrawal, fewer than fifteen troops were stationed at the Hawkesbury, but detachments from Sydney or Parramatta were sent to the frontier when required.[9]

The Darug continued to attack. The warrior Pemulwuy led many farm raids, and in March 1797 even challenged a party of soldiers and settlers to a fight in the dusty streets of Parramatta. Pemulwuy received several musket wounds in this skirmish, but survived. Following this, some Darug believed that Pemulwuy could not be harmed by firearms. When Pemulwuy was eventually shot by settlers in 1802, Governor King sent his pickled head to Sir Joseph Banks in England, though what happened to this grisly present is a mystery.[10]

Settlers and Darug killed each other in a spiral of retribution. In the most notorious case, a settler named Wimbolt kidnapped a Darug woman in 1799. In retaliation, the leader of this woman's group, the Darug man known to the British as 'Major White', killed Wimbolt and another settler, Thomas Hodgkinson, while they sat around a fire at night. When Hodgkinson's widow demanded revenge, five settlers grabbed three Darug youths working on Edward Powell's farm. They tied the youths' hands, at which point one of the three broke free and jumped into the river. Though his hands were still bound, he swam to safety using his feet. The settlers then got out their swords and killed the other two, a twelve-year-old boy known as 'Little George' and a fifteen-year-old youth known as

'Jemmy'. The settlers, Edward Powell, Simon Freebody, James Metcalfe, William Timms, and William Butler, were tried for the murder of the two boys and were convicted, but the court was unable to decide on the sentence, and they went unpunished for the murders.[11]

While tit-for-tat killings such as these were certainly part of the frontier war, the Darug's attacks against the settlers' property have greater significance. The Darug were the first Aboriginal people to develop new tactics for use specifically in frontier warfare. In these frontier warfare tactics the focus of attack shifted from settlers — sensibly avoided as they often carried firearms — to easier targets such as the settlers' crops and farmhouses. The Darug used these tactics in a sustained campaign of raids against farms and farmhouses that continued until 1805.[12]

The Darug developed three main tactics to fight the British on the frontier. The first of these was the corn raid. The settlers' corn had a special appeal for the Darug: it was easy to take and, unlike other introduced grains such as wheat and barley, could be eaten without the need for husking and grinding. These raids, while a form of food gathering, were also a type of warfare in the same way that cattle raids were a characteristic form of early Irish warfare. The corn harvest in late autumn and early winter was recognised by the settlers as bringing with it an increase in the number of Darug attacks. As the *Sydney Gazette* commented in May 1805: 'Until the crop of maize shall be wholly gathered the natives will be more or less troublesome'.[13] The Darug's corn raids on the Hawkesbury from 1795 to 1805 were notable for being carried out by large groups of up to 150 men, women and children. Numbers like this show several Darug groups must have been involved, and that the raids required a high degree of negotiation and coordination. These parties could easily outnumber the settlers because farms were dispersed and in 1795 already spread over 50 kilometres on both sides of the river. The sheer size of these raiding parties was normally sufficient to enable the Darug to carry out these raids without violence, but weapons were used if the settlers resisted. The settlers' corn was not even safe after it had been harvested and was on the long voyage down river to Sydney. In 1797 Darug captured a boat on the Hawkesbury, killed the crew, and took the corn.[14] The continual nature of the Darug's raids at harvest time was the surest sign of their success. The Darug needed blankets and nets to carry off all their booty, and were taking so much corn that they were able to live off it and did not have to interrupt their attacks to collect traditional foods. This enabled them to take even more corn, which they stored. When Pemulwuy's son Tedbury was captured at Pennant Hills during the harvest of 1805 (when, according to the

Sydney Gazette, 'few, if any of the out-farms have escaped pillage'), he showed his captors a cache of 40 bushels of grain.[15]

The Darug's second tactical innovation was their method of attacking farmhouses. To carry out a successful farmhouse raid, they first needed to collect intelligence on the number of people living in the farmhouse, how they were armed, what they owned, and the best times to attack. The Darug patiently observed the settlers moving around their huts and tiny fields from the cover of the trees. When a party led by the man known as 'Branch Jack' raided William Knight's farm at Portland Head on 15 June 1805, the raiding party waited for Knight and his servant to leave before plundering the hut. Farmhouse raids could involve large numbers of people — up to 200 people took part in the raid on Wilshire's farm at Lane Cove in 1804 — but generally farmhouse raiding parties required fewer participants than corn raids because household goods taken from huts were not as bulky as corn. The average size of a Darug farmhouse raiding party was between fifteen and twenty people.[16]

Once the Darug learnt English it increased their ability to gather intelligence and carry out raids. In 1804 the *Sydney Gazette* complained that the Darug learned English only to 'apply the talent in mischief and deception'. A good example of Darug deception took place in 1804, when some Darug visited a George's River farm and struck up a conversation with a woman. This distracted her while the rest of the group stripped an acre of corn. The ability to understand English also meant the Darug could now collect intelligence by visiting farms and listening to conversations. For example, three attacks at Portland Head in 1805 were carried out using intelligence gathered from the farms by an English-speaking, thirteen-year-old Darug girl. Incidents like these led to a Government Order warning settlers of the dangers of allowing Darug to 'lurk about their farms'.[17]

The third tactic developed by the Darug was the use of fire. This was an important innovation: while the Darug used fire for hunting kangaroos and other animals, they had not used it in traditional warfare.[18] The Darug used fire in frontier warfare against two different targets at two different times of the year. The first was to attack farmhouses, mostly in autumn and winter, and the second was to destroy wheat crops in late spring and summer

The first recorded incendiary attack on a British farmhouse took place on the Hawkesbury in April 1797 and such attacks soon became a popular tactic. At first attacks took place at night, by Darug warriors using the cover of darkness to approach the house stealthily and, with a hand-held torch, to set ablaze the wattled walls and thatched roof. Thomas Yardley was incinerated in his house on the lower Hawkesbury when it was attacked in this way.[19]

This method of incendiary attack had to be carried out at night because a raiding party would rarely be able to get so close to the farmhouse in daylight without being detected. The Darug then may have developed a way to set fire to farmhouses during daytime in which they did not have to approach the target, as shown in the following two reports from the *Sydney Gazette* of the attack of 30 May 1805 on Henry Lamb's farmhouse and sheds at Portland Head on the Hawkesbury:

> Last Wednesday a number of natives assembled near the farm of Henry Lamb, at Portland Head, who was absent from home. After remaining some considerable time without manifesting any disposition to violence, they all ascended a ridge of rocks at a trifling distance from the house, where they kindled their fires; and rising suddenly commenced an assault upon the settler's little property against which it is impossible to devise any means of security. A number of fire-brands were showered about the house and different sheds, which were thrown a considerable distance by means of the *moutang* or *fish-gig* [a spear used for catching fish]; and the premises being by this device set fire to, were in a short time wholly consumed.
>
> Mrs Lamb was at a small distance from the dwelling in which she left an infant asleep; and perceiving the smoke issue from the roof, hastened back to the house, which was in a blaze before she entered it, and scarcely permitted her with safety to herself to release the child from the flames. Two labouring servants at work in an adjacent field ran to her assistance; but the fire raged with such violence as to render every exertion to save a single article ineffectual.[20]

A follow-up story suggested that the fire was actually lit by the thirteen-year-old Darug girl mentioned previously. The image of warriors hurling fiery missiles may be nothing more than the figment of the settlers' fears, although the explanation that the Darug girl carried a burning torch unnoticed in broad daylight to set fire to the house is perhaps just as incredible.[21] What cannot be argued is that Darug incendiary attacks wrought great disruption and fixed panic in the settlers' minds.

During the dry heat of late spring and summer, the Darug used fire against the settlers' yellowing wheat crops.[22] The Darug lost nothing by this because they ate corn and not wheat. The settlers, however, relied on the wheat for their survival, so the threat of the crop going up in flames filled them with dread. When the Darug threatened to set fire to the wheat crops in 1799 (after the five settlers convicted of murdering 'Little George' and 'Jemmy' returned to the Hawkesbury to await sentencing), Collins commented: 'Fire, in the hands of a body of irritated and hostile natives, might, with but little trouble to them, ruin the prospect of an abundant harvest; and it appeared by this threat, that they were not ignorant of having this power in their hands ...'.[23]

When Pemulwuy's attacks on the George's River farms in November 1801 led to fears that the crops there could be set alight, Governor Philip Gidley King ordered that a detachment of the New South Wales Corps consisting of one sergeant, a corporal and six privates be stationed on two of the farms with the specific duty of preventing Aborigines setting fire to the settlers' wheat crop. To this end, the detachment's orders detailed that the farm boundaries were to be patrolled from dawn until 9:00 PM, while a sentry was to stand guard during the night.[24]

The Darug found that location and terrain protected some farms while exposing others to attack. Once the farms facing the Hawkesbury in the main settlements were consolidated, the Darug rarely raided them, but they continued to attack both the 'back farms', which bordered the forest on the edge of the main settlements, and the scattered farms on the lower Hawkesbury.[25] In fact, the Darug's frontier warfare tactics found their greatest success on the lower Hawkesbury below Portland Head. Here the lower Hawkesbury meanders through a narrow valley confined by sandstone cliffs. The crumbling sandstone created a sandy soil on the ridges; such soil, while supporting eucalypt forest and a thick scrubby undergrowth, was unsuitable for farming. Rich alluvial soil was, however, deposited on small river-flats on the bends.[26] Settlers had tried to farm these flats in 1795 but they found themselves under constant attack from Darug who came down from the heavily wooded ridges. The settlers carried out their own attacks in reply, and in December 1795 killed four men and a woman, wounded a child and captured four women. However, the position of the farms was untenable and the Darug attacks forced the British to abandon the lower Hawkesbury during 1796. The following year Governor Hunter visited the area by boat to see if settlers could be located in such a way as to enable mutual assistance when attacked. However, Hunter found the river-flats, though consisting of 'excellent' soil, were 'much too narrow' to allow safe settlement.[27]

When settlement of the lower Hawkesbury was next attempted, Darug attacks during the corn harvest of 1804 led to the area being abandoned again. In an attempt to end these raids, Governor King talked to three Darug men, who told him that they were raiding the farms because they had been driven from the river upstream and were simply attempting to retain some land with river access. King thought the Darug's 'request appear[ed] to be so just and so equitable' that he promised them that no more settlements would be made on the lower Hawkesbury.[28] While some point out that King's reservation of land for the Darug was not particularly generous — as most of lower Hawkesbury consisted of a non-arable sandstone plateau[29] — this does not take away from the fact that the area also included river-flats of rich, arable land. What is important is that the Darug held the military advantage on the lower Hawkesbury and King, unable to impose his will on the Darug by force, had no choice but to compromise. While settlers did return to the lower Hawkesbury in 1805, a combination of Darug hostility and Hawkesbury floods continued to limit their numbers. As late as 1810 Macquarie noted that there were few settlers below Portland Head.[30]

While the Darug developed new tactics to fight frontier warfare, they also continued to fight in their traditional way with other Aborigines and to use tactics developed in traditional Aboriginal warfare to fight the British. Darug men continued to take part in ritual trials. Tedbury, for example, suffered a spear wound at a trial at the Brickfields near Sydney in December 1805. Revenge attacks also continued. When a Darug woman died of spear wounds on 26 March 1805, the *Sydney Gazette* wrote: 'Vengeance against the infamous assassin agitates the tribes in the vicinity of the Hawkesbury', and, approving of this Darug practice, called for the killer to be put to death.[31] The enmities of traditional Aboriginal warfare were much longer lasting than the Aborigines' conflict with the newly arrived British, as indicated by reports of traditional warfare on the Hawkesbury in 1818, two years after the frontier war is generally considered to have ended. In November 1818 the Reverend William Lawry met a group of Darug at Portland Head, who were 'preparing for war with another tribe, making swords of timber, and womaras (a sort of club), and spears in great number for the combat'.[32]

The Darug used revenge attacks against settlers on the Hawkesbury, and the British recognised these killings as such. When Robert Luttrill died from club wounds on 7 November 1811, the jury at his inquest found 'that the deceased came to his death by means of a blow from a native; which blow was given in consequence of the deceased breaking the spears of the native, and taking away their women'. The tactics Darug raiding parties used to avoid British pursuers also came from traditional warfare. The range of these tactics can be seen by examining three separate actions in April and May 1805. In the first, the angry Henry Lamb pursued the Darug men he thought had set fire to his farmhouse but they evaded him by first laying a false trail west towards the Blue Mountains before making their escape south to the Nepean. In the second, a Darug camp at North Rocks had watch-dogs which barked in alarm when a settler party tried to attack, enabling the Darug to escape. In the third, a Darug group led by Yaragowby built fires on the west bank of the Nepean to give the impression of a camp in order to lure the pursuing Richmond Hill settlers into an ambush. In this incident, the settlers were accompanied by two men of the Burraberongal group. They warned the settlers that it was an ambush and the settlers were able to stealthily encircle Yaragowby's party instead, killing him and about seven or eight others.[33]

This last incident highlights an important feature of Darug warfare on the Hawkesbury. Because Darug groups were fighting traditional Aboriginal warfare and frontier warfare simultaneously, they sometimes formed alliances with settlers against other Aborigines to gain the benefits of combining against a common enemy. The most striking example of this on the Hawkesbury was the cooperation between the Burraberongal group of the Darug and the Richmond Hill settlers during 1804 and 1805. On 11 June 1804 between thirty and forty of the Burraberongal came to the Richmond Hill farms offering friendship and expressing their willingness to fight the 'Portland Head tribe' (probably the Kurrajong group of the Darug), who were at that time raiding the farms.[34] In the pursuit of Yaragowby's party described above, the two Burraberongal men had asked to join the settler party in exchange for being able to take women from Yaragowby's group. Both sides would have been happy with this agreement. The Burraberongal gained the assistance of the Richmond Hill settlers and their firearms in carrying out a traditional raid for women. The settlers gained the Burraberongal men's skills in tracking down Yaragowby's group for their punitive expedition, and the Burraberongal saved the settlers from a potentially disastrous ambush. The alliance between the Richmond Hill settlers and the Burraberongal even extended to settlers giving the Burraberongal access to muskets. The most notable example of this took place when two Burraberongal men joined settler John Warby and six soldiers of the New South Wales Corps in pursuit of six Aborigines who had killed some settlers. One of the Burraberongal men, known as 'Tuesday', was loaned a musket, which he used to shoot and kill one of the wanted men.[35] Other Aborigines at various times cooperated with the British by capturing and bringing in escaped convicts, and by providing guides for punitive expeditions.[36] Brook and Kohen believe that Aboriginal guides viewed the people they were pursuing as 'compatriots' and led British expeditions away from the groups they were trying to pursue; however, to suggest a pan-Aboriginal identity existed at this time is probably anachronistic. Guides may have led the British away from their quarry out of fear of a revenge attack, but this is a quite different motivation.[37]

An alliance of a more personal kind was formed in the friendship between Pemulwuy's son, Tedbury, and the famous army officer turned grazier John Macarthur. Tedbury knew of the hostility between Governor William Bligh and Macarthur, and, when he heard the news that Bligh had been arrested by the New South

Wales Corps on 26 January 1808, he arrived in Sydney the following day carrying his bundle of spears. According to what Tedbury told Macarthur, he feared Bligh might have harmed Macarthur, and had this been the case he would have speared Bligh.[38]

From 1805 there was little warfare on the Hawkesbury frontier until 1808, when Tedbury led a number of raids. These attacks ended on 19 November 1809, when the main Darug leaders met William Paterson (who had become lieutenant-governor again, following the arrest of Bligh) and were pardoned in exchange for promising to cease their attacks.[39] After this, the frontier was relatively quiet and the corn harvests from 1809 to 1814 were not attacked.[40] This seems to have been a consequnce of the decline in the Darug population due to disease and warfare. As numbers dropped there were no longer enough people to mount corn raids.

When frontier warfare broke out again, the fighting took place on the Nepean River to the south. British settlers had started occupying land on the Nepean from about 1809. In this phase of the frontier war, which began in May 1814, the Darug were joined by the Darawal and Gandangara peoples. The Darawal and Gandangara had traditional lands in this area, and they had also begun to move onto what was previously Darug land which had become empty with the decline in the Darug population.[41] Brook and Kohen argue that the renewal of corn raids in 1814 was forced on the Darawal and Gandangara by drought and the shortage of traditional foods. While drought probably had some causal effect on raids, it cannot be the only cause as the 1810–11 drought had not led to corn raids.[42]

The Darawal and Gandangara were able to carry out corn raids because their populations were large enough to allow them to form raiding parties of sixty or eighty. Like the Darug before them, the Darawal and Gandangara carried out farm raids and forced some settlers to abandon their farms and flee from the river.[43] Traditional and frontier warfare also continued to be fought simultaneously. Gandangara raiding parties attacking British farms also raided Darug and Darawal communities, so it was logical for the Darug and the Darawal to cooperate with the British against the Gandangara. Karada of the Darug would warn the British when Gandangara raiding parties were approaching the Nepean, while in 1814 Darawal people sought protection from the Gandangara at settlers' farms.[44] However, as the fighting continued at least some of the Darawal and Gandangara formed an alliance against the British, since Gandangara and Darawal warriors were known to have shared camps during 1816.[45]

The British Army continued to use the same tactics against Aboriginal raiding parties on the Hawkesbury-Nepean during both the first phase (1795–1805) and the second phase (1814–16) of frontier warfare. This was to send 'arm'd parties … to scower the country' and track down the raiders. The soldiers' muskets meant they could exact serious casualties on raiding parties if they made contact. For example, a New South Wales Corps punitive expedition killed two of 'the most violent and ferocious' Darug warriors in 1804. However, skirmishes of this nature rarely happened. Darug warriors travelled more lightly than British soldiers and knew the country better. This meant they generally moved faster through the bush and British soldiers could not catch them. George Caley, the government botanist, wrote in 1801 how troops on the Hawkesbury 'went out in quest of them [Darug] several times, but were not able to meet with them', while in 1805 Governor King complained of 'the Velocity with which these people Remove from One place to another'.[46]

When the frontier raids on the Nepean began in 1814, members of the Veteran Company were sent to the frontier. The Veteran Company consisted of men of the New South Wales Corps who wished to remain in the colony when the regiment left in 1810, but were no longer fit for active service. Governor Lachlan Macquarie considered these men suitable for less strenuous tasks such as guard duty and in 1813, two lieutenants and forty-five men were stationed on the Hawkesbury and forty-two men at Liverpool.[47] However, in 1816 the attacks had increased to such an extent that Macquarie was forced to stiffen these garrisons with small detachments of regulars from the 46th Regiment to be 'Guards of Protection for those Farms which are Most exposed to the Incursions of the Natives'. While these small frontier garrisons provided a sense of security for settlers and acted as some deterrent to Aboriginal attacks, they were not an efficient use of manpower. As Macquarie noted, it was impossible to protect every farm[48], and even small frontier detachments spread the limited resources of the colonial garrison too thinly.

While the Eora's method of dealing with firearms was simply to avoid armed men, the Darug, Darawal and Gandangara developed tactics based on knowledge of the length of time it required to reload a musket. By February 1796 Collins noted that the Darug knew 'how little use a musket was when once discharged', and added that this 'effectually removed that terror of our fire-arms with which it had been our constant endeavour to inspire them'. Collins claimed that the Darug had learned this from two ex-convicts, John Wilson and William Knight, who were living with them[49], but it is just as likely that the Darug were able to discover this fact for themselves.

The Darawal and the Gandangara developed two tactics against armed settlers or soldiers. The first new tactic was to take cover when a musket was about to be fired. This was used by Aborigines in March 1816 at Camden to rout a settler party of forty men, of whom only a few had muskets. A settler, Samuel Hassall, wrote that 'the natives would fall down as soon as the men would present theire muskets at them and then get up and dance'.[50] The second tactic was to rush the man after he had discharged his musket and before he could reload. This was used on 7 May 1814: a Gandangara party, taking corn from Milehouse's farm at Appin, rushed three privates of the Veteran Company once they had fired their muskets. According to the *Sydney Gazette*, the Gandangara charged the soldiers 'with a promptitude that put it out of their power to reload', killed Private Isaac Eustace, and forced the other two to flee.[51]

The Darug, Darawal and Gandangara took muskets during raids on farmhouses, but they did not take them with the regularity that they took corn and other goods. Pemulwuy's raiding parties took musket balls in 1797, and in 1805, 'Branch Jack' brandished a musket during farmhouse raids, but there is no record of him discharging it. Settler rumour claimed Aborigines on the George's River had several muskets, though again there is no record of their being used.[52] The Darug sometimes left muskets when they raided farmhouses and sometimes they even returned ones they had taken. In 1804 a raiding party attacked Gilbert's farm on the George's River. After knocking Mrs Gilbert unconscious, they took practically everything except her musket. In 1799, after Thomas Hodgkinson was killed by 'Major White', another Darug man arranged for Hodgkinson's musket to be returned to his widow.[53]

The only recorded incident in which Aborigines fired on settlers took place on the Nepean River on 2 March 1816. A party of seven settlers who crossed the Nepean on a punitive expedition was surprised in an ambush by Aborigines, who took the men's muskets and 'commenced a terrible attack, as well by a discharge of the arms they had captured, as by an innumerable shower of spears'. Three of the seven settlers, Patrick McHugh, Denis Hagan and John Lewis were killed either by muskets or spears, while the four survivors fled back across the river.[54]

The British governors knew that their troops lacked mobility when serving on the Hawkesbury-Nepean and made various attempts to improve this. In 1805 New South Wales Corps detachments were given native guides and used boats as transports.[55] In 1814 Macquarie, perhaps in the belief that settlers with Aboriginal guides could move faster than any soldiers, sent out a punitive expedition consisting entirely of black and white civilians armed and equipped from Government Stores. However, there is no record of the result of this expedition and the experiment was not repeated.[56] Horses, a logical way to improve mobility on the frontier, do not appear to have been used either by settlers or soldiers, probably owing to the small number of horses then in the colony.[57]

In the first four months of 1816, there was a spate of Aboriginal raids along the Nepean River, and on one occasion a raiding party even crossed the Blue Mountains to attack the government cattle herd at Cox's River (near what is now Hartley on the Great Western Highway).[58] Along the frontier, settlers fled their farms, and Macquarie felt he was 'compelled' to send 'a Strong Detachment of Troops' against the Darug, Darawal and Gandangara to 'Strike them with Terror against Committing Similar Acts of Violence in future'.[59] This expedition would be one of the most elaborate operations ever carried out by the British Army on the Australian frontier.

Macquarie attempted to improve the mobility of these troops in four ways. First, he used six officers and approximately sixty-eight other ranks from the 46th Regiment's light infantry and grenadier companies because these companies consisted of the fittest and best troops in the regiment. Second, he provided the commanders of the two main detachments, Captain WJB Schaw and Captain James Wallis with mounted messengers to enable them to communicate with each other. Third, he provided the detachments with Aboriginal and settler guides. And fourth, he gave both Schaw's and Wallis's columns a two-horse cart to carry the troops' baggage and enable them to move more quickly (the third detachment, commanded by Lieutenant Charles Dawe, had no cart as it was to be a static blocking force at Camden).[60]

Macquarie ordered Captain Schaw and Lieutenant Dawe to take detachments of the light infantry company on 9 April 1816 and patrol the river and its surrounds from Windsor and Richmond in the north to Camden and Bargo in the south. Macquarie expected Schaw's march along the river would force the raiders 'from the lurking places' and enable them to be captured by Dawe, waiting at the Macarthur property at Camden. Before Schaw and Dawe left, however, reports reached Sydney on the night of 8 April of a series of killings of both settlers and Aborigines around Appin. This led Macquarie to add a third detachment, commanded by Captain James Wallis, from the regiment's grenadier company, to move through Appin and then coordinate with the other detachments once Schaw had moved south (see map 3.2a).[61]

In contrast to previous British expeditions on the Hawkesbury-Nepean, in which it was thought enough simply to kill any Aborigines they came across, Macquarie told his officers that the aim of this operation should be 'to Punish the guilty with as little injury as possible to the innocent Natives'. A list of men accused of carrying out the raids who were to be arrested or killed was issued, and

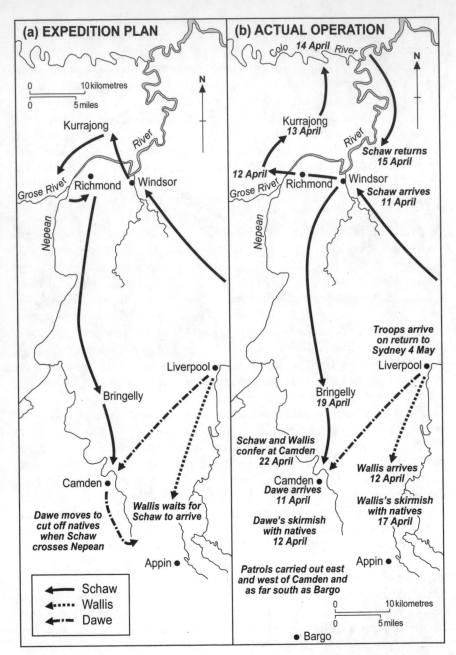

MAP 3.2
British punitive expedition, 1816

SOURCES Letters — Macquarie to Schaw, 9 April 1816, Macquarie to Wallis, 9 April 1816, NLA mfm N257 Reel 6045 AONSW CSO 4/1734. Letters — Schaw to Macquarie, 8 May 1816, Dawe to Macquarie, 4 May 1816, Wallis to Macquarie, 9 May 1816, NLA mfm N257 Reel 6045 AONSW CSO 4/1735.

Macquarie stated that the 'Five Islands Tribe' (the Illawarra group of the Darawal people) had not taken part in the attacks and was therefore not to be molested.

The rules of engagement were also very specific. Macquarie told his officers:

> On any occasion of seeing or falling in with the Natives, either in Bodies or Singly, they are to be called on, by your friendly Native Guides, to surrender themselves to you as Prisoners of War. If they refuse to do so, make the least show of resistance, or attempt to run away from you, you will fire upon and compell them to surrender, breaking and destroying the Spears, Clubs and Waddies of all those you take prisoners. Such Natives as happen to be killed on such occasions, if grown up men, are to be hanged up on Trees in Conspicuous Situations, to Strike the Survivors with the greater terror.

He further ordered the expedition that, if it was required to open fire, 'you will use every possible precaution to save the lives of the Native Women and Children'.[62]

Macquarie had written his orders with much thought and a sincere desire to limit frontier violence. Unfortunately, they were almost impossible to implement in frontier conditions. The only way British troops could get close to Aboriginal groups was to look for their campfires at night and surprise them in their sleep. In these circumstances it was very difficult for soldiers to differentiate between men, women and children.

This problem was shown during the course of the expedition. Schaw's detachment followed the route as specified in his orders (see map 3.2b) and did not kill or capture any Aborigines. Dawe's detachment arrived at the Macarthur farm at Camden on 11 April to be informed that a group of Aborigines was camped nearby. At 3:00 AM the next morning Dawe's troops set out for the camp aiming to reach it at dawn, but about 100 metres from the camp, the alarm was raised and the inhabitants fled. The soldiers fired and hit one man, who later died of wounds. The only one captured was a teenage boy.[63]

The third party, commanded by Wallis, reached Broughton's farm west of the George's River at Appin, and early on the morning of 17 April came across an Aboriginal camp on the cliffs above a creek. Wallis ordered his troops into a line and advanced into the camp in the moonlight, killing seven Aborigines. Tragically, Wallis did not send any men around the camp to cut off people fleeing the advancing line and a further seven 'met their fate by rushing in despair over the precipice'. Two women and three children were captured. Wallis later wrote to Macquarie, 't'was a melancholy but a necessary duty'. The bodies of two men, Durelle and Kanabygal, were hauled from the creek and hung up on McGee's Hill near Broughton's farm.[64]

Following these encounters, the troops mounted a series of fruit-less patrols until ordered on 30 April to return with their prisoners to Sydney. By then, the detachments' rations were almost exhausted, but Macquarie was satisfied that the troops had 'inflicted exemplary Punishment on the Hostile Natives'.[65] In reward for their service, Schaw and Wallis received 15 gallons of spirits, and Lieutenants Dawe, Grant and Parker, and Assistant Surgeon Bush received 10 gallons each. Each soldier received a new pair of shoes and half-a-pint of spirits, and the British and Aboriginal guides were similarly rewarded. All but one of the Aboriginal prisoners were released after a month's detention.[66]

Wallis praised his grenadiers for 'their steadiness and patient endurance of long marches & privations of every kind'. However, while the British troops carried out their duties to the best of their ability, the 1816 expedition showed the limitations of British tactics. Schaw's detachment had pursued a party of fifteen Darug men around Windsor for five hours but could not make any ground on them. Even the best British troops in the colony could not move as fast as Darug warriors. As well, the level of logistics was insufficient for effective operations in the bush. Wallis's detachment was forced to hire two extra carts from local landholders to provide adequate transport, while Schaw complained that the poor state of the frontier tracks meant that his cart, rather than helping his troops move faster, actually slowed them down.[67]

While raids re-commenced after this punitive expedition and a further smaller punitive expedition was sent out, by November 1816 the frontier situation had stabilised. In December 1816 Aboriginal leaders promised to end their attacks, and in April 1817 Macquarie informed the British Colonial Secretary that 'all Hostility on both Sides has long since Ceased'.[68]

4

THE BATHURST AND HUNTER VALLEY DISTRICTS, 1822–1826

As the sun dipped beneath the horizon Sergeant John Baker halted his men and ordered them to use the remaining daylight to make camp on the banks of the Macquarie River, just north of Bathurst. It was late June 1824 and the short winter day was made even shorter by the looming hills that hemmed in the river and blocked the sun from the valley. The Bathurst commandant, Major James Morisset, had sent Baker out accompanied both by a guide to find a Wiradjuri camp and by a constable to arrest certain men for raiding settlers' cattle and stock huts. Baker and the rest of the party, soldiers of the 40th Regiment, were to assist in the arrest and to guard the prisoners. Baker had been a soldier for eleven years and had fought against the French in the Peninsular campaign, but he had never before been ordered to do such a pointless task. They had not seen a single native all day! Baker cursed as an old soldier should and pulled his blanket around him to keep out the frosty air. The party returned to Bathurst the next day and Baker reported his failure. Morisset knew that his tiny garrison had no chance of stopping Wiradjuri attacks on the dispersed properties around Bathurst unless he could make his troops more mobile. Within days of Baker's return, Morisset wrote to Sydney asking for horses.[1] The army's failure on the Bathurst frontier led in 1825 to the formation of the New South Wales Mounted Police — British soldiers mounted on horses provided by the colony. The deployment of Mounted Police to the Hunter Valley frontier the next year led to an escalation in frontier violence. Ensign Archibald Robertson used the soldiers' new mobility to pursue and attack raiding parties, while Lieutenant Nathaniel Lowe's execution of Aboriginal prisoners led to his being tried for murder.

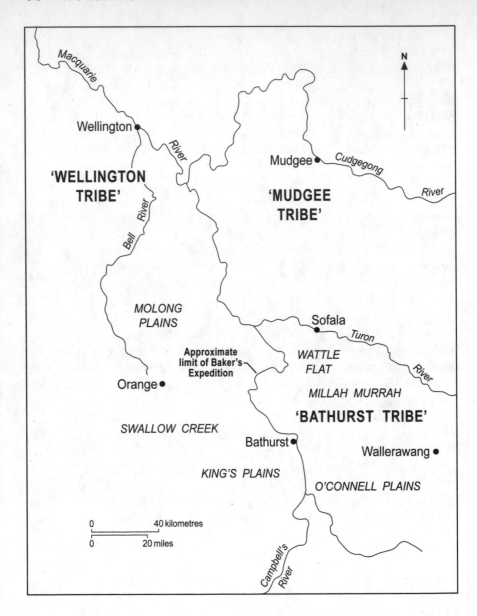

MAP 4.1
Wiradjuri lands on the Macquarie River, 1822

SOURCE After Michael Pearson, 'Bathurst Plains and Beyond: European Colonisation and Aboriginal Resistance', *Aboriginal History*, 8(1), 1984, p 67.

The Wiradjuri people's traditional land covers an extensive area of inland New South Wales embracing the Macquarie, Lachlan and Murrumbidgee rivers. The Wiradjuri knew the Macquarie as the Wambool and probably three separate Wiradjuri groups lived on the river upstream of Wellington: the 'Bathurst tribe' on the upper Macquarie around what is now Bathurst, the 'Mudgee tribe' on the Cudgegong River around what is now Mudgee, while the 'Wellington tribe' lived on the Bell River and the Macquarie River downstream of Bathurst (see map 4.1). At the time the British crossed the Blue Mountains, the combined population of these three groups is estimated to have been between 500 and 600 people, a considerably lower population density than that of the Eora and Darug.[2]

The British built a road across the Blue Mountains in 1814, and established the settlement at Bathurst the following year. Unlike at the Hawkesbury, the initial settlement at Bathurst was strictly controlled. Governor Macquarie used the Bathurst district to run government sheep and cattle and the small British population consisted of convicts employed as shepherds and stockmen, with a few officials and soldiers to oversee them. The Bathurst frontier was relatively peaceful between 1815 and 1822. The small number of people, and their limited use of the land to run sheep and cattle, meant that the chance of conflict with the Wiradjuri was lessened. There are only four recorded violent incidents during this seven-year period: the possible killing of an escaped convict in 1815, a cattle raid at Cox's River in 1816 by coastal Aborigines who had crossed the Blue Mountains, the spearing of one of Lieutenant William Lawson's horses in 1819, and the Wiradjuri killing — the circumstances are unknown — of Private James King of the 48th Regiment on 6 February 1821.[3]

The relative peace of the Bathurst frontier ended with the arrival in New South Wales of Governor Sir Thomas Brisbane in December 1821. In accordance with the recommendations of the Bigge Report, Brisbane 'privatised' the convict system, and ended Macquarie's limit on inland settlement, granting settlers large tracts of land around Bathurst and assigning them convicts with which to work their land. Between 1821 and 1825, the number of cattle and sheep in the Bathurst district increased from 33,733 to 113,973, while the amount of alienated land increased from 2520 acres to 91,636 acres (1010 ha to 36,650 ha). In 1822 Bathurst was so small that it did not have a public house, but by 1827 the population had grown so much that the town now supported a brewery, and eleven public houses — ten of them unlicensed.[4]

The ever-increasing number of settlers and stock animals put traditional Wiradjuri land-use under threat. The Wiradjuri began attacks at Mudgee and at Swallow Creek, west of Bathurst in 1822. Previously the good relationship between Wiradjuri leaders and the Bathurst commandant, Lieutenant William Lawson (of Blaxland, Lawson and Wentworth fame), had minimised conflict, and in December 1823 Lawson and another long-term settler suggested to Wiradjuri men that they should visit Bathurst to meet the new commandant, Major James Morisset, in the hope that negotiation could stop the attacks.[5] However, the scale of the British encroachment onto Wiradjuri land made compromise impossible and the raids continued.

The Wiradjuri used a variety of old and new tactics to attack stockmen and their stock. They took advantage of the dispersed nature of the pastoral frontier to ambush individual stockmen in a traditional fashion, while their innovation was to target cattle and sheep. According to John Maxwell, the superintendent of Government Stock at Bathurst, the Wiradjuri 'got into the practice of eating Beef', and the New South Wales judge-advocate, John Wylde, whose properties west and south of Bathurst were often attacked, observed that the constant nature of the raids meant they had become a regular means for gathering food. The mountainous terrain on the edges of the Bathurst Plains and around Mudgee assisted the Wiradjuri warriors in their attacks and gave them what the *Sydney Gazette* described as 'an interminable extent of country to retire back upon'.[6]

The Wiradjuri raiding campaign succeeded in stopping British pastoral expansion. Attacks in November 1823 on the government station at Swallow Creek forced it to be abandoned. Maxwell wrote that the Wiradjuri had 'so intimidated' the stockmen at Swallow Creek that they 'dare not stop at their station without protection' and had retreated with their stock into Bathurst. Plans to set up a government station further west at Molong were cancelled. Wylde pleaded for 'the *appearance* even of a small military detachment' to prevent the raids 'so very injurious to private Property and Security'. British troops were sent to protect settlers' cattle runs; however, these deployments were limited to parties of no more than four men, as the Bathurst garrison at this time consisted of only twelve soldiers.[7]

The best-known Wiradjuri leader in these raids was Windradyne, called 'Saturday' by the British, though he was only one of several Wiradjuri leaders. Traditional enmities between the different Wiradjuri-speaking groups meant they were unable to combine to fight the British as one group. As late as 1836 Charles Darwin, who visited Bathurst during his visit to Australia, noted that the Wiradjuri had kept up 'their ancient distinctions, and sometimes go to war with each other'. As Goodall points out, 'the limitation of authority to one's country' meant that no one leader could coordinate all the Wiradjuri groups, and, as the British advanced through the vast Wiradjuri lands, each group fought the invasion in their turn, 'country by country'.[8]

Settlers claimed the Wiradjuri captured some muskets during their raids, but there is no record of them using firearms in frontier conflict. The Wiradjuri's use of spears meant that they needed a large numerical advantage — estimated by one settler as ten-to-one — and could target only individuals or small groups of stockmen (no more than three or four) to have any chance of success.[9] On the British side, most punitive expeditions failed because the parties were unable to make contact with the Wiradjuri. However, on the few occasions when the British did make contact, they could bring their superior firepower to bear. Following a raid on a hut on 19 March 1824 by about sixty Wiradjuri men at the re-occupied Swallow Creek government station, Private Softly and Private Epslom of the 3rd Regiment, who were protecting Wylde's station nearby, went to investigate. Accompanied by Andrew Dunn, Wylde's overseer, and Michael McKegney, who had raised the alarm, the two soldiers reached the hut at about 2:00 AM the following morning to find several Wiradjuri still there. When Softly entered the hut, most of the men inside tried to escape but one caught hold of his musket. When Epslom followed, a Wiradjuri man tried to hit him over the head with a spade. Epslom raised his musket to protect himself, but after two blows it broke in two. With one functioning musket between them, the two soldiers killed two men and captured three others: 'Taylor', Columbummoro and Cullalbegary.[10]

During May 1824 the Wiradjuri killed seven stockmen in an audacious series of attacks, which shocked the settlers. William Lawson Junior wrote that, though drought had destroyed his pasture, fear of the Aborigines meant he dare not graze his animals further inland, while a letter to the *Sydney Gazette* sympathised with the convict stockmen in isolated huts, where 'every sound conveys to the unfortunate the horror of a bloody and cruel death'. William Cox stated that the Wiradjuri 'may now be called at war with the Europeans'. British retaliation was inevitable, and on 31 May after the Wiradjuri had speared a stockman, five of the victim's workmates, John Johnston, William Clark, John Nicholson, Henry Castles and John Crear, asked their overseer William Lane for weapons and horses. They rode out armed with four muskets and a sword, but returned that evening claiming they had not seen any Aborigines. The discovery two weeks later of three bodies led to the men's admission that they had killed them in a skirmish with thirty spear-wielding warriors. The five were charged with manslaughter and found not guilty, though Saxe Bannister, the New South Wales attorney-general, wondered why, if they had truly fought a group of men, the bodies found were of three women.[11]

On 14 August 1824, a week after the acquittal, Governor Brisbane proclaimed martial law west of the Blue Mountains.[12] He did this because Aborigines were considered to have automatically become British subjects when the British claimed Australia. Soldiers who shot British subjects during civil disturbances such as riots could be charged with murder unless their action had been sanctioned by a magistrate or by the declaration of martial law, and several officers and men had faced trial in England over such matters during the eighteenth century. Martial law had been previously declared in New South Wales during the 1804 convict revolt, while Governor Macquarie had provided legal protection to the troops by ensuring they were accompanied by magistrates or civil police during the 1816 punitive expedition. Brisbane's declaration of martial law was made similarly to prevent soldiers or settlers who killed Wiradjuri being charged with murder.

The British claim that Aborigines were British subjects meant that frontier conflict was defined as civil disorder rather than as war against a foreign enemy. The British government would never accept that Aborigines had sovereign rights to their land as this would undermine the Crown's claim to all of Australia. The British government argued that settlers and soldiers killing Aborigines on the frontier was not warfare; but prior to 1824 few settlers had been tried for killing Aborigines and only one — the convict John Kirby at Newcastle in 1820 — had been hanged for the crime.[13] The great difficulty in gaining murder convictions against settlers was that any Aboriginal witnesses could not give evidence because, as non-Christians, they could not take the oath. Difficulties also arose in putting Aborigines on trial. In 1805 the New South Wales judge-advocate, Richard Atkins, produced the legal opinion that, while Aborigines were British subjects, they could not understand British law, and so the only way to apply the law to them was, 'when they deserve it, … to pursue and inflict such punishment as they may merit'. Corporal Peter Farrell of the New South Wales Corps was rebuked by Governor John Hunter in 1799 for capturing the Darug man known as 'Charley' for farm raids on the Hawkesbury River and bringing him to Sydney for trial. Because 'Charley' did not understand British law, Hunter refused to try him and told Corporal Farrell that, instead of making the arrest, he should have shot 'Charley'.[14]

Governor Brisbane's martial law proclamation was one of three measures introduced to end the Wiradjuri raids. He also, at Morisset's request, increased the Bathurst garrison to seventy-five men, and asked Earl Bathurst, the British Colonial Secretary, for permission to raise 'a Troop of Colonial Cavalry'. Following the failure of Sergeant Baker's expedition (referred to at the beginning of the chapter), and a party sent on 24 June 1824 to Mudgee, 100 kilometres from Bathurst, Morisset complained to Major Frederick Goulburn, the New South Wales Colonial Secretary, that 'it is impossible to march the Military and Constables after the Natives' unless they were provided with pack-horses to make them faster. Governor Brisbane went one step further when he told London that 'Infantry have no chance of success' against the Wiradjuri and asked for mounted troops. However, neither Morisset's requisition for horses and pack-saddles, nor Brisbane's request to create a mounted unit received replies before Morisset's expedition departed in September 1824.[15]

The reinforcement of the Bathurst garrison enabled Morriset to deploy an elaborate expedition. Despite the importance of this operation, no official report of its conduct exists, probably because Morisset travelled to Sydney soon afterwards and gave Governor Brisbane a verbal report. The expedition probably consisted of Morisset, four magistrates, six mounted settlers, some Aboriginal guides and a detachment of about forty soldiers of the 40th Regiment. Carts were probably used to transport supplies. There were eighty-three government horses in Bathurst in 1824, but a lack of pack-saddles probably meant they could not be used as pack-horses following Morisset's idea, and the unavailability of soldiers able to ride probably meant that soldiers assigned to the expedition were not mounted, as in Brisbane's proposal.[16]

The expedition was divided into four parties, each led by a magistrate. Leaving Bathurst in the first week of September, each travelled north by a separate route to the first rendezvous at Mudgee (see map 4.2). The speed of the parties was determined by the marching pace of the troops. Clem Sargent estimates that they probably took five days to reach Mudgee. The parties then left Mudgee around 17 September for a ten-day sweep beyond Mudgee, in which Morisset's party headed north, James Walker's party headed west, and Lawson's and George Ranken's parties went east. Ranken's party travelled as far as the Hunter Valley and made camp-fires out of coal. According to Ranken, by this stage, the expedition had not killed any Wiradjuri. In fact, the parties between them had only seen two people. Returning to Mudgee on 27 September, the parties again separated for a sweep towards Wallerawang, after which the expedition ended. Governor Brisbane stated that no Wiradjuri were killed on this part of the expedition either.[17] Wiradjuri attacks ceased and during October and November Wiradjuri leaders came into Bathurst to ask for peace. Morisset visited Sydney on 20 November to report his success personally to Governor Brisbane, and Brisbane

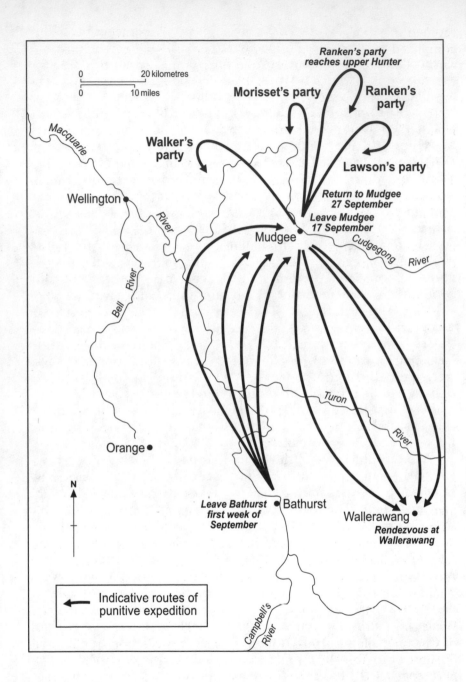

MAP 4.2
British punitive expedition, 1824

SOURCE Letter — George Ranken to Janet Ranken, 28 September 1824, quoted in WB Ranken, *The Rankens of Bathurst*, Townsend, Sydney, 1916, p 20.

revoked martial law on 11 December 1824. The peace process was completed in December, when a Wiradjuri delegation travelled across the Blue Mountains to attend the annual governor's feast for the Sydney Aborigines. Windradyne attended the feast and was introduced to the governor.[18]

It is known that twenty-two settlers were killed on the Bathurst frontier[19], but estimating the number of Wiradjuri deaths has become the subject of dispute. Salisbury and Gresser assert that Morisset's expedition massacred Wiradjuri at Bells Falls on the Turon River near Sofala, and their assertion has been repeated in books written by Grassby and Hill, Coe, Day, Elder and Fry. A Museum of Australia exhibit refers to a massacre at Bells Falls, though the Wiradjuri oral tradition quoted by the exhibit talks of a massacre committed by settlers, rather than soldiers. Fry suggests that writers who say the massacre occurred are 'sympathetic to the Kooris', and Roberts says these authors' books are about 'recognising past atrocity … admitting that it happened and agreeing how immoral it was'. However, the evidence for a massacre at Bells Falls is weak, Windschuttle going as far to call it 'spurious'. While these writers acted with the best of intentions, Roberts suggests that their repeating the story means that an incident that may not have occurred 'is now in the process of being accepted as bona fide history'.[20]

The Wiradjuri's quick surrender following Morisset's expedition may suggest a massacre at Bells Falls took place, but the Wiradjuri's actions can be explained without relying on this incident. About a week before Morisset's expedition passed through the Mudgee area a man named Chamberlane, who was William Cox's overseer at Mudgee, and two stockmen killed sixteen Wiradjuri, probably all men, including a leader known by the settlers as 'Blucher'. While this number of men killed might seem low, for a small group like the 'Mudgee tribe', it was a high percentage casualty rate for a single action. The appearance a few days afterwards of Morisset's four coordinated parties must have sent a wave of terror through the Wiradjuri. It forced them to move constantly to keep out of sight of the British patrols, and, as Governor Brisbane wrote, kept the Wiradjuri 'in a constant state of alarm'.[21] The devastating casualties of Chamberlane's skirmish followed in swift succession by the total disruption to food gathering caused by Morisset's parties would have convinced the Wiradjuri that negotiating peace was the only option to ensure their survival.

The Bathurst frontier was peaceful after 1824. Earl Bathurst rejected Governor Brisbane's first request for mounted troops — made when the fighting was at its height — because Brisbane had not provided enough information on why the unit was needed.

However, he accepted Brisbane's second proposal, made with the backing of the New South Wales Legislative Council, in 1825. The New South Wales Mounted Police was the first unit of mounted infantry formed in Australia, and can be seen as the precursor of the Light Horsemen, which rode into legend during the First World War. Members of the Mounted Police were soldiers, not civilian police. They remained on their regiment's pay lists, but the expense of their horses was borne, not by the British government, but by the colony. This was a significant cost for the colonial government: each horse cost £50, while each set of saddles and gear were manufactured in Sydney for a further £6.[22] Van Diemen's Land formed a mounted police detachment a year later, in 1826, but as the colony had less revenue to spend on horses, the detachment was much smaller. In New South Wales Colonel William Stewart, the commanding officer of the 3rd Regiment, formed the Mounted Police by hand-picking two officers, two sergeants and twenty-two other ranks from his regiment.[23] The first detachment, armed with short muskets known as carbines, and consisting of Lieutenant Richard Everard, a sergeant, three corporals and seven privates, left Sydney on 4 November 1825 for immediate operations against bushrangers around Bathurst. The Mounted Police was universally recognised as both an effective and an efficient use of resources. The Bathurst settlers praised the 'horse soldiers' for protecting them from bushrangers, while the New South Wales Colonial Secretary was able to deny a request from the Wellington commandant for more troops on the grounds that the Mounted Police at Bathurst could quickly ride to his aid if required.[24]

The remaining half of the Mounted Police was sent to Wallis Plains (now Maitland), the highest navigable point on the Hunter River. The men in this detachment did not reach their camp until February 1826 owing to difficulties in purchasing suitable horses; the mounts they took to the Hunter Valley were later criticised for being too old. However, this detachment was the first deployed for frontier warfare. The Wonnarua people owned most of the upper Hunter, while some groups of the Kamilaroi lived at the very top of the valley. The land on the Hunter River above Wallis Plains and Patrick Plains (now Singleton) was described by settler Peter Cunningham as 'well adapted for cultivation or pasture', and settlers streamed into the valley following Henry Dangar's survey in 1824.[25]

MAP 4.3
Wonnarua and Kamilaroi lands on the upper Hunter Valley, 1826

SOURCE After Roger Milliss, *Waterloo Creek: The Australia Day Massacre of 1838, George Gipps and the British Conquest of New South Wales*, McPhee Gribble, Ringwood, Victoria, 1992, pp 52–53.

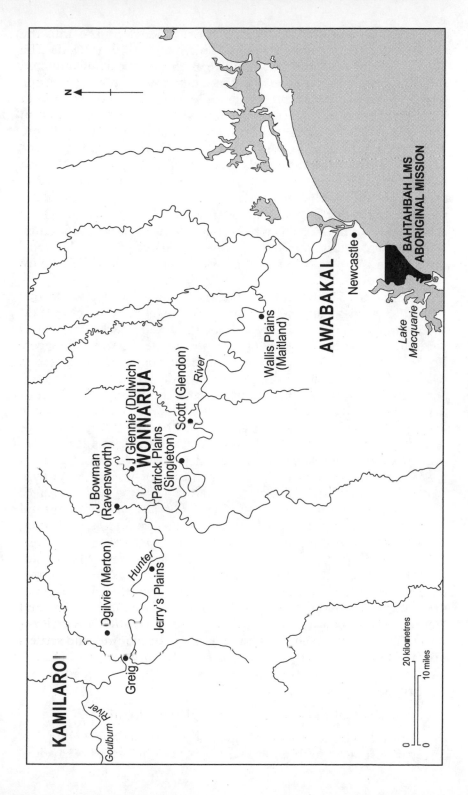

KAMILAROI

Goulburn River

Greig

Ogilvie (Merton)

Hunter River

Jerry's Plains

J Bowman (Ravensworth)

J Glennie (Dulwich)

WONNARUA

Patrick Plains (Singleton)

Scott (Glendon)

River

Wallis Plains (Maitland)

AWABAKAL

Newcastle

Lake Macquarie

BAHTAHBAH LMS ABORIGINAL MISSION

N

20 kilometres

10 miles

0

0

There were good relations between the Wonnarua and Kamilaroi and some settlers, most notably Lieutenant William Ogilvie at Merton station (see map 4.3). Unlike Bathurst, the Hunter Valley was temperate enough to grow corn, and some natives helped the settlers harvest corn in exchange for meals of sweetened boiled pumpkin. However, other settlers, such as James Greig, whose property was at the important junction of the Hunter and Goulburn rivers, tried to block Aboriginal access to the land. Greig was absent when Wonnarua warriors attacked his farm in October 1825, but they killed his cousin Robert, just out from Scotland, and Greig's convict servant. When neighbours came to the farm after the raid, they found Greig's sheep safe and unscattered, under the watchful eye of Greig's sheepdog. As well as such revenge attacks, Aborigines also plundered huts, took corn and attacked sheep. The 'Mudgee tribe' of the Wiradjuri joined the Wonnarua and the Kamilaroi in these raids.[26]

In June 1826, following the deaths of two labourers at Doctor James Bowman's station, Lieutenant Nathaniel Lowe of the 40th Regiment and the entire Hunter Valley Mounted Police detachment were ordered to the frontier. Of course, by the time the Mounted Police had ridden up the valley, the Wonnarua raiders had long gone, so Lowe returned to Wallis Plains almost immediately, leaving Sergeant Lewis Moore and four privates on the frontier. In late July a man known as 'Jackey Jackey' was arrested for the attack on Bowman's station and handed over to the Mounted Police. Two soldiers took 'Jackey Jackey' to Lieutenant Lowe at Wallis Plains and presented the prisoner to him. Lowe ordered his men to take 'Jackey Jackey' into the bush and kill him. The men tied their prisoner to a tree and obeyed their order.[27]

The execution of 'Jackey Jackey' was just one incident in Lieutenant Lowe's campaign of terror on the upper Hunter. During the first half of August a further three Aboriginal men were 'shot while trying to escape' by the Mounted Police. Selesky points out that the use of brutality in frontier warfare was justified in other parts of the British Empire on the grounds that terror broke resistance and ended fighting sooner.[28] This attitude certainly existed in New South Wales at this time. In June the *Australian* argued that the best course in dealing with the Hunter Valley Aborigines was: 'To strike these with terror, by the discriminating application of firearms, [which] will ultimately prove a saving of human life, and leave the people in the quiet enjoyment of their farms'.[29]

When news of Lowe's murderous activities reached Sydney in early August, Governor Ralph Darling immediately ordered an inquiry and recalled Lowe. Despite the obstructions of Hunter Valley magistrates and of settlers who approved of Lowe's behaviour,

Darling eventually collected sufficient evidence to put the mounted police officer on trial the following year.[30] It is important to note that Darling did not put Lowe on trial for shooting Aborigines without the legal sanction of a magistrate or martial law. He put Lowe on trial because, by shooting a prisoner, he had committed what would now be termed a 'war crime'. Earl Bathurst had told Darling when he began his term as governor that if Aborigines attacked British settlements he should 'oppose force by force, and to repel such Aggressions in the same manner, as if they proceeded from subjects of an accredited State'. This is the closest the British government ever came to accepting the reality that the Aborigines were not misbehaving British subjects, but were sovereign peoples defending their lands in war. Though Saxe Bannister, the New South Wales attorney-general, told him that Bathurst's advice was 'illegal', Darling followed it and viewed the fighting on the Hunter as warfare that did not need to be legalised by the declaration of martial law. Darling's comment that 'prompt measures in dealing with such people may be the most efficacious' implies approval of the use of some terror tactics in frontier warfare. However, Darling stated that 'it is impossible to subscribe to the massacre of prisoners in cold blood as a measure of justifiable policy', and this is the reason he pursued the case against Lowe.[31]

Meanwhile, on the frontier the Mounted Police, reinforced with more men from Sydney, kept trying to break Aboriginal resistance with arbitrary arrests. In early August 1826 two privates visited Ogilvie's station at Merton and arrested Tolou and Mirroul (also known as 'Ben' and 'Denis') for the raids at Greig's and Bowman's stations. Lieutenant Ogilvie was absent, but his wife Mary told the soldiers the two men, who worked on the farm, were innocent. Mrs Ogilvie's pleas were in vain; Tolou and Mirroul were imprisoned in Newcastle. One or two weeks later a soldier and a constable returned to Merton and asked for Aboriginal guides in order to track bushrangers. When some men came forward, the soldiers seized two Aborigines, one of whom was a local leader 'Jerry', whom the mounted policeman mistook for another man, also known as 'Jerry'. Mrs Ogilvie pointed out to the soldier that he had the wrong 'Jerry' and this time they released him. Realising that the Wonnarua would seek revenge for the treacherous way they had been treated, the soldier and the constable fled, leaving Mrs Ogilvie to deal the next day with a large and angry gathering of well-armed warriors. With her son Peter, who could speak the Wonnarua's language, Mary Ogilvie reminded 'Jerry' how her family had always been friends with him and, to her great relief, 'Jerry' persuaded the warriors to leave without attacking either the Ogilvies or their farm.[32]

Soon afterwards, on 28 August, about sixteen armed Wonnarua arrived at Richard Alcorn's hut on the farm of Captain Robert Lethbridge, RN. At the little two-roomed hut were Mrs Charlotte Alcorn, her baby and her younger brother and three assigned servants. Mrs Alcorn provided the Wonnarua with food and all was peaceful until Richard Alcorn arrived at the hut and ordered the Aborigines to go away. At this, the warriors attacked. The settlers fled into the hut, which the Aborigines besieged. The hut windows had no glass or shutters, so spears rained through the gap. A spear pierced Henry Cottle's arm and entered his chest. He cried 'I'm a dying man!', and died almost immediately. While Charlotte and the baby huddled in fear under the bed, Alcorn held a box against the open window to block spears until the Aborigines smashed it apart. When their spears ran out, the warriors began hurling stones into the hut, one killed Marty Hermon while another knocked Alcorn out. John Woodbury, the last man left standing, had been speared in one hand. He could not reach the shot, but laboriously loaded his musket one-handed with powder in the fervent hope that the sound would scare the Aborigines away. When Woodbury fired, the Aborigines chanted in English, 'fire away, fire away'. The noise attracted a shepherd, however; on seeing the siege of the hut, he started running to James Glennie's nearby station. The Aborigines saw the shepherd, and realising that mounted policemen were at Glennie's station, broke off their attack and withdrew.[33]

That there was a Mounted Police outpost strategically placed at Glennie's station was due to the planning of Ensign Archibald Robertson of the 57th Regiment, who had led the Mounted Police reinforcements to the Hunter. Robertson was a skilful horseman and carefully deployed the troops under his command so they covered both sides of the river and could quickly react to raids.[34] A party was quickly formed to pursue the Aborigines who had raided Alcorn's hut. Led by Robert Scott, the local justice of the peace, the party included mounted policemen, armed settlers and armed Aborigines. Scott's party tracked the raiders for two days over about 30 kilometres and came across them as they were making camp for the night. The British fired into the camp and the Aborigines replied with spears, wounding one man in the cheek. There are two accounts of this skirmish: one states that two Aborigines were killed and several were wounded; the second account, just as plausible, was that Scott's men fired a volley into the camp, reloaded from tree cover and, before withdrawing, fired a second volley, killing eighteen Aborigines.[35]

Scott's pursuit and the ensuing action can be used to illustrate two points. The first is Charles Callwell's classic phrase that the best soldiers for frontier warfare were '[s]mall bodies of mounted troops'. The second is Malcolm Kennedy's thesis that it was the British use of horses which 'tilted the balance' on the Australian frontier. This was the case for several reasons. First, Aborigines who had never seen these large animals before were naturally intimidated at the sight of a man on horseback. Second, horses finally gave the British the extra mobility, both in speed and range, necessary to pursue raiding parties effectively. No matter how quickly Aborigines could move through the bush, mounted policemen or settlers could move faster, and this enabled the British advantage in firearms to be brought to its full effect. Third, a mounted man's height advantage over a man on foot gave the mounted policeman a greater field of vision, and it was difficult for Aboriginal warriors to defeat a man on a horse. Finally, the bulk of the horse itself could be used as a weapon, especially effective when attacking camps.[36]

The fighting on the upper Hunter intensified in September 1826. The Reverend Lancelot Threlkeld at Lake Macquarie, south of Newcastle, informed the London Missionary Society that 'war has commenced and still continues against the Aboriginals of this land'. A group of Hunter Valley pastoralists petitioned Governor Darling to declare martial law, but he bluntly replied that: 'Martial Law could not be a necessity to put down a few naked Savages'. Darling told the settlers they had to defend themselves and had already sent twenty muskets to the upper Hunter to arm them. However, the fighting was so intense that Darling was forced to reinforce the Mounted Police with about twenty soldiers from the Newcastle garrison. After some 'brisk conflict', the Wonnarua and the Kamilaroi were forced to yield, though resistance continued into 1827.[37]

Lowe's trial took place on 18 May 1827.[38] His legal counsel, Robert Wardell and WC Wentworth, publishers of the *Australian*, argued that, if Aborigines could not be tried for murder as they did not understand the legal system, then Lowe could not be tried in a British court for murdering an Aborigine. Francis Forbes, the New South Wales chief justice, rejected the argument on legal grounds, but Wardell and Wentworth were also factually incorrect, as four Aborigines had been hanged for murder in Van Diemen's Land in 1825 and 1826. The witnesses called in Lowe's defence did not refute the details of the allegation against him but attacked the character of the prosecution witnesses. In summing up, the chief justice told the jury — who were all military officers — that if Lowe had acted in the way described then he should be found guilty. The pro-government *Sydney Gazette* praised the trial as an 'act of justice on the part of the black natives'. However, the jury chose to disbelieve the evidence and acquitted Lowe within five minutes. When his supporters in the court realised that Lieutenant Lowe had literally got away with murder, they burst into applause.[39]

5

NORTHERN AND WESTERN AUSTRALIA, 1824–1834

In later years two friends with the names of Green and Gold would be the victims of nothing more dangerous than endless jokes about being fanatical supporters of Australian sporting teams, but in 1827 John Green and John Gold faced the perils of frontier warfare. Green was the twenty-year-old commissariat officer, and Gold was the doctor, at the tiny British outpost of Fort Dundas on Melville Island in northern Australia. Green and Gold regularly went walking in the relative cool of the tropical evening. Close to the equator, the sun sets quickly, and Lieutenant William Bate warned them as they left the fort on 2 November 1827 that dusk was approaching and they should not walk too far for fear of being ambushed by Tiwi warriors. Green was armed, so the two men shrugged off Bate's warning and strolled into the bush. About twenty minutes later a cry of pain pierced the darkness. Soldiers and convicts rushed towards the sound and found Green was dead. Gold's body was found after a search the next day. Both men had been the victims of an expertly laid Tiwi ambush. Examination of the bodies found that Green suffered a total of nineteen wounds including a fractured skull, while Gold had been wounded thirty-one times. A barbed Tiwi spearhead was found still stuck in his right thigh, and a spear had been thrust in one ear and through his head.[1] The Tiwi's aggressive defence of their land against both the British garrison at Fort Dundas and the Macassan trepang-gatherers was so successful that it forced the British to abandon the Melville Island outpost in 1829. In Western Australia the long series of frontier wars began with fighting around Perth in the early 1830s, including the encounter between a British expedition and the Pinjarup at Pinjarra in October 1834.

The Tiwi of Melville and Bathurst Islands, the Iwaidja of the Cobourg Peninsula of eastern Arnhem Land[2], and other coastal peoples of northern Australia were the only Aborigines to have regular contact with foreigners before the British invasion. From about 1700 Macassans from southwest Sulawesi (see map 5.1) sailed their boats, known as praus, to northern Australia to collect trepang (sea-slug). The Macassans processed the trepang ashore and then returned north. The trepang eventually reached ports in southern China, where it had become a fashionable food with a reputation as an aphrodisiac. The Macassans introduced tobacco and pipes to Aborigines, and some Aborigines sailed with Macassans to Sulawesi. Macassar had been under Dutch rule since 1669 and some Aboriginal languages borrowed the term 'balanda' for Europeans from the Macassan use of the word 'Hollander'.[3]

The British made three attempts to establish outposts on Tiwi and Iwaidja lands: Fort Dundas in 1824, Fort Wellington in 1827 and Fort Victoria in 1838 (see map 5.2). One reason for these settlements was to enforce British sovereignty over the entire Australian continent against Dutch or French claims. As the French naval officer Jules Dumont d'Urville wrote in 1839: 'The British consider themselves the owners of the whole of New Holland. It is merely to indicate that assumption of ownership and to secure this vast territory that they are so persistent about establishing an outpost on these inhospitable shores.'[4]

However, the British had another reason for trying to establish a northern Australian settlement: to develop a port for trade with Asia. The English East India Company imported tea from China to satisfy Europe's unquenchable thirst for this new beverage. The Chinese had no interest in British goods and would trade only for gold and silver. Running short of specie, the East India Company decided that it needed to increase trade in South-East Asia as a way of funding the Chinese tea trade, and began looking for a suitable site in the region outside Spanish or Dutch control. In 1773 the Company made an agreement with the Filipino Sultan of Sulu to establish a settlement at Balambangan Island, off Borneo, but this outpost was destroyed in 1775. The Sultan of Kedah allowed a trading post to be set up at Penang in 1784, but this was initially a poor site for trade. In 1793 Fort Coronation was constructed at Dore Bay in what is now West Papua, but it was abandoned two years later. Another attempt to settle Balambangan began in 1803 and ended in failure in 1805. Finally in 1819 Sir Stamford Raffles gained the approval of the Sultan of Johore to establish a port at Singapore, and this quickly became one of the main trading centres in South-East Asia.[5]

Following the foundation of Singapore, small British traders, not part of the East India Company, also wanted a trading port.

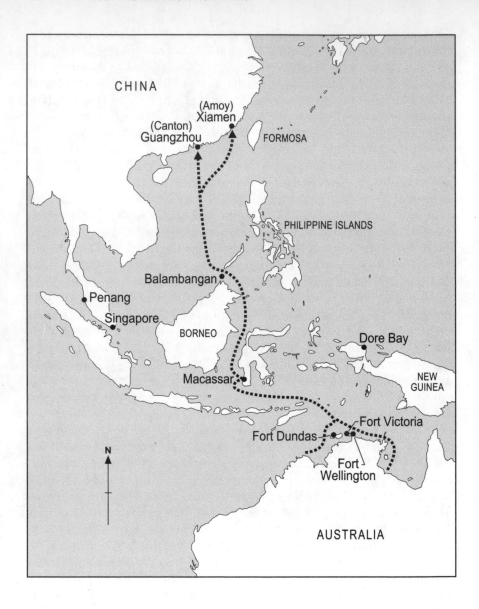

MAP 5.1
British trading posts and the trepang trade to China

SOURCES CC MacKnight, *The Voyage to Marege': Macassan trepangers in northern Australia,* Melbourne University Press, Melbourne, 1976; Andrew Griffin, 'London, Bengal, the China Trade and the Unfrequented Extremities of Asia: The East India Company's Settlement in New Guinea, 1793–95', *British Library Journal,* 16, 1990, pp 151–73.

Organising themselves as the East India Trade Committee, they petitioned the British Colonial Secretary, Earl Bathurst, in 1823 to establish a settlement in northern Australia. Matthew Flinders and Captain Phillip Parker King had met Macassan trepangers when they visited the north coast, and it was hoped that a British port here would link up with the Macassan trade into China. As Major John Campbell, one-time commandant of Fort Dundas wrote, the aim of such a settlement was to be 'the friendly hand of Australia, stretched out towards the north', where Asian traders 'may deposit the productions of their native inter-tropical islands; and receive in exchange the more improved manufactures of the natives of the temperate zone'. Earl Bathurst agreed to the East India Trade Committee's proposal, and in February 1824 told the Admiralty to make plans to establish two settlements on the northern coast of the colony of New South Wales: the first at either Bathurst Island or Melville Island, the second at Port Essington.[6]

Captain James Bremer, RN, who was given the task of conveying the garrisons, had been warned that the Tiwi would be hostile. Following discussions in Sydney with Governor Brisbane, Bremer decided that it would be 'most imprudent' to divide the small number of troops and established only one outpost: Fort Dundas on Melville Island on 26 September 1824. Craig Wilcox has written that in British Australia, unlike British North America, forts 'dotted the coastline, not the interior and faced out to sea, for their enemies were foreign navies, not warlike natives'. With two exceptions, this is true. For example, Fort Victoria, built at Port Essington in 1838, was described by Dumont d'Urville as being 'wide open to the landward', but with walls in the shape of a half octagon and four gun positions covering the jetty and port 'to protect from foreign invasion'. However, Fort Dundas and Fort Wellington were the only British Army fortifications built in Australia for protection from Aboriginal attack. Fort Dundas was rectangular, 75 by 50 yards (68 x 45 m) with walls 5 feet (1.5 m) thick at the base. The fort was surrounded by a ditch 10 feet deep and 15 feet wide (3 x 4.5 m) and was armed with two 9-pounder guns, one 12-pounder gun, and four 18-pounder guns, each provided with fifty rounds of round shot and eight rounds of grape-shot.[7] This ammunition came off HMS *Tamar*, but ammunition used on ships in this period was suitable for land warfare. Contemporary cannon could not sink wooden sailing ships so anti-personnel ammunition was used in naval warfare to incapacitate enough of the opposing crew so they were unable to man their ship.[8] The Fort Dundas garrison was commanded by Captain Maurice Barlow: it consisted of thirty-four members of the 3rd Regiment augmented by a Royal Marine detachment of twenty-seven commanded by Lieutenant Williams, a surgeon, two commissariat officers and forty convicts.[9]

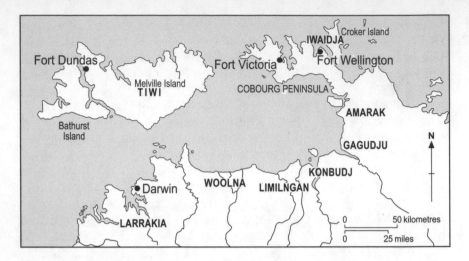

MAP 5.2
Tiwi and Iwaidja lands, 1824

SOURCES After David Horton (ed.), *The Encyclopaedia of Aboriginal Australia: Aboriginal & Torres Strait Islander history, society and culture*, 2 vols, Aboriginal Studies Press in association with the Australian Institute of Aboriginal and Torres Strait Islander Studies, Canberra, 1994, 2: 802; Collet Barker (eds John Mulvaney & Neville Green), *Commandant of Solitude: The Journals of Captain Collet Barker 1828–1831*, Melbourne University Press, Melbourne, 1992, p 40.

JMR Cameron gives a plausible reconstruction of Tiwi tactics during the period immediately after the British arrival. As soon as the British ships arrived offshore, the women and children of the Munupula band of the Tiwi went to safe havens and the men watched the British. While expecting the ships to sail away as others had in the past, the Munupula men took the precaution of beginning negotiations with the neighbouring Malauila, Minguila and Wilrangwila bands on combining, if necessary, to fight the invaders. When — with the construction of Fort Dundas — the British had made their intention of staying obvious, the Munupula confronted them on 25 October 1824. Deciding that a number of steel axes would be an appropriate recompense for the British trespass, they surrounded two men cutting timber and took their axes, and then went to Fort Dundas to demand the other axes they felt were due to them. Captain Bremer, who was still at the fort, gave them three more axes, so the Munupula men camped near the fort overnight with the expectation of receiving more axes in the morning. Bremer presented no further axes and then used the garrison, with bayonets fixed, to force the Munupula away. Following the British rebuff of the Munupula's efforts at negotiation, the Tiwi bands formed a combined force of about 100 warriors painted for war and, on 30 October, carried out a series of three coordinated ambushes on small British parties away from the fort. In the first, about sixty men ambushed five marines cutting grass. The marines responded to the Tiwi spears with musket fire and soon forced them to retreat. In the second, the Tiwi confronted sailors filling ship's casks with water, but they sensibly withdrew when they saw the British were armed. In the third, a midshipman and Corporal Gwillam of the Royal Marines were surrounded. Gwillam fired his musket, which enabled them to retreat to the shore, where the sailors were collecting water and all clambered into their boat to escape. The Tiwi pursued them to the beach, hurling spears, one of which grazed the midshipman. Gwillam fired at close range at the leading Tiwi warrior and killed him.[10]

This was just the beginning of a Tiwi campaign that would keep Fort Dundas under virtual siege for its entire existence. Corporal Gwillam was killed, probably in revenge for the Tiwi man he had shot. On 26 October 1826 a twenty-strong, painted Tiwi party ambushed two convicts, killing Julius Campbell and wounding Edward Lowther, and, as mentioned at the beginning of the chapter, Green and Gold were killed in November 1827. As well, the Tiwi 'constantly hovered through the forest', regularly raiding outbuildings and livestock. They speared pigs, drove away cattle, burnt haystacks and even scaled a 6-foot (1.8 m) fence to take clothes from the hospital.[11] The British posted sentries but, as Major Campbell (Barlow's successor as commandant) explained, the Tiwi were 'too cunning and warey for our vigilance'. Campbell's successor, Captain Humphrey Hartley was no doubt greatly relieved when he received the order to abandon Fort Dundas, while the Tiwi no doubt celebrated a great victory. Fort Dundas was doomed to fail from the very start. It was designed to trade with Macassan trepangers, but the Macassans had found the Tiwi so hostile that they avoided Melville Island. No praus visited Fort Dundas during its five-year existence.[12]

The second British outpost was established in Iwaidja country at Raffles Bay on 18 June 1827. As this was the anniversary of the Battle of Waterloo, the settlement was named Fort Wellington in honour of the British commander in that battle. The fort was hexagonal in shape with walls 7 feet (2 m) high with four 18-pounder cannons. Inside the walls was a tower 20 feet (6 m) high; outside the walls, the barracks were placed to protect the fort's flanks. The garrison consisted of soldiers and some soldiers' wives of the 39th Regiment, fourteen Royal Marines, a surgeon, a commissariat officer, a Malay interpreter and family, and twenty-two convicts. The commandant, Captain Henry Smyth of the 39th Regiment, was praised by Captain James Stirling, RN (soon to be the founder of

Perth), as 'a Gentleman of good sense, great zeal and experience'.[13] Sadly this would prove not to be the case.

From early on Smyth permitted his men to fire from the tower and walls at passing Iwaidja. On 28 July 1827 the Iwaidja gained their revenge by wounding Private James Taylor after he became separated from a fishing party. Smyth decided to do two things in reply: the first was to capture an Iwaidja and teach him or her English to enable communication; secondly, he decided to 'put a serious stop' to the Iwaidja's 'growing audacity'. On 30 July Smyth, in the only known use by the British Army of artillery on the Australian frontier[14], ordered a round to be fired from an 18-pounder cannon at Iwaidja gathered around the fort. The Iwaidja fled, and though Smyth had sent troops out to capture one or more, they failed to outflank the Iwaidja. The soldiers did fire into the panicked crowd running past, and killed one and wounded others. Not surprisingly, the Iwaidja did not approach Fort Wellington for several months.[15]

During August 1827 scurvy and other diseases broke out in the fort, and illness may have begun to impair Smyth's judgement. In September he erected a sign at the head of Raffles Bay because he was afraid supply ships would not find Fort Wellington's 'sequestered position'. He ordered more muskets from Sydney even though the garrison already had enough. Doctor Cornelius Wood became ill and tried to commit suicide before finally succumbing to fever on 15 October. With no medical officer, the garrison's health declined even further. Lieutenant William Coke of the 39th Regiment wrote that five men, evacuated from Fort Wellington owing to illness, arrived in Sydney 'reduced to skeletons & cripples'.[16]

The low point of Smyth's command came when, having issued an order that he would give a £5 bounty to any individual or group who could capture an Aborigine, he allowed an armed group of three convicts and three soldiers to go out on 28 December 1827. Seeing some Iwaidja in a canoe offshore, the armed group trailed them until they landed and went to a campsite, where there were about sixty people. The British decided to drive the Iwaidja towards the beach to enable their capture. They waited until about 2:00 AM, when the three soldiers, Privates Charles Miller, John Norton and Thomas Smith, went forward and fired into the sleeping camp. A few men threw spears in reply and then the two convicts with muskets stepped forward and fired their muskets. The Iwaidja ran towards their canoes to escape. The convict James Murray ran to the beach and saw a woman trying to bring two children, one of whom was wounded, to the safety of the canoes. He bayoneted the woman. The wounded child soon died. There was also a man on the beach with a stomach wound. The British party decided, in the words of Private Charles Miller, that it was 'better to put him out of his misery at once' and killed him. Firing occasionally into the night to cover their retreat, they returned to Fort Wellington with their one captive. This was a six-year-old girl called Riveral, who Smyth renamed 'Mary Waterloo Raffles'.[17]

Both the New South Wales governor and the British Colonial Secretary rebuked Smyth when they heard what he had done. Governor Darling had Smyth relieved in April 1828, ostensibly on grounds of ill-health, while Sir George Murray wrote that Smyth had done wrong both 'to the unfortunate people, whose lives have been taken away, and to the honor of the British name'.[18] Lieutenant George Sleeman of the 39th Regiment acted as commandant until the arrival, on 13 September 1828, of Captain Collet Barker of the same regiment.

Barker brought an immediate change to Fort Wellington. He addressed the garrison on 'the importance of avoiding cruelty towards the natives'. He ensured the issue of lime-juice and the men's health improved. Most remarkable was the way he turned British–Iwaidja relations around. On 25 November Barker made contact with an Iwaidja man called Merriak. By 7 December Merriak and others were sufficiently convinced of Barker's good intentions that they came into the settlement. On 14 December Barker reciprocated by visiting Merriak's camp, though the Iwaidja did not recognise him when he first arrived because he had changed from his uniform into a more casual 'Flannel cricket jacket and straw Hat'. On 29 January 1829 relations had improved so much that two men named Alobo and Mago came into the settlement and entertained the British with an evening of singing, dancing and didgeridoo playing, probably the first time any Europeans had heard the instrument.[19]

Macassan praus visited Fort Wellington during the 1828 and 1829 trepanging seasons. One man named Pamoono told Barker that he had been to Singapore and 'described it as like this with respect to the number of Europeans, but the bay was full of Junks and Proas [praus]'. However, Fort Wellington would never get the chance to develop into a second Singapore. The British government decided that there was no 'prospect of advantage sufficiently strong to warrant a continuance of the Expense and risk of life', and Barker received orders to abandon Raffles Bay on 21 July 1829. He ordered a Union Jack be nailed to the Fort Wellington flag-pole as the garrison sailed away on 29 August.[20] The final British attempt at a northern trading port was in 1838 with the establishment of Fort Victoria on Port Essington. This, too, would end in failure — in 1845.[21]

Barker's next posting was as commandant at King George Sound in Western Australia. A British outpost had been established here in 1826 to prevent the French claiming territory. As mentioned in chapter 2, King George Sound was a peaceful 'beachhead frontier', where there were good relations between the members of the small British settlement and the local Minang people.[22] Barker continued this policy, even issuing an order on 15 November 1830 banning the mention of deceased Aborigines' names so as to respect Minang beliefs. Barker was later ordered to explore the mouth of the Murray River; there, on 30 April 1831, some Njarrindjeri men mistook Barker for one of the sealers who had been abducting Njarrindjeri women and killed him.[23]

The second British settlement in Western Australia was established with the founding of Perth on 12 August 1829, and it was British expansion from here that led to the outbreak of frontier warfare in Western Australia. The traditional owners of the Perth area were the Wajuk, who like the Minang and the other Aborigines of the southwest, all spoke dialects of the Nyungar language (see map 5.3).[24] There was little violence in the first years of the Swan River colony, but fighting began when the British began encroaching on Aboriginal land. The Wajuk's staple food was a type of yam; but, as the settler Robert Lyon wrote, by 1833: 'Most of the places where this grows are now in the occupation of the settlers'.[25]

The Nyungar peoples continued to practise traditional Aboriginal warfare[26], and occasionally groups asked the British to form alliances against other Aborigines.[27] The Nyungar peoples also included the British in their system of revenge attacks. When Domjim of the Wajuk was shot at Fremantle on 29 April 1833, Yagan avenged his death by leading an ambush on the Velvick brothers as they accompanied a cart into the bush. The British posted a reward for Yagan, and William and James Keates, eighteen and thirteen years old respectively, killed Yagan for the reward money. William was also killed in the fight, and, while young James received the money, he was sent from the colony to prevent his becoming the victim of a Wajuk revenge attack.[28]

The Nyungar peoples also developed new tactics to fight the British in frontier warfare. As Lyon wrote, the Aborigines 'carry on the war against us in the [agricultural] heart of the settlement, after their own manner, not only with the spear, but the torch; that most dangerous of all weapons in a country so full of combustibles'. They tried to drive settlers off their land by spearing sheep and cattle, with a woman apparently leading one sheep raid at York in February 1833.[29] They set fire to houses and haystacks. Raiding parties of thirty or fifty warriors took flour and potatoes, sometimes escaping with remarkable hauls. On one occasion two men managed to take

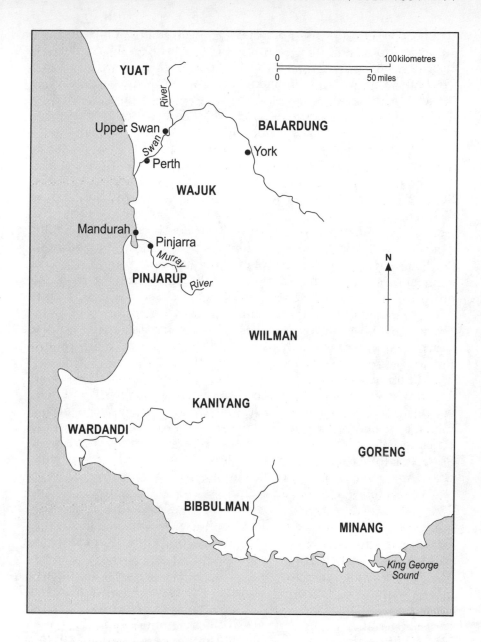

MAP 5.3
Nyungar lands, 1829

SOURCE After David Horton (ed.), *The Encyclopaedia of Aboriginal Australia: Aboriginal & Torres Strait Islander history, society and culture*, 2 vols, Aboriginal Studies Press in association with the Australian Institute of Aboriginal and Torres Strait Islander Studies, Canberra, 1994, 2: 1011.

2 hundredweight (102 kg) of potatoes; on another, a Pinjarup raiding party from the Murray River came to Perth on 24 April 1834 and took 980 pounds (444 kg) of flour from George Shenton's windmill. This was a well-planned and well-executed attack. The Pinjarup had carefully observed the mill beforehand; they tried to draw Shenton out of the mill before the raid by offering him some freshly baked damper, and, though the Pinjarup warriors held Shenton down while they plundered the flour, they did not harm him.[30]

The flour-mill raid was part of an ongoing conflict between the Pinjarup and the British. The first British death in the Swan River Colony had been when Pinjarup men killed nineteen-year-old George Mackenzie on the Murray River south of Perth in 1830. Thomas Peel, a driving force in founding the colony and cousin of the British Home Secretary, Robert Peel, attempted to occupy land upstream on the Murray River and Stirling provided a garrison to protect him. When this settlement failed, Peel and the troops withdrew to Mandurah at the mouth of the river. In July 1832 the Pinjarup had wounded a soldier of the 63rd Regiment on the Murray, which led to a British punitive expedition in which five Pinjarup were killed and many wounded.[31]

The immediate British response to the flour-mill raid was to send a detachment of troops to the Murray under cover of darkness, which arrested the Pinjarup leader Calyute and some other Pinjarup men for the raids. After the detachment's return to Perth, two of the Pinjarup who were in their late teens, Yeydong and Gummol, were flogged; another man, Wamba, was immediately pardoned; Calyute was held for about six weeks, however, before he was released.[32]

On 24 July 1834 the Pinjarup led Private Hugh Nesbit of the 21st Regiment and Edward Barron, an ex-soldier, into an ambush while claiming to help them find a lost horse. Nesbit was killed while Barron barely escaped with his life, riding to safety with three spears sticking out of him. The superintendent of Natives, Captain Theophilus Tighe Ellis (formerly of the 14th Dragoons), led a party to capture the men Barron identified as taking part in the attack, but it was unsuccessful.[33]

In September 1834 Governor Stirling announced that he would 'extend protection and assistance' to enable Peel to make another attempt to occupy land upstream on the Murray.[34] Stirling was able to make this offer because he now had the military resources to take the fight to the Pinjarup on their own land. From the colony's foundation (in 1829) to 1833 the garrison — consisting of just one company of the 63rd Regiment, with sixty-four officers and men — had been totally over-stretched. In 1832 Stirling had even proposed asking the Cape Colony in South Africa to send a Cape Mounted Rifles detachment to help defeat Aboriginal attacks. However, on 14 September 1833 the garrison doubled when the 63rd Regiment company was replaced with two companies of the 21st Regiment, consisting of six officers, eight NCOs, and 116 other ranks.[35] As well, around September 1834 Stirling established the Western Australian Mounted Police. Unlike the Mounted Police in New South Wales and Van Diemen's Land, the Western Australian unit was not recruited from the British garrison. This was probably because the 21st Regiment could not spare any men, though at least some of the initial intake were former soldiers of the 63rd Regiment who had taken their discharge in the colony. While the new constables were still training, the *Perth Gazette* commented that the Mounted Police would be a 'a most essential protection to the colonists against the attacks of the Natives'.[36]

On 25 October 1834 Stirling went south with a party to meet Peel. Windschuttle has written that the only reason for Stirling's expedition was to arrest the Pinjarup men who had killed Nesbit, but Stirling also intended to establish an outpost on the Murray to protect Peel's planned settlement. He waited for the two corporals and eight privates who were to form the garrison to arrive with wagons carrying their supplies, and then headed towards the Murray on 27 October.[37] After camping overnight, Stirling's party of twenty-five, which included Peel, Captain Ellis and five mounted policemen as well as the soldiers, arrived at Pinjarra early on the morning of 28 October. Here, as the *Perth Gazette* wrote, the British had an 'encounter with the Natives of the Murray'.[38]

The choice of word used to describe the 'encounter' at Pinjarra has become controversial in itself. George Moore, the Western Australian advocate-general used the term 'battle of Pinjarra' in his diary entry of 1 November 1834; while some historians have followed Moore and used 'battle', others have described it as a 'massacre'.[39] As we will see, to call Pinjarra a 'massacre' denies recognition of the Pinjarup warriors' heroic actions. The best analysis of the day's events is provided by Geoff Blackburn in his history of the 21st Regiment in Western Australia.[40] The British party had just crossed the ford on Murray River where they intended to establish the military outpost when they realised there was a Pinjarup camp on the side of the river they had just left.

Stirling ordered Ellis to take Norcott, the Mounted Police officer, and three constables to recross the ford and ride towards the camp, while the rest of the party quickly spread out along an 800-metre frontage of the river (see map. 5.4). As Ellis's small party rode towards the camp of about seventy Pinjarup, Norcott recognised Noonar, who was wanted for killing Private Nesbit. The fighting began with Noonar throwing a spear at Norcott, who shot back at

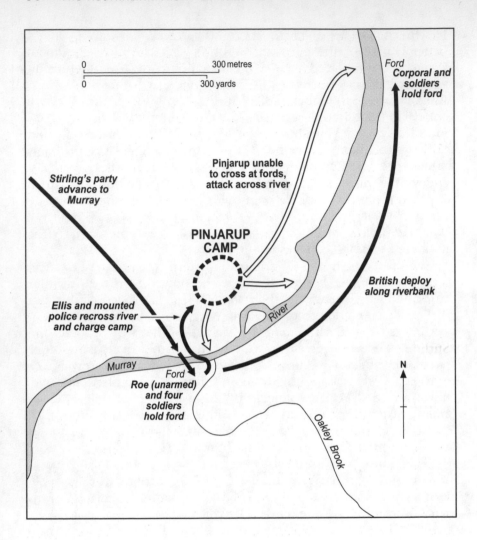

MAP 5.4
Pinjarra encounter, 28 October 1834

SOURCE After Geoff Blackburn, *Conquest and Settlement: The 21st Regiment of Foot (North British Fusiliers) in Western Australia 1833–1840*, Perth, Hesperian Press, 1999, p 58.

Noonar. Ellis's party galloped into the camp, but the Pinjarup got the better of the initial encounter. Of the five men who had charged, the Pinjarup unhorsed three, including Ellis, who later died of his wounds. The normal Aboriginal reaction to the appearance of a British punitive party would have been to evade them. The Pinjarup could have easily escaped into the bush away from the British. However, on this morning, the Pinjarup chose not to. They could see Stirling's men on the other side of the Murray, lining the bank about 40 metres apart. It appears that, having seen off Ellis's mounted charge, the Pinjarup decided, as Stirling later told Moore, that they were 'in a position which I dare say the natives thought was most favourable for their manœuvres'. Stirling had laid a trap for them but the Pinjarup, by bravely crossing the river to attack the British, chose to enter it. Neville Green writes that the mounted British party 'pressed the stragglers towards the river'; but, as only two of the men were still on their horses, it seems unlikely they could have forced a large number of people in a direction against their will.[41]

The Pinjarup ran to the fords to cross the Murray, but found that Stirling had posted blocking parties at these choke points. When Stirling's men opened fire, the Pinjarup jumped into the river and hid among the tree roots and branches, looking for opportunities to hurl spears at the British. This was a serious mistake, as taking a static position in frontier warfare surrenders the initiative to one's enemy.[42] With the Pinjarup caught in the river, the British systematically shot at the bobbing heads until Stirling decided that 'sufficient punishment' had been inflicted and ordered the bugler to call cease fire. Stirling was moved by the Pinjarup's bravery and informed the Colonial Secretary: 'The natives very resolutely stood their ground'. Within days someone in the colony had written a song about the action: unfortunately, the words have not survived but it was entitled 'The Jackets of Green', after the uniforms of the Mounted Police.[43]

There are two questions that arise about Pinjarra: how many Pinjarup were killed? and is the encounter best described as a 'battle' or a 'massacre'? Contemporary British estimates of Aboriginal casualties ranged from fifteen to thirty-five. Considering that the camp was reported to have held about seventy people, casualties in this order would have been devastating to the Pinjarup. The journalist Tom Austen also refers to a figure of about eighty killed, mentioned by Jane Elizabeth Grose in 1927 based on childhood memories of her parents' conversations. While Aboriginal traditions refer to deaths in their hundreds, these numbers should be seen more as symbolising the disastrous effect of Pinjarra on the Murray River Aborigines than as a realistic assessment of the size of an average Pinjarup camp.[44]

In deciding whether Pinjarra was a 'battle' or a 'massacre', it is useful to look at Bill Thorpe's definition of these words. Thorpe argues three points about the word 'battle'. The first is that an encounter in which one side is armed with guns and the other with spears cannot be a 'battle'. The second is that the word 'battle' implies 'a more or less equivalent struggle between contending forces'. The third is that an action in which one side's casualties are much higher than the other cannot be a 'battle', with Thorpe posing the question: 'If, for example, one group of combatants happens to be mown down in the line of fire, however, "bravely" or "valiantly" they have fought, is it appropriate simply to refer to this as a "battle"?'.[45]

All of these definitions of 'battle' can be refuted using historical examples. While British soldiers mostly armed with Martini-Henry rifles inflicted many casualties on Zulu warriors mostly armed with *iklwa* stabbing spears during the Zulu War of 1879, I am not aware of any claims that either Isandhlwana (a Zulu victory) or Rorke's Drift (a British victory) is not a 'battle'. To argue that battles are only fought when forces are evenly matched goes against the aim of generals to make battles as one-sided as possible in their own favour. During the landings at Balikpapan in Borneo in July 1945, the Australian commander, Major-General Edward Milford, used the Allied superiority in firepower to his advantage against the Japanese defenders. This landing is a 'battle' even though it was preceded by a twenty-day naval and air bombardment, the longest of any Second World War amphibious landing. Finally, a battle is still a 'battle' even if one group of combatants suffers many more casualties than the other. The Turks lost no men, while 372 out of 600 Australians were killed or wounded during the attack on the Nek in August 1915, but again I am not aware of any claims that this event, though tragic, is not a 'battle'.[46]

Thorpe, in an article written with Raymond Evans, argues 'that a "battle" (particularly between technologically uneven forces) can turn into a "rout" and then a "massacre"'. However, this claim relies on a loose definition of 'massacre' as meaning nothing more than 'killing a large number of people'. A better definition is provided by Broome, who writes that a 'massacre' is the 'mass killing of defenceless [people]'. Broome's definition means that killing armed people in combat, like the attack at the Nek, is not a 'massacre', but killing unarmed civilians or disarmed prisoners-of-war is. The settler killing of unarmed Aborigines at Myall Creek in 1838 (see chapter 7) and the Japanese killing of about 160 Australian prisoners at Tol Plantation near Rabaul in January 1942 are rightly known as massacres.[47] While the British killed non-combatants at Pinjarra, it was as part of a fight with Pinjarup warriors which can legitimately be described as a 'battle'.

Grassby and Hill's account of the Battle of Pinjarra has the men of the 21st Regiment wondering why the Aborigines did not try to surrender. This is just a piece of imaginative description, as there is no evidence of what the troops were thinking; but it raises two points. The first is that we do not know whether the Pinjarup had a concept of surrendering during a battle, or whether warriors in this situation had a duty to fight to the death. The second is that, as Mark Johnston has shown for the Australian Army in the Second World War, in the heat of battle soldiers often kill enemy combatants trying to surrender. Governor Stirling reported that his men stopped shooting when he signalled them to do so; considering that the Pinjarup had recently killed their comrade Private Nesbit, it would not be surprising, however, if the troops kept firing for a time after the cease-fire had been called.[48]

After the devastating losses of Pinjarra, the Pinjarup met with Governor Stirling for negotiations in March 1835. The next main theatre for frontier fighting in Western Australia was around York on the Avon River. The York garrison originally consisted of only eight men, but after a number of farm raids by the Wajuk and the Balardung, it was increased in July 1836 to an officer's command with a sergeant and thirty-five other ranks, and Lieutenant Henry Bunbury was sent from Perth with orders 'to make war upon the natives'. Bunbury's men were scattered on farms along the Avon River on an 80-kilometre front. With continual attacks, more troops were sent, and by 1837 one-third of the Western Australian garrison was stationed around York.[49]

This was only the beginning of decades of conflict in the West. The Avon River would be contested into the 1840s, while frontier warfare would continue in Western Australia into the twentieth century.[50]

6

VAN DIEMEN'S LAND, 1826–1831

On the lazy summer Sunday afternoon of 21 February 1830 three Big River warriors lay still and silent on the tree-lined hills above John Sherwin's property on the Clyde River in Van Diemen's Land. Two other Big River men were already hidden on the other side of the narrow valley. Once they were in position they knew it was simply a matter of waiting patiently for the right moment to attack. Following lunch, Sherwin's family and his assigned convicts stayed around or inside the house and the separate servants' quarters. Now was the time. A Big River man bearing a fiery torch ran from cover and sprinted across the cleared fields towards the farm buildings. His two comrades watched his perilous journey anxiously from the hill. He reached the buildings without detection and, going straight to the back of the farmhouse, set fire to the thatched roof before running to the back of the servants' quarters to set them alight as well. His mission accomplished, the Big River man began rushing back to the safety of the trees. It was only at this point that the settlers realised that they were under attack. A servant cried 'Fire!' and Sherwin, who had been in the front room of his house, ordered the men to draw water to douse the flames. Soon realising that it was futile to try to save the house, Sherwin ordered his men to carry out furniture and whatever else could be salvaged before the whole structure became an inferno. In the meantime, the Big River man who had carried out the incendiary attack reached safety, and the two men who had been with him now took torches and walked calmly along Sherwin's wooden fences, setting fires at intervals along their entire length. The two men on the far side of the Clyde came down to the riverbank and stood on a rock to provide cover for the men igniting the fence, who, as planned, completed their journey of destruction at the river, and crossed over to join their comrades. Distracted by trying to save what was left of his possessions, Sherwin only now noticed that his fences were in flames, and that the warriors on the far bank of the Clyde were dancing and shouting in English, 'Go away you white buggers — what business have you here?'. A servant grabbed a musket and ran to the river, but Sherwin, dazed and demoralised by the raid, shouted at him to come back. At this the Big River men called out to Sherwin that he was a coward and continued their dance. The raid was a masterpiece of surprise, in which the Big River men had used no weapons apart from their firesticks. Sherwin's family were forced to spend several undignified months living in the open while they rebuilt their house.[1] Between 1826 and 1830 Tasmanian Aborigines, especially the Big River people, used farmhouse raids like this to wage an effective war against British settlers. Van Diemen's Land saw some of the bitterest fighting of any Australian war, and the largest deployment of British troops to an Australian frontier, which culminated in Lieutenant-Governor George Arthur's[2] 'Black Line' operation of 1830.

For the first twenty years of the British colony, relations between the invaders and the Aborigines had been relatively peaceful. Some Aboriginal men enforced traditional law on settlers with ritual spearings; more often, shepherds and sealers abducted Aboriginal women and children to work as forced labour. Generally, though, the small size of the British enclaves around Hobart and Launceston meant the two sides were able to coexist. British-introduced disease devastated Aboriginal communities, but the British also brought dogs, flour and tea, which revolutionised Aboriginal life. Tasmanian Aborigines eagerly adopted all three, because dogs made hunting kangaroos easier and became watch-dogs at night guarding against attack, and flour and tea were tastier and more convenient than traditional foods.[3]

The frontier war began in earnest in Van Diemen's Land in the mid-1820s, when the British attempted to occupy all the limited amount of arable land on the island (almost two-thirds of Van Diemen's Land being rugged mountains). By 1823 land grants stretched in an unbroken line across the island from north to south (see map 6.1). Monpeliatta, a man of the Lairmairrener or Big River people, wryly commented that if Aborigines 'left any place to go ahunting elsewhere … when they returned in the course of eight days, they found a hut erected'. The French doctor Jean-René Quoy, who visited Hobart in 1827, wrote: 'A sort of war to the death … has broken out between the English and the natives'.[4] As Plomley's study of Aboriginal–settler clashes in Van Diemen's Land shows (see table 6.1), the number of incidents rose steeply in 1827.

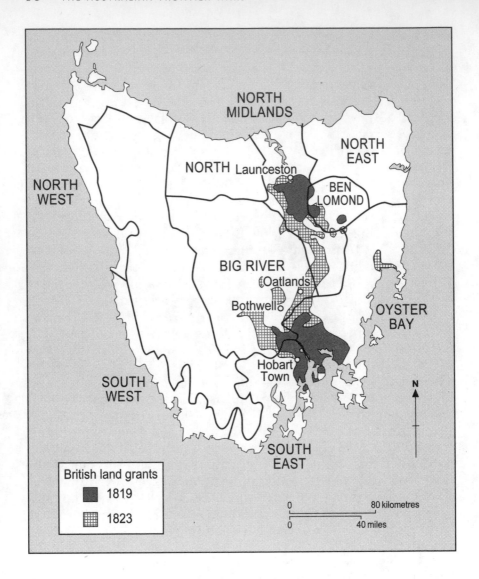

MAP 6.1
Van Diemen's Land: Aboriginal lands and British expansion

SOURCES After Lyndall Ryan, *The Aboriginal Tasmanians*, 2nd edn [1981], Allen & Unwin, Sydney, 1996, p 15; Sharon Morgan, *Land Settlement in Early Tasmania: Creating an Antipodean England*, Cambridge University Press, Cambridge, 1992, pp 18, 21.

TABLE 6.1
ABORIGINAL–SETTLER CLASHES, VAN DIEMEN'S LAND: 1824–31[5]

Year	Number of incidents
1824	11
1825	14
1826	24
1827	72
1828	144
1829	148
1830	222
1831	6

The casualty estimates for the Vandemonian war made by the Ryan in *The Aboriginal Tasmanians* and Reynolds in *Fate of a Free People* differ but they illustrate three main trends. The first is that between one-and-a-half and four times as many Aborigines were killed as settlers. Ryan estimates that the Big River people killed sixty settlers and settlers killed 240 Big River people between 1824 and 1831, and that a total of 700 Aborigines were killed over the entire frontier between 1804 to 1831. Reynolds suggested in 1987 that 800 Aborigines were killed on the frontier, but now both he and Windschuttle believe that Ryan's total number is too high. Reynolds estimates that between 250 and 400 Tasmanian Aborigines and 170 British settlers were killed during the 1804–31 period, making the ratio of British to Aboriginal deaths between 1:1.47 and 1:2.35. Windschuttle estimates the ratio to be 1:1.6.[6] The second casualty trend is that the number of settlers killed each year between 1828 and 1830 did not increase even though the number of Aboriginal raids increased, showing that the Aboriginal tactic was to take goods rather than kill people. As settler Roderic O'Connor commented at the time, the raiders 'were more anxious to plunder than to murder'. The third trend is that, by contrast, the number of Aborigines killed rose dramatically in the middle of the 1820s, indicating that the settlers' response to the increasing number of Aboriginal raids was deadly retaliation.[7]

One soldier of the 40th Regiment pleaded with settlers not to kill 'the poor natives' because he had been unhappy ever since he had taken part in a punitive expedition, but others felt no such remorse. George Augustus Robinson wrote that William Gunshannon, who murdered several Aborigines on the west coast had an 'astonishing' indifference to his crime.[8] The wealthy landowning settlers overlooked the fact that their occupation of Aboriginal land was the cause of the conflict and blamed all violence against Aborigines on 'bushrangers, run-away Convicts and others of a dissolute & desperate character'.[9] Lieutenant-Governor Arthur hanged four Aboriginal men in 1825 and 1826 for murdering settlers, but no settler in Van Diemen's Land, not even a serial killer like Gunshannon, was ever charged, let alone tried for the murder of Aborigines — though when Gunshannon was speared in 1830 Robinson commented that 'the justice of God was apparent in this instance'.[10]

Some Tasmanian Aborigines united to fight the British[11], but traditional warfare continued. The Committee for the Care of Captured Aborigines, taking evidence on the frontier war, was told in 1830 that Aborigines fought each other at the same time they were fighting settlers, and the Ben Lomond and Big River peoples continued their 'determined hostilities' against each other even when they were both at the Flinders Island mission in the mid-1830s.[12] Revenge attacks on settlers continued alongside farmhouse raids and remained the predominant form of attack in the north of the colony. In one incident, two settlers were attacked but their hut was left untouched. In another, a man at Piper's Lagoon was speared and clubbed to death in punishment for burning an Aboriginal woman to death.[13] Settlers told stories of Tasmanian Aboriginal women exacting revenge for settler brutality by torturing wounded men 'with sharp stones upon secret parts'.[14]

Aboriginal warriors continued to use their traditional spears and clubs because they could be easily manufactured. When Tasmanian Aboriginal men needed spears, they had only to find a stand of ti-tree, select the best pieces, straighten them in a camp-fire and create a spear-point by sharpening one end. Aborigines pursued by British parties could always abandon their weapons to aid their escape, knowing that they could quickly make replacements.[15] Plomley calculates that spears were used in 77 per cent of Aboriginal attacks from 1824 to 1831.[16] However, the point of the Tasmanian spear was not barbed, so the wound it inflicted was rarely mortal. There are examples of British men and women who, on being speared, pulled out the weapon and then used it against their assailants![17] Plomley estimates that clubs were used in only about 20 per cent of attacks, but this was the weapon most used to kill settlers.[18]

By the 1820s Tasmanian Aborigines had a thorough knowledge of British firearms and had some in their possession. Aboriginal women, through their contact with sealers, were an important conduit of information on firearms. Tasmanian Aborigines learned to rush settlers after they had fired muskets and before they could reload. Robinson recorded an Aboriginal song about stealing muskets from the settlers and concealing them, and Plomley believes that this concealment of firearms was an end in itself, as it prevented their further use against Aborigines.[19] However, at least some firearms were kept for future use. Aborigines carefully stored these weapons to prevent rust and made replacement flints for them.[20]

Tasmanian Aborigines used firearms for three purposes. The first and, according to Reynolds, the most common use was for hunting. A blunderbuss, with its barrel designed to scatter small shot, was a favourite for hunting birds.[21] The second use for firearms was in inter-tribal warfare. Robinson lists several incidents where Aborigines used or threatened to use firearms against other Aborigines.[22] The final and least common use was in frontier warfare. Aborigines fired at stockmen in November 1827 and brandished guns in a raid on a hut in October 1831, but the only known incident in which a Tasmanian Aborigine used a firearm and it led to a settler's death took place in September 1831, when some Big River men attacked James Parker, a farm overseer, near Port Sorell. One of the men stole Parker's gun and shot him with it, after which Parker was speared to death.[23]

Fighting the frontier war required the Tasmanian Aborigines to change many aspects of their daily life. To avoid detection they abandoned traditional campsites and tracks and established hidden sanctuaries and new pathways which hugged high wooded ridges or scrub-covered gullies. Blankets became prized items in farmhouse raids as using them to keep warm at night avoided the need for fires which might disclose a camp's location to British patrols.[24]

While the number of Aboriginal raids increased during the late 1820s, this increase was not uniform over the entire frontier. In northern Van Diemen's Land there was no change and the increase took place mainly in the Big River people's lands around Bothwell and Oatlands[25], because the terrain here was especially conducive to farmhouse raids. Unlike the areas of Van Diemen's Land first occupied by settlers, the Bothwell and Oatlands districts consisted of a series of narrow river valleys. The farms were small pockets of cleared land on the valley floors enclosed by forest, or as Sherwin's Clyde River farm was described at the time, 'a sequestered meadow surrounded with hills'.[26] As settlers advanced into these valleys they created farms in exposed positions impossible to defend from Aboriginal raids. The tree-covered ridges provided cover for raiding parties, while the narrow width of the valleys made it possible for them to cross the cleared ground and reach farmhouses before settlers could react. The valleys also isolated each settler from their neighbour over the ridge, enabling Aboriginal raiding parties to create a local numerical superiority against a particular farm. Raiding parties returned to farms again and again. Sherwin's farm, for example, was attacked four times in the ten months between August 1829 and May 1830.[27] The frequent raids on the Clyde forced some settlers to flee from their properties and ask for land grants in a less exposed area. Lieutenant Henry Boden Torlesse, after being raided several times on the Clyde, asked to exchange his grant for one closer to the protection of the town of Hamilton, adding 'Mrs Torlesse being in so very an uneasy state of mind, our lives are really in jeopardy'.[28]

Aboriginal raids were most prevalent in late spring and early summer and, as table 6.2 shows, the most common form of attack was the farmhouse raid. Women played an important role in spying on farms, and one woman, Walyer, led attacks in the north of the colony armed with a blunderbuss. Raiding parties generally consisted of between twenty and fifty warriors, and most raids were completed without resorting to violence. Of the sixteen farmhouse raids referred to in table 6.2, only two involved the wounding of settlers. A variety of goods was taken ranging from flour and tea to blankets and muskets. Tasmanian Aborigines killed entire flocks of sheep to destroy settlers' livelihoods and during the dry summer months torched farmhouses, other farm buildings and fences.[29]

TABLE 6.2
ABORIGINAL ATTACKS, BY TYPE: 1 JANUARY – 9 MARCH 1830[30]

Type of attack	Number of attacks
Farmhouse raids	16
Farmhouse / buildings burnt	6
Attacks on sheep	2 (120 sheep killed)
Settlers killed	7
Settlers wounded	6

Settlers tried to protect themselves by fortifying their huts. Robinson described one of the huts on George Espie's property as: 'like most stock huts, a formidable construction. It is made by piling large solid logs horizontally upon each other halved together at the ends, with portholes to fire out of. The roof is barked and covered in turf so as not to ignite.'[31] Bob Scott, Espie's overseer, withstood a day-long siege at this hut on his own. He kept off the attack by continually changing his clothes to make it seem like there was more than one man in the hut.[32]

The settlers made demands for the garrison to be used to protect them and their property. Lieutenant-Governor George Arthur had previously deployed troops in aid to the civil power during a spate of bushranging in 1825, and his first response to the frontier war was to use the same tactics that had defeated the bushrangers.[33] On 29 November 1826 he ordered the troops stationed in the inland military districts (soon renamed police districts) to begin operations against Aboriginal raiding parties. When Aboriginal raids increased, Arthur sent more troops and police to the police districts. John McMahon estimates that in 1827 up to 220 soldiers (out of a garrison of 712 other ranks) were deployed on the frontier.[34] The escalation in Aboriginal raids led first to Arthur's shrill proclamation on 15 April 1828 making it illegal for Aborigines to enter the settled districts, and finally to the declaration of martial law over parts of Van Diemen's Land on 1 November 1828.[35]

The military operations against the Aborigines placed a strain on both resources and men. The transport system was initially unable to supply the increased requirements at the inland military stations, and soldiers went short of clothing, boots and muskets.[36] Arthur understood the need to keep up the morale and discipline of troops scattered in small detachments. He asked officers to visit their men constantly, not only to 'minutely inquire into the conduct of the men', but also to make each soldier feel 'that his own individual efforts are essential towards the general security'.[37]

As on other frontiers, deploying small detachments of troops to defend farmhouses had limited success. In 1827 soldiers saved a settler family from a raiding party that had set fire to their hut, but in February 1830 a settler named Brodie on the Clyde River was raided and speared four times even though he was only 300 metres from a military outpost. His attackers escaped before troops arrived.[38] After visiting the frontier in 1830, Arthur reported to the British Colonial Secretary that 'unless a safety-guard were placed in every dwelling, a thing which is impossible', the 'only effectual security' was for settlers to defend themselves.[39]

Following the declaration of martial law, Arthur established two types of patrols to operate against Aboriginal raiding parties. There were combined patrols of soldiers and police known as 'Pursuing Parties', which operated throughout the area under martial law. In the Oatlands Police District, which bore the brunt of the fighting against the Big River people, the Pursuing Parties were joined by other patrols, which were civilian 'Roving Parties' organised by the police magistrate, Thomas Anstey.[40]

Pursuing Parties consisted of eight to ten men carrying fourteen to sixteen days' rations, who patrolled the bush to prevent the Aboriginal raiding parties attacking farms.[41] Pursuing Party tactics are shown by a patrol led by the settler Gilbert Robertson, which consisted of six soldiers of the 40th Regiment, three settlers and an Aboriginal guide. The party patrolled at night so it could find Aboriginal camps by looking for camp-fires. When the party saw a flickering light in bush near Little Swan Port, Robertson ordered three soldiers to each flank and advanced with the civilians in the centre. On reaching the fire, it was found to be a decoy, but from it a second fire could be seen about 100 metres away. Robertson stealthily circled around to the opposite side of this camp and then fired his musket to wake those sleeping around the fire and make them run away from the gunfire towards the rest of his party. Robertson's tactic was successful and one Aborigine was shot and the rest were captured.[42]

Pursuing Parties were unable to lay ambushes for raiding parties because they had little intelligence on which paths Aborigines took. Attempts were made to keep the natives 'in a constant state of alarm' by a regime of constant patrolling, but troop shortages meant this could not be sustained. Pursuing Parties were therefore reduced to generally futile attempts to track down Aboriginal parties after they had carried out attacks.[43]

The Pursuing Parties were criticised on several grounds. Officers and the colonial upper class doubted the ability of private soldiers to act effectively without officer supervision. Malcolm Laing Smith, the police magistrate at Norfolk Plains, wrote in 1827 that 'unless Military are judiciously stationed and commanded, at least by an intelligent non-commissioned officer and frequently visited by a Superior, I consider detachments of two or three men highly objectionable'.[44] The settler FGB Browne stated more bluntly: 'A Private Soldier without a leader, is like a man without a head'.[45] While it is true that soldiers were often uneducated and lacked initiative, this was not always the case. Private Charles Westwood of the 40th Regiment, an acting corporal in command of a detachment, was described by the police magistrate at Bothwell as 'a very steady and well behaved man', and used his initiative to investigate rumoured movements of Aborigines.[46] Even Browne found during his time in Pursuing Parties that soldiers retained their discipline on patrol.

Other criticisms of the Pursuing Parties were more valid. Combining soldiers with police, who in Van Diemen's Land were normally former convicts, led to argument within patrols as each group disliked the other. Soldiers were lazy in their pursuit of Aborigines. Gilbert Robertson complained that soldiers were useless because 'they will not exert themselves'. However, Browne explained that this was owing to the shortage of government-issue boots and clothing at the inland stations, which meant that the soldiers had to wear their own clothing on patrol. Understandably, they did not want to ruin their own meagre possessions 'running about the Hills after Blacks'. As well, the shortage of muskets at military stations meant that soldiers were required to have the weapon they had taken on patrol in a condition suitable for an inspection parade the next day, so they did not want to take their muskets on patrols, in which they would become battered or rusty. Browne noted that 'a slight shower or a heavy dew' always became 'the certain harbinger of complaint and disagreement' in a Pursuing Party. The wearing of bright clothing by soldiers (including, but not only, their red uniform jacket), the smoking of tobacco and the noise they made on patrol made Pursuing Parties highly visible and easy for Aborigines to avoid. Browne also pointed out that the long muzzle of Brown Bess muskets made them 'very inconvenient in the Bush' and suggested that smaller carbines or muskets with shortened barrels be issued.[47]

Most of the criticisms made against the Pursuing Parties could also be made of Anstey's all-civilian Roving Parties operating out of Oatlands. The aim of the Roving Parties was to capture Aborigines, but in the two years from November 1828 to November 1830, only thirty — just over one a month — were captured.[48] The report of the Aborigines Committee commented that these parties, like the Pursuing Parties, showed 'great want of caution' while on patrol.[49]

In December 1829 Arthur told Anstey that he felt 'much discouraged at the total want of success of all the parties who have been employed ... against the Aborigines' and in February 1830, Arthur revived the Committee for the Care of Captured Aborigines to review the conflict and made a public appeal for suggestions on how to defeat the Aboriginal attacks. Suggestions in response to Arthur's appeal ranged from the introduction of rewards for the capture of Aborigines (which Arthur instituted) to the importation of hunting dogs, which would '*Set* the natives as they would a Quail!'. The latter suggestion was not taken up.[50]

In April 1830 the British Colonial Secretary, Sir George Murray, wrote to Arthur laying the blame for the frontier conflict in Van Diemen's Land squarely with the settlers and demanded that all settlers who killed Aborigines should be put on trial.[51] Murray's analysis of the cause of the fighting was sound, and his call for Arthur to enforce the law commendable. However, Murray's letter met with a hostile reaction when it arrived in Hobart Town in August. During the year, the number of Aboriginal raids had risen dramatically and at least fifteen settlers had been killed.[52] The prominent settlers of the Van Diemen's Land Executive Council told Arthur on 27 August that settlers were only doing what was necessary to defend their farms, and that it would be 'extremely impolitic' to try settlers for killing Aborigines. Arthur himself was a humane man who later wrote that he regretted that the British had not negotiated a treaty with the Aborigines when they first arrived. While superintendent of British Honduras he had fought the slaveholders over the rights of their slaves, and perhaps the bitter experience of that defeat led him to conclude that he could not oppose the settlers on this issue.[53]

Arthur decided that he had to take the initiative to end the frontier war or else the settlers would destroy the Aborigines in a 'War of Extermination'. On 27 August 1830 the Executive Council agreed that Arthur should call on the civilian population to join the military and the police in a large-scale operation — which became known as the 'Black Line' — to capture and remove all the Aborigines from the settled districts.[54] Arthur commissioned Major Sholto Douglas of the 63rd Regiment as a justice of the peace so he would have both the civil and military authority to command a combined force and called for volunteers on 9 September.

The origin of the 'Black Line' can be found in Arthur's 1828 comment that 'if sufficient force could be found', it would be possible to 'occupy the country by Parts' and capture the Aborigines.[55] Others — such as William Gray, a former major, and John Helder Wedge, a surveyor — proposed plans similar to the 'Black Line', but the idea of using civilians to create a line stretching across the colony appears to have been Arthur's alone.[56] The Van Diemen's Land garrison of fewer than 1000 men was, according to Arthur, 'quite unequal' for the task; if civilian volunteers could be used to augment the troops, however, Arthur felt he could put his plan into effect. The 'Black Line' was a very simple concept (see map 6.2). Parties would form on the northern and western ends of the settled districts and advance across the colony, driving the Aborigines into the Forestier and Tasman peninsulas, which would become a reservation from where they would be unable to escape.[57]

Calling for volunteers from the civilian population (a *levée en masse*) is not unusual, but the use of a human line to clear the enemy from an area of land was. The closest comparisons in recent history are the British Army's mounted drives against the Boers during the South African War (1899–1902) and the Indonesian Army's use of long lines of coerced civilians, known as 'human fences' to disturb guerillas during the Darul Islam uprising in west Java in 1960 and during the occupation of East Timor.[58]

The call for a *levée en masse* caused much excitement in the colony. Free settlers volunteered both for the 'Black Line' and for temporary militias formed in Launceston and Hobart, which took over military duties and enabled troops to be released for the operation.[59] Colonial Auditor GTWB Boyes wrote how 'Clerks in public Offices have put the knapsack upon their backs, rations in their pouches and guns upon their shoulders and have marched in charge of ten or twelve men, each to the destined scene of action'.[60] Ticket-of-leave convicts were compelled by the governor to either join the line or provide a substitute, and Melville described the parties taking part in the 'Black Line' as 'a curious melange of masters and servants'.[61]

Arthur soon had 2200 men with which to commence the operation. The majority were civilians, to which were added a few police and 550 troops of the 63rd, 57th and 17th Regiments (out of a total garrison of 965 officers and men). As the British population of the Van Diemen's Land was only 22,556 people[62], Arthur was intending to deploy and supply for an extended period in the field a force equivalent to 10 per cent of the colony's population.

Arthur was able to mobilise the civilian infrastructure of the colony for this military operation because he was both colonial governor and commander of the military garrison.[63] Two civilian organisations, the Survey Department and the Commissariat[64], played a vital role in planning the 'Black Line' and organising its supply. The chief surveyor, George Frankland, was a former army officer and worked as Arthur's staff officer, becoming so intimately involved in the detail of the operation that some referred to it as 'Mr Frankland's Plan'. The assistant surveyors worked with officers and police magistrates to devise the best lines of march for the various parties[65], while the Commissariat — which normally supplied the garrison and the large convict population — drew on its ample stocks of clothing to dress the civilian volunteers. The thick bush would tear clothing to shreds so jackets and shoes were taken out of store by the hundreds and an extra 640 pairs of trousers were specially made by the inmates of the female prison.[66]

The planning for the 'Black Line' showed the importance of logistics to British frontier warfare. Arthur ordered that only two out of every five men should be armed, so that 'the remaining three can very advantageously assist their comrades in carrying provisions &c'.[67] In accordance with this ratio, nine hundred muskets were issued. Civilians joining the Line were most unhappy to find that most of them would not be armed. The police constable at Bagdad, just north of Hobart Town, found that the local men 'positively refuse to turn out unless they have Arms' and pleaded for a cartload of muskets and pistols to be sent.[68]

On 1 October 1830 Arthur extended martial law to the whole of Van Diemen's Land, so as to enable the 'active and extended system of military operations against the Natives'. Following some preliminary patrols on 4 October[69], the 'Black Line' commenced its advance on a 120-mile (195 km) front on 7 October. The force was divided into three divisions — commanded by Major Douglas of the 63rd Regiment, and Captain D'arcey Wentworth of the 63rd and Captain VY Donaldson of the 57th — with each division being divided into corps commanded by army officers. Civilians were organised into parties of ten with leaders chosen by the local magistrates, but were ultimately under military command. The parties moved forward in extended order with no attempt at stealth. The aim was to 'beat the bush in a systematic manner' and drive the Aborigines ahead of them towards the coast. To ensure each party kept to its line of advance, Arthur allocated each a number and ordered that they continually confirm their relative position by shouting their number, firing muskets and blowing bugles.[70]

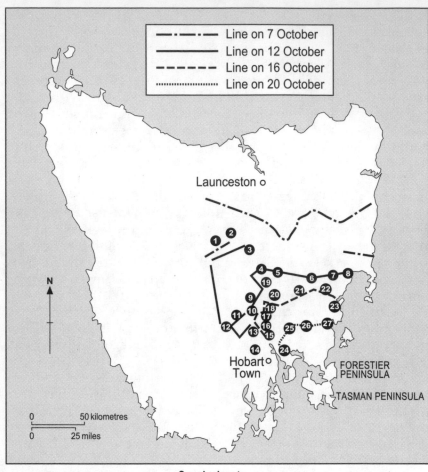

Supply depots

1 Jones's Hut, St Patrick's Plains
2 Captain Wood's Hut, Regent Plains
3 Kemp's Hut, Lake Sorell
4 Table Mountain
5 Lackey's Mill
6 Maloney's Sugar Loaf
7 Tier West of Waterloo Point
8 Waterloo Point
9 Nicholas's Farm, Ouse River
10 Bothwell
11 Lieutenant Torlesse's Farm, Clyde River
12 Hamilton
13 Murdoch's Farm, Jordan River
14 New Norfolk

15 Brighton
16 Green Ponds
17 Cross Marsh
18 Bisdee's Farm
19 Michael Howe's Marsh
20 Oatlands
21 Hobb's Farm
22 Little Swan Port River
23 Lieutenant Hawkins's Farm, Little Swan Port River
24 Richmond
25 Reis's Farm, Kangaroo River
26 Olding's Farm, Prosser's Plains
27 Captain McLaine's Farm, Spring Bay

MAP 6.2
The 'Black Line', 1830

SOURCE *British Parliamentary Papers*, Colonies, Australia, Irish University Press, Shannon, Ireland, 1968–70, 4.

The daily ration for a man on the 'Black Line' was 2 pounds (900 g) of flour, 1½ pounds (680 g) of meat, 3 ounces (85 g) of sugar and half an ounce (15 g) of tea.[71] Each man commenced the operation carrying only one week's ration, so it was vital that they reached the first line of ration stations before their food ran out. The carts carrying supplies to the stations began their journey on the day the Line commenced, to ensure that the depots would be stocked in time for the men's arrival. Tea and sugar came from Commissariat stocks, while the assistant surveyors purchased flour and meat from local farmers and organised its transport to the ration stations.[72]

Despite having to hack their way through rugged, unexplored country, most parties reached their rendezvous points weary but in good humour. The rough going meant, however, that many of the men's shoes had already begun to wear out. Arthur ordered the Commissariat to urgently provide several hundred shoes from the stores in Hobart and Oatlands. Anticipating that this demand for shoes would continue for the remainder of the operation, Affleck Moodie, the chief commissary officer in Hobart, placed a tender on 16 October for 2000 extra pairs, while George Hill, the commissary officer in Launceston, the colony's second main centre, bought 'all the Shoes in Launceston', about 800 pairs at ten shillings each.[73]

The Line continued to advance, and on 20 October the Northern and Western Divisions joined, forming a continuous cordon for the first time. After a halt on the 22nd to allow stragglers to catch up, the Line moved forward again until, on 24 October, the force had concentrated on a 30-mile (50 km) front. Arthur then ordered another halt, this time due to torrential rain. During this pause Arthur sent patrols forward to look for Aborigines which he believed were being driven ahead of the Line. One of these civilian patrols led by Edward Walpole found a camp of Big River and Oyster Bay people, and at dawn on 25 October tried to capture them. In the ensuing skirmish, the settlers killed two and captured a man and a boy named Ronekeennarener and Tremebonenerp. The other Aborigines escaped through the Line.[74] Arthur later claimed that Walpole should not have tried to seize the Aborigines, but McMahon has shown that Arthur had indeed sent the patrols forward to effect a capture and that Arthur's charge against Walpole was an attempt after the event to find a scapegoat for the Line's failure.[75] The rain continued, making the forward movement of men and supplies over rough bush tracks impossible. Arthur was forced to halt for three weeks and during this time ordered extra sentries and dogs and the construction of fences and obstacles in an attempt to strengthen the perimeter and prevent further break-outs.[76] The rain, however, did not prevent the arrival of the ship *Tamar* at

Prosser's Bay to resupply the Line's eastern flank. The *Tamar*'s captain encouraged the footsore men on the Line with the words, 'Go it you cripples!'.[77]

Arthur realised that the majority of his force were civilian volunteers and made efforts to retain their good will. For example, when civilians complained about the monotony of their rations, Arthur took note and added tobacco and salt to the provisions issued.[78] To ensure the men received fresh meat, Moodie's deputy, Joseph Browne, set up a supply depot behind the Line; the depot employed about ten convicts and purchased live cattle and sheep, which he termed 'a reserve disposable to any part of the Line' because they could be herded directly to the required place and butchered on the spot.[79] Morale and discipline remained high until the last stages of the Line. Only three convicts had their tickets-of-leave revoked for desertion, and one free settler, John Crouch, was sent home for 'endeavouring to create a spirit of Discontent amongst the Free Substitutes [men substituting for ticket-of-leave convicts] and others by his examples'.[80] With the Line stationary for three weeks, the local farmers saw the opportunity to exploit a captive market and substantially increased their prices. While flour cost $2\frac{1}{2}$d per pound in Hobart Town, it was sold to the Commissariat for the Line at 4d a pound. As the Hobart *Colonial Times* commented: 'We believe all our friends at Pitt-water will coincide in our views when we wish that the line had continued its operations another month or two'.[81]

The final advance to the neck of the Forestier Peninsula began on 17 November. No Aborigines were encountered and Arthur ordered the end of the operation on 24 November 1830.[82] The Line had been a prodigious organisational and logistical effort for a small colony. The scale of the operation is conveyed in Robinson's description of an area through which the Line had passed:

> The ground was torn up by the trafficking of carts, horses, bullocks &c in conveying supplies. Shoes of a light description, worn out, were strewn about. It had all the appearance of a great assemblage of persons having met, and vast destruction was effected among the trees of the forest. Stripped of their covering they were left to droop and die, a monument to a well intended but ill-devised plan.[83]

The 'Black Line' was also an expensive operation. The financial statement for Van Diemen's Land for 1830 stated that the operation had resulted in a 'most serious augmentation ... against the Colonial Government' of at least £30,000, and, as the total revenue collected by Van Diemen's Land colonial government in 1830 amounted to only £65,000, the cost had to be paid out of the British Treasury's £105,000 funding that year of the colony's convict department.[84]

Arthur's motives in planning and carrying out the 'Black Line' have remained a matter of dispute. Some have argued that he deployed the Line knowing it would fail, but the entries in Arthur's private diary show that until the end he still believed a large number of Aborigines lay ahead of the Line.[85] The best explanation is that Arthur deployed the Line in the belief that an operation of this scale was necessary to break the cycle of frontier violence in the colony. By removing the Aborigines from the settled districts, the settlers would be freed from raids, while placing the Aborigines in a reservation would protect them from settler attacks and enable them to be reconciled with the British and converted to Christianity.

The 'Black Line' failed for three reasons. First and most important, the Aborigines had sufficient bushcraft to enable them to pass through the Line undetected. Second, the British planned the operation believing there was a large number of Aborigines to capture in the settled districts, but Ryan estimates there were probably only about thirty.[86] The third reason the Line failed is that the British could not form an effective cordon either on the march or encamped at night. Even if there had been more Aborigines in the path of the Line, they could still have passed through the cordon. Though the aim of the Line was to pass over every yard of the settled districts, it by-passed several areas either because the terrain was too rough, or because commanders allowed their parties to march in column along a track or road and not in extended order.[87] As the Hobart *Colonial Times* commented at the time, while the plan might have worked in a flat, open country like Holland, 'marching on good Macadamised roads is one thing, and scrambling through the rocky tiers and scrubby underwood is another'.[88] At night it was impossible to create an effective cordon using only bonfires and sentries. The darkness allowed Aborigines to pass through without being observed. Even the extra precautions instituted by Arthur while the Line was stationary for three weeks probably would not have succeeded. Aborigines who examined these structures after the operation laughed at the idea that the fences could have prevented them slipping through.[89] Callwell refers to this problem when discussing the large British mounted drives used against Boer guerillas during 1901–02 in South Africa: 'There was always the risk of a gap being left somewhere, or of the enemy breaking through lines which were necessarily stretched almost to breaking point'.[90] Before the invention of barbed wire and searchlights there was no way to quickly form an effective cordon. The only options available to Arthur with the technology then available would have been to either dig a ditch or build a wall the entire length of the cordon every night. Both tasks were obviously impossible.

One could argue that the 'Black Line' failed simply because its scale was too big, and a shorter line organised in the same manner might have been an effective barrier. However, an incident which took place on the Freycinet Peninsula a year after the Line showed that Aborigines could even pass through a cordon across the narrow neck of a peninsula only one mile wide. In October 1831 an expedition was formed to capture a group of between twelve and twenty Aborigines on the Freycinet Peninsula. The operation had all the attributes of the 'Black Line'. Ten soldiers and seventy-four civilians were supplied with rations from the military station at Waterloo Point on the same scale as that used during the 'Black Line'. Across the peninsula a mile-long line was formed, which was guarded by sentries and illuminated by bonfires at night. The line was held in expectation of reinforcements arriving which would allow scouring parties to be sent beyond the cordon onto the peninsula. However, before reinforcements arrived, the Aborigines slipped through the line in the darkness between dusk and moon rise. The gap through which they passed lay between the two huts of soldiers in the middle of the perimeter, and was less than 80 metres wide.[91] Settlers formed a party to pursue the natives, but there is no record of their capture.

The 'Black Line' operation failed to clear the Aborigines from the settled districts: other than the two captured, Aborigines easily evaded the Line. Arthur's political opponents — including Henry Melville, who published his *History of Van Diemen's Land* soon afterwards — described the Line as a 'fiasco', and this view has been perpetuated by writers to the present day.[92] However, while the Line may have failed in its immediate aim, it was too well-organised to be described as a fiasco, and it indirectly contributed to ending the frontier war. Arthur pursued a two-pronged policy towards the Aborigines, in which military coercion was balanced by attempts at conciliation made by George Augustus Robinson, the one man in the colony who could speak to the Aborigines in their own languages. Contemporary observers claimed that the Line's demonstration of British power aided Robinson in his mission, and when one Aboriginal party near Launceston heard about the Line, the whole group wept for the entire day.[93] Each of the various Aboriginal groups decided in turn to negotiate with Robinson, and willingly came out of the bush and went to a reservation on Flinders Island in Bass Strait.[94] The Line must have been one of the contributing factors in the decision by each Aboriginal group to begin talks with Robinson.

The most serious failing in Arthur's military strategy during the frontier war was that he did not use mounted forces. Though horses were scarce in Van Diemen's Land, settlers had used them with some success in punitive expeditions.[95] Tasmanian Aborigines understood the advantage in mobility horses gave to settlers, and devised a dance which told the story of an Aboriginal man so fast that he could out-run an armed horseman.[96] Reynolds has claimed that the Vandemonian terrain was unsuitable for horses, but this is not the case. Lieutenant-Governor William Sorell, Arthur's predecessor, had thought mounted militia would be 'well adapted to this country'; in 1860, when light-horse units were formed in Tasmania, the *Launceston Examiner* pointed out that mounted infantry 'would be invaluable' in 'a country like Tasmania, densely wooded and full of broken ground and mountain gorges'.[97] Arthur had formed a twelve-man mounted police detachment from soldiers of the 40th Regiment in 1826 for operations against bushrangers. These men helped capture the gang-leader Matthew Brady and Arthur was pleased with their effectiveness.[98] When the Aborigines Committee asked in 1830 for the size of the Mounted Police detachment to be increased and for it to be used against Aboriginal raiding parties, it is therefore surprising to find that Arthur refused. However, Arthur made this decision on financial, rather than strategic grounds, stating: 'The Mounted Police is a very expensive force, and certainly should not be augmented without great caution'. The cost of mounting British troops on horses had to be borne by the colony and the British Colonial Secretary warned Arthur that the Van Diemen's Land mounted police could not be increased 'without incurring a charge to which the finances of the colony would not be equal'.[99] Cape Colony, at the tip of South Africa, was at this time also a colony with little revenue; unlike Van Diemen's Land, however, it had strategic importance as the key to the British route to India. This meant that while the British government was not willing to pay for mounted troops in Van Diemen's Land, they did fund the Cape Mounted Rifles as well as the cost of mounting British infantry when required. During the Sixth Cape Frontier War of 1835, mounted troops defeated Xhosa raids against the settlers' cattle in mountainous terrain by using cordon and search tactics to gradually clear the Xhosa from the frontier, valley by valley.[100] Ironically, Arthur, having rejected the use of mounted troops for fiscal reasons, used 2000 men on foot during the 'Black Line' and blew out the colonial budget. A small unit of mounted troops operating in the settled districts could have sufficiently harassed the Tasmanian Aborigines to force them into negotiations and done this more effectively and with less cost than the Line operation.

7

THE LIVERPOOL PLAINS AND PORT PHILLIP DISTRICTS, 1838

About 3:30 PM, on 10 June 1838 a group of stockmen rode into Myall Creek station near the Gwydir River in what is now northern New South Wales. This group had joined together with the aim of killing Aborigines, and at Myall Creek they found their prey. For almost two weeks, about fifty unarmed people, probably Ngarabal[1], had camped peacefully at the station. The stockmen dismounted and tied all the Aborigines present, about thirty men, women and children, to a long rope normally used for tethering horses at night. The Aborigines pleaded with the Myall Creek station men to protect them. 'Davy', a Kamilaroi stockman, and George Anderson bargained for the release of two women and hid three children. Charles Kilmeister, in contrast, got his pistols and horse and joined the mounted party as they led the captives to their fate. About fifteen minutes later, the massacre started. Two pistol shots were fired, but the rest of the killing was done with swords. All the Aborigines were murdered except for one young woman, whom the stockmen spared for a fate not disclosed but easily assumed. The men later claimed that they did not know it was against the law to murder Aborigines, but they showed they knew they had done an evil thing by trying several times to hide it. They decapitated the bodies and burnt them to make identification difficult. Then they removed the charred remains from the site, sweeping the ground clean with brooms to erase the evidence. Many settlers approved of the men's action, but others were appalled and reported the massacre to the authorities. When Police Magistrate Edward Denny Day visited the murder site, he found a few bone fragments missed in the clean-up and arrested eleven of the twelve men involved. Seven of the eleven charged were eventually found guilty and were hanged in Sydney on 18 December 1838. For only the second time in the fifty-year history of New South Wales, British men had been found guilty and had been punished for murdering Aborigines.[2]

As British pastoralists advanced rapidly towards the Gwydir River and out of Melbourne, Aborigines perfected tactics for attacking cattle and sheep, and frontier warfare intensified. Despite this, the British government still refused to accept that wars were being fought in its Australian colonies. The last major British Army deployments to the frontier took place in 1838 when Major James Nunn of the 80th Regiment led long Mounted Police patrols to the Gwydir River in the Liverpool Plains District and to the Melbourne road in the Port Phillip District (now Victoria). After 1838 the army left frontier fighting to settlers and civilian police, but warfare would continue for another ninety years until the British had occupied the entire continent from Gippsland to the Kimberleys.

During the 1820s British squatters rapidly occupied vast tracts of Aboriginal land to run sheep and cattle. The settlers' advance left the government surveyors, who were supposed to map land before it was granted, far in the rear. In 1826 Governor Darling attempted to temporarily halt the settlers' movement and enable the surveyors to catch up. He did this by limiting settlement to the Nineteen Counties of New South Wales, an area stretching from Taree in the north to Moruya in the south and inland to Yass, Wellington and Coolah (see map 7.1). However, the squatters ignored the so-called 'Limits of Location' and continued to push inland with flocks and herds far beyond the area of government control. The same year Governor Darling tried to stop their movement, settlers from both the Hunter Valley and Mudgee arrived on the Liverpool Plains, described by one contemporary writer as being 'like a green ocean, of unbounded extent'.[3]

In 1826 there was an estimated 12,000 Aborigines living in this district, mostly of the large Kamilaroi language group (see map 7.2), but including other peoples such as the Ngarabal.[4] There was no British authority to curb the excesses of the settlers and frontier warfare had commenced by 1827. The Kamilaroi became adept at cattle raids, even forming an alliance with the bushranger George Clarke, alias 'the Barber', and constructing a stock-yard with his assistance on the Namoi River near what is now Boggabri.[5] The missionary Lancelot Threlkeld suggests that a combined party of settlers and Mounted Police killed eighty Kamilaroi in a single action in 1836. Bob Reece and Roger Milliss point out that this particular claim is unlikely, but settlers certainly did pursue and kill Kamilaroi.[6] After a few years of conflict, settlers and the Kamilaroi of the Namoi

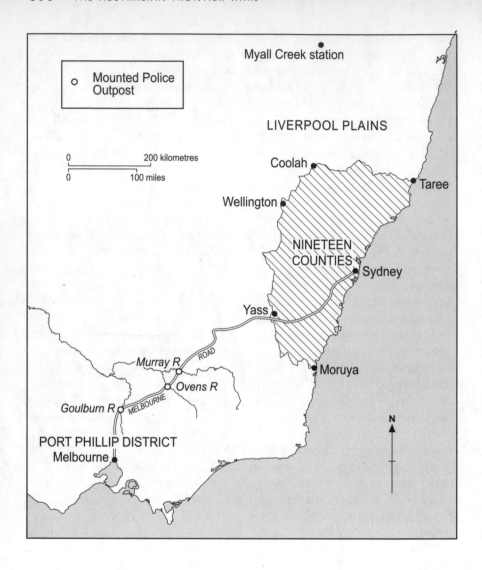

MAP 7.1
The Nineteen Counties, Liverpool Plains and Port Phillip

SOURCE *British Parliamentary Papers*, Colonies, Australia, Irish University Press, Shannon, Ireland, 1968–70, 5.

and Peel rivers came to an accommodation. The Kamilaroi man 'Charley', who had led cattle raids on the Namoi and had been pursued by settlers, later told the Reverend William Ridley that one day he came across a settler leading a horse too exhausted to be ridden. Taking advantage of the settler's immobility, 'Charley' and his group surrounded the settler and offered to spare his life in exchange for tobacco and an ongoing friendship. Settlers started to employ Kamilaroi as stockmen. Two of the stockmen at Myall Creek station when the killing party visited were Kamilaroi men from the Peel.[7]

In 1836 settlers pushed beyond the Peel and Namoi to the Gwydir, then known as the 'Big River'. The local Kamilaroi groups resisted the invasion almost immediately, and the dispersed nature of the stations enabled them to easily isolate and attack stockmen and cattle. Henry Bingham and Alexander Paterson, Crown Lands commissioners, both reported the warfare between settlers and Aborigines back to Sydney in the second half of 1837. Paterson listed five British killed and stated that the stockmen at Loder's station, the westernmost on the Namoi, were so afraid of Kamilaroi raids that they had abandoned their cattle to roam unattended in the bush.[8] In November James Glennie asked fellow squatter Robert Scott, who was visiting Sydney, to lobby for a Mounted Police detachment to be sent to the Gwydir. Glennie wrote that he had enough flour, sugar and tobacco to supply the troops and that he would 'ration them at contract price [that is, at a loss] rather than be obliged to quit my stations'.[9] The colonial government responded to these calls by despatching the Mounted Police.

By 1837 the New South Wales Mounted Police had grown to a force of 120 men stationed at twenty outposts with headquarters and clerical staff in Sydney and divisional commands at Bathurst, Goulburn and the Hunter Valley. The Mounted Police was still 'composed entirely of the Military', who were paid by the British government.[10] As Lieutenant-Colonel Henry Breton of the 4th Regiment told a House of Commons Select Committee in 1837, when a regiment arrived in New South Wales, the officers selected for Mounted Police duty 'the best behaved men and the smartest, free from incumbrance, unmarried, light and active; that is to say, the very best men we have'. Breton admitted that the high standard of its personnel made the Mounted Police very effective, but complained that a man serving in the force became used to using his own initiative and this ruined him as a soldier: 'that man is hardly any longer amenable to discipline; he becomes careless and slovenly and unclean, and is insolent; that is to say, he dislikes coercion'.[11] The men were issued with blue, and later green uniforms 'to render them as little conspicuous as possible', though, when operating in the bush, they often wore straw hats and 'any other convenient dress'.[12]

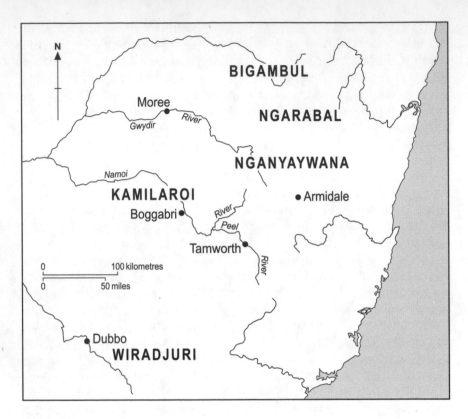

MAP 7.2
Kamilaroi lands, 1826

SOURCE After David Horton (ed.), *The Encyclopaedia of Aboriginal Australia: Aboriginal & Torres Strait Islander history, society and culture,* 2 vols, Aboriginal Studies Press in association with the Australian Institute of Aboriginal and Torres Strait Islander Studies, Canberra, 1994, 2: 946, 1009.

Each soldier was armed with a carbine, pistol and sword, and shooting was practised more diligently than in the regular garrison.[13] Men joining the Mounted Police were described as having 'just enough [riding skill] to enable them to sit on a horse' and highly detailed regulations issued to the soldiers suggest they also had little initial knowledge of how to care for their animals.[14]

Officers hoped in time that their saddlesore infantrymen would become skilled riders with a detailed knowledge of the country in their district. A surprisingly lyrical order of 1832 stated:

> The Home of a Mounted Policeman should be in the Bush, he should consider Barracks merely as a place where he can obtain rations & supplies or receive orders & where he may be allowed to take shelter in continued wet weather, but it should be his delight as it is his interest

& duty to wander about the Bush in his District, & by the uncertainty & rapidity of his movements to render the escape of the Bushranger almost impossible.[15]

As this order also indicates, during the 1830s the Mounted Police operated mostly against bushrangers and escaped convicts.[16] Most of this work took place within the Nineteen Counties, though Captain John Forbes and Captain James Williams both led detachments to the Nandewar Ranges to search for a bushranger hideout. The Mounted Police force was rarely used against Aborigines during this time because settlers had moved the frontier far beyond the Limits of Location, although Lieutenant Zouch of the 4th Regiment led a detachment onto the Liverpool Plains in 1835 to find and arrest the Kamilaroi accused of killing Richard Cunningham, the botanist accompanying Thomas Mitchell's exploring expedition.[17]

The Mounted Police joined the frontier war on the Liverpool Plains in 1837. Kamilaroi women were being abducted by stockmen and this probably led Kamilaroi men to kill Frederick Harrington in June at Charles Purcell's station in the Warrumbungles. On 21 September Lieutenant George Cobban of the 50th Regiment, commanding the Hunter River division of the Mounted Police, was ordered to look for Harrington's killers. Cobban's party did not leave Jerry's Plains (the detachment's headquarters since moving from Maitland in 1833) until early October. So many months after the attack, the trail was cold, and the men returned home on 24 October without success. Cobban estimated during this ride that he reached a point 400 kilometres from Jerry's Plains.[18] Despite the expedition's failure, Cobban showed that the Mounted Police could quickly cover long distances to reach the frontier and could remain in the field for weeks on end.

Lieutenant-Colonel Kenneth Snodgrass, acting governor of New South Wales between the departure of Governor Bourke and the arrival of the new incumbent, Sir George Gipps, read Alexander Paterson's report of Aboriginal attacks on the Gwydir on Saturday, 16 December 1837. Snodgrass decided that a large Mounted Police party needed to be sent north 'for the purpose of enquiring into, and repressing as far as possible the aggressions complained of' and had orders written up, which he presented personally to Major James Nunn, the Mounted Police commander, on 19 December.[19]

Nunn's report of this deployment lacks many details and contrasts badly with the despatches written by officers of the 46th Regiment concerning the 1816 punitive expedition to the Hawkesbury River. Milliss says that to piece together what happened on Nunn's expedition requires 'a fair amount of hypothesis and educated guesswork'. While Windschuttle suggests that Milliss's route for the Mounted Police party 'exist[s] solely in Milliss's imagination',

Milliss's account is based on a painstaking review of the existing evidence and should be considered as generally credible unless other conflicting material comes to light. Nunn did not even include in his report basic details such as exactly how many men took part in the expedition. He states that he left Jerry's Plains on 29 December with Lieutenant Cobban, two sergeants and twenty other ranks, but this number does not include Sergeant John Lee and several mounted policemen who joined the party as it passed through Invermein (now Scone) and probably swelled the group to just under thirty.[20]

On reaching the Liverpool Plains (see map 7.3), Nunn passed the Australian Agricultural Company's large holding on the Peel around what is now Tamworth and arrived on 4 January 1838 at a station just south of the Namoi owned by Charles Smith, but which Nunn referred to by the name of Smith's overseer, Joseph Greenhatch. While the men and horses rested from their ride in the summer heat, Nunn sent Sergeant James McNally to a nearby station to gather intelligence and he soon returned with news of a large number of Aborigines nearby on the Namoi. Nunn decided to confront them and had stockmen guide the Mounted Police party to the Kamilaroi camp. During this night-time journey the men walked their horses, instead of riding them, probably because the horses had not been fully rested. They arrived early the next morning.[21]

Nunn ordered the men to use their swords rather than firearms, probably to prevent casualties from 'friendly fire' in the pale dawn light, and arranged his force on both sides of the Namoi to surround the camp and prevent any escapes. Cobban and some men mounted their horses and galloped into the camp, and about 100 bleary-eyed Kamilaroi woke to find themselves captives. The camp included Kamilaroi-speakers from two groups. Through his interpreter 'Jacky', Nunn demanded the surrender of any men involved in killing stockmen or raiding cattle, and members of the local group, who knew it was vital to keep good relations with nearby settlers, pointed out about fifteen of the other group. One of these men, known as 'Doherty', was accused of killing a stockman eighteen months previously; later he was conveniently shot while trying to escape, Cobban commenting that 'the death of the man who had been shot may deter them from committing further outrages'. The remaining men were released, except for one man who was kept to be a guide.[22]

Nunn then led his men on a four-day ride to Bells' station on the Horton River. Mounted troops were well-suited to patrolling large areas efficiently. Nunn may have taken advantage of this and sent out patrols to carefully 'scour' the surrounding country while they moved north, as the expedition made this journey at the slow pace of 25 kilometres per day. Nunn met one of the Bell brothers, who

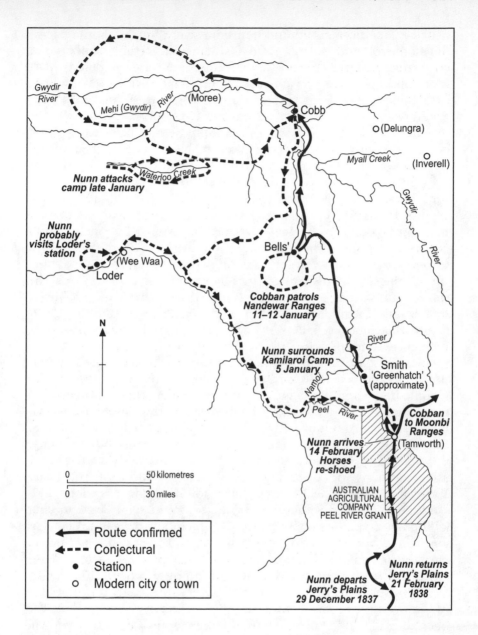

MAP 7.3
British punitive expedition, 1838

SOURCE After Roger Milliss, *Waterloo Creek: The Australia Day Massacre of 1838, George Gipps and the British Conquest of New South Wales*, McPhee Gribble, Ringwood, Victoria, 1992, p 193.

owned this station, and found him 'in a state of great alarm' due to the Kamilaroi attacks. To ease Bell's fears, Nunn sent Cobban and some men on a two-day sortie in search of Aboriginal raiding parties. Cobban seems to have headed south to the Nandewar Ranges, as he spoke of being in rugged country, where the Mounted Police saw Aborigines but were unable to pursue them.[23]

After leaving Bells' station, the Mounted Police detachment took four days to ride at a slow pace, presumably again using 'scouring' parties, to Cobb's station on the Gwydir River. Nunn saw that Aboriginal raids had placed the entire station in 'the greatest confusion'. The sheep were starving because they had eaten all the grass around the station huts and the shepherds were too afraid to take them further out. Nunn says that men at Cobb's station told him that the Aborigines who had killed two shepherds were now inland on the Gwydir River. However, as Milliss points out, the initial pursuit of the shepherds' killers had been to the east towards the Masterman Ranges, not to the west along the Gwydir. Milliss writes: 'In heading downstream, Nunn was thus planning a punitive expedition not against the killers of Cobb's shepherds but any Aborigines he happened to come across'.[24]

Nunn organised fifteen days' provisions for his men from the station stores and began his ride west. Some stockmen accompanied the Mounted Police. Milliss suggests between ten or twenty civilians may have joined the expedition, but the prevailing atmosphere on the stations fearful of Aboriginal attacks probably meant that few men were spared. Four days after leaving the furthest inland station then on the Gwydir, Nunn's men captured a small group of Aborigines who, either willingly or unwillingly, gave the location of the main Aboriginal camp. The British soldiers followed the directions, and about noon on the second day of riding, came across a large number of Aborigines on the opposite side of a large body of water. Milliss has conclusively identified this place as Waterloo Creek, 50 kilometres southwest of what is now Moree, and — rather less conclusively — suggests that the date, a day or two on the either side of 26 January, was in fact by 'a supreme accident of history' that exact day: the fiftieth anniversary of the British landing at Sydney Cove.[25] Why the Aborigines did not know Nunn's party was nearby is not known. Perhaps they did not expect to be attacked by the British so far beyond the frontier. If this is the case, it shows how horses gave the British the military advantage on the Australian frontier.

Cobban was the first to see the Aborigines because he was riding ahead of the main group with an advance guard of five or so men with the best horses. Cobban's party immediately backtracked to a place they had just seen where they could cross the creek. Cobban ordered his men to form an extended line, draw their swords and charge towards the Aborigines so as to force them towards the water and the main party. The Mounted Police galloped in and soon 'encountered the blacks face to face'. Corporal Patrick Hannan apparently pursued a man. When he had ridden him down, Hannan tried to grab him, but the man thrust his spear into Hannan's calf. Sergeant John Lee said he heard Hannan's scream of pain and this led him to open fire. Others joined in the shooting, which Lee says continued 'for some time'.[26]

Nunn made no attempt to count the bodies, so there is no way of knowing how many people were killed in this attack. Nunn's estimates of the casualties his men inflicted ranged from 'a few' in his official report to an unlikely 200 to 300 in dinner-party boastings. Sergeant Lee's estimate of forty or fifty killed seems the best calculation.[27]

The Aborigines Nunn killed at Waterloo Creek had been armed, unlike the victims of the later Myall Creek massacre, but Nunn's attack on them was unprovoked. There is no evidence for Nunn's motives at Waterloo Creek, but it appears he mounted an attack against the first Aboriginal group he came across in the belief that terrorising the Gwydir Aborigines would stop them attacking British settlers and their livestock.

The expedition returned to Cobb's station for supplies and three days' rest before heading back to Jerry's Plains. Again, Nunn gave little detail of this part of the expedition, although he commented that he visited the Australian Agricultural Company station on the Peel even though it was out of his way. As Milliss points out, travelling directly from the Gwydir River to Jerry's Plains would have taken Nunn right past the Australian Agricultural Company station, which suggests that Nunn must have taken a detour from the direct route on the return journey. Milliss reasonably speculates that Nunn led his men westwards along the Namoi River. Alexander Paterson's report of the embattled conditions at Loder's station on the Namoi was one of the reasons Nunn's expedition had been ordered in the first place, and it seems natural that Nunn would have visited that station. On 14 February the Mounted Police detachment arrived at the Australian Agricultural Company station and had their horses re-shoed. The flexibility of mounted troops was shown here when Nunn received news that Aborigines had killed two members of a survey party in the Moonbi Ranges to the north. Nunn ordered Cobban to take a detachment to the Moonbis and then on 21 February 1838 returned with the remainder of the expedition to Jerry's Plains after fifty-three days in the field. Nunn's expedition enabled settlers to consolidate their hold on the Gwydir and advance north to the Barwon and Macintyre rivers. However, this occupation would be short-lived as drought and a collapse in wool prices forced settlers to abandon their stations in the early 1840s.[28]

In March 1838 the newly arrived governor, Sir George Gipps read Nunn's report of his expedition to the Gwydir with some alarm because Nunn's action ran contrary to the instructions Gipps had received from the Colonial Office. The British government at this time was going through a period of reformist zeal. Catholics had regained their political rights in 1829, parliament was reformed in 1832, slaves had been freed in 1833, and in 1835 the House of Commons convened a Select Committee on the conditions of indigenous people throughout the empire. The Committee's deliberations coincided with the Sixth Cape Frontier War, so the evidence it took concentrated on the situation in South Africa. The Committee report's most important recommendation was for the British to withdraw from land it had annexed from the Xhosa at the end of the Cape Frontier War.[29]

Henry Reynolds argued in *The Law of the Land* that the Select Committee report recognised Australian Aboriginal land rights in its general statement that 'the native inhabitants of any land have an incontrovertible right to their own soil'. However, as David Philips points out, Reynolds does not refer to the report's specific comments on Australia.[30] Here Aborigines were dismissed as:

> forming probably the least-instructed portion of the human race in all the arts of social life. Such, indeed, is the barbarous state of these people, and so entirely destitute are they even of the rudest forms of civil polity, that their claims, whether as sovereigns or proprietors of the soil, have been utterly disregarded.

While the report admitted that the British had taken the Aborigines' land from them 'without the assertion of any other title than that of superior force', it went on to say that '[w]hatever may have been the injustice of this encroachment, there is no reason to suppose that either justice or humanity would now be consulted by receding from it'. According to the Select Committee, what the Aborigines needed was, not land rights, but British missionaries to convert them to Christianity and government officials to manage their relations with settlers.[31]

In fact, British reformers, such as the Select Committee members and Lord Glenelg, the Colonial Secretary, argued that Aborigines had a status the exact opposite of what it was in reality. The Select Committee report stated that 'the Aborigines of the whole territory [of Australia] must be considered as within the allegiance of the Queen, and as entitled to her protection'.[32] The reality was that Aborigines on, or beyond the frontier were not British subjects; they were sovereign peoples fighting to defend their lands. Lord Glenelg denied this in 1837, telling Governor Bourke:

Hence I conceive it follows that all the natives inhabiting those Territories must be considered as Subjects of the Queen, and as within H.M.'s Allegiance. To regard them as Aliens with whom a War can exist, and against whom H.M.'s Troops may exercise belligerent right, is to deny them that protection to which they derive the highest possible claim from the Sovereignty which has been assumed over the whole of their Ancient Possession.[33]

Glenelg told Governor Gipps in 1838 that his solution for preventing frontier conflict was to 'impress' the Aborigines 'with the conviction that the laws of the colony will be equally administered for their protection from wrong and injury as for that of the European settlers'.[34] However, the idea that Aborigines should have faith in the legal system was incredible when the British government denied Aborigines the basic legal right of land ownership. There was a war being fought on the frontier, even if Glenelg said this was legally impossible. The British government, by encouraging settlers to occupy Aboriginal land, and then refusing to view the resultant fighting for that land as 'war', created the conditions that led settlers to act secretly and brutally against Aborigines in actions such as the Myall Creek massacre.

Gipps faced a dilemma in attempting to reconcile his Colonial Office instructions with Nunn's actions on the frontier. He ordered that Nunn and his men should be questioned about the Gwydir expedition by the police magistrate at Invermein (now Scone), but knew he would face opposition if he tried to take action against the Mounted Police. The New South Wales Executive Council warned Gipps that, if he charged any member of the Mounted Police, the officers and men who were 'Volunteers from Regiments of the Line serving in New South Wales' would all 'resign their Police duties and return to their Regiment', leaving the colony defenceless against both bushrangers and Aborigines. As a result of delays, Nunn, Cobban, Sergeant Lee and Corporal Hannan were not questioned until 1839, and Gipps and the Executive Council then decided that it would be impolitic to pursue charges. Gipps justified Major Nunn's actions by stating that considering he 'was a Military man, acting under Military orders', it was appropriate that, having come across a large group of Aborigines, 'he should have considered it his duty to disperse them'.[35]

The delays in dealing with Nunn and the Mounted Police were caused by the Myall Creek massacre, and an escalation in frontier conflict in the southernmost part of the colony of New South Wales, the Port Phillip District (now Victoria). The first British attempts to occupy this coastline were the short-lived military outposts at Port Phillip (1803) and Westernport (1826–28). Next came the sealers and whalers, who began calling along the coast from 1828, and land-hungry settlers from Van Diemen's Land, who sailed across Bass Strait with sheep and cattle and commenced permanent settlements at Portland Bay in 1834 and Melbourne in 1835. Both the Vandemonian settlers and the British government tried to learn lessons from the frontier war in Van Diemen's Land to prevent conflict around Port Phillip. Batman and the settlers tried to make a treaty with the local Aborigines, which was disallowed by Governor Bourke. Subsequently, the British government instructed Governor Gipps to appoint a Chief Protector of Aborigines in the Port Phillip District — preferably George Robinson, who had worked with Aborigines in Van Diemen's Land.[36]

By 1838 the British were contesting the lands of several Aboriginal peoples in the vicinity of Port Phillip District — including the Wathaurong, west of Geelong, and the Woiworung, north of Melbourne (see map 7.4).[37] Aborigines in the Port Phillip District continued traditional warfare both against other Aboriginal groups and British settlers. Critchett's study of the fighting west of Geelong shows that the nine settlers killed on that frontier to the end of 1838 were all victims of revenge attacks. While there was little conflict in the immediate area around Melbourne[38], Aborigines in other parts of the District developed effective tactics to raid farmhouses and the settlers' sheep.

The Aboriginal warriors' ability to isolate and attack individual farmhouses was assisted by the settlers' initial decision to site their pastoral runs at least 3 miles (4.8 km) apart. Critchett points out that few stockmen were killed in farmhouse raids, but raiding parties of thirty or forty Aborigines took goods and bedding.[39] Settlers initially lent firearms to Aborigines so they could go hunting, but settlers soon found the guns turned against them and used in attacks on pastoral stations. On 22 May 1838 Wathaurong men armed with two muskets attacked Thomas Rickett's station on the Barwon River and took a further gun they found there.[40] Authorities in the Port Phillip District asked Governor Gipps to prohibit Aborigines possessing firearms without a magistrate's permission. Gipps passed such a law in 1840, which the British government disallowed: it was considered to be unfair to create a 'distinction' between Aborigines, whom the British government regarded as British subjects, and 'their White brethren'.[41]

The most common form of Australian frontier warfare practised in the Port Phillip District was raids on sheep. As Captain William Lonsdale, the Melbourne police magistrate, complained in 1838, Aboriginal sheep raids 'have been numerous, and their attacks can seldom be guarded against'. By doing this, Aborigines were in fact targeting the settler's most prized possessions: each sheep on the Port Phillip frontier in 1837 had cost up to £3 to purchase and

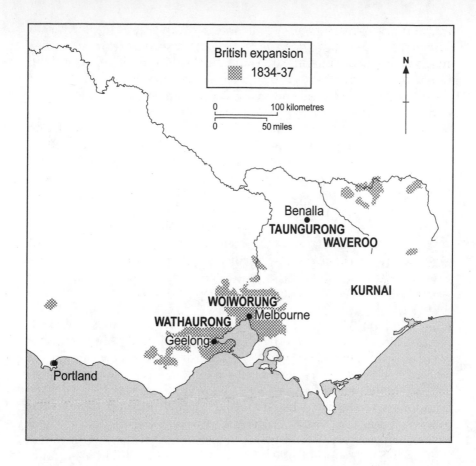

MAP 7.4
Port Phillip District: Aboriginal lands and British expansion

SOURCES After David Horton (ed.), *The Encyclopaedia of Aboriginal Australia: Aboriginal & Torres Strait Islander history, society and culture,* 2 vols, Aboriginal Studies Press in association with the Australian Institute of Aboriginal and Torres Strait Islander Studies, Canberra, 1994, 2: 946, 1009; MF Christie, *Aborigines in Colonial Victoria 1835–86,* Sydney University Press, Sydney, 1979, p 58.

transport to the District.[42] According to settler Hugh Murray, Aboriginal tactics developed over time. At first raids took only a few sheep while they were penned in for the night, but then Aborigines learned they could take more sheep by attacking flocks while they were out grazing during the day. To carry out a daylight sheep raid, raiding parties, consisting of as few as four men, distracted or chased away the shepherd and then tried, sometimes with dogs, to herd the unattended flock to a safe place. While the settler generally retrieved at least some of their sheep, the raiding party would butcher some for a meal, as well as breaking the legs of some animals and killing others they did not eat, possibly in an attempt to ruin the settler's flock.[43]

In one notable attack, on 9 June 1838, about twenty men with dogs chased away shepherd Samuel Fuller and captured his flock. This raiding party formed a circular formation, perhaps originally used for kangaroo hunting, to surround the sheep.[44] The Aborigines herded the sheep to a camp and placed them in yards which they had constructed themselves 'after the manner of the white shepherds'. Fuller reported the loss to his station overseer, John Coppock, who formed a party of eight or nine armed men and tracked the sheep for about 5 kilometres until they came to the camp. The British party was still about 400 metres away from the camp when the fifty Aborigines there were alerted. The settlers tried to make for the penned sheep, but the Aborigines, who had made rudimentary fortifications out of tree trunks and bark sheets, discharged such a volley of spears that they forced the British to halt and find shelter among trees. What Coppock described as a 'regular engagement' then took place for about forty-five minutes. The muskets' roar startled the sheep and they escaped out of the yards. Despite the settlers' continuous fire, Aborigines coolly herded up the sheep and took them to safety. The settlers charged and occupied the camp, only to find that the Aborigines had already withdrawn. By now it was dark, so the British party retreated. Seven or eight Aborigines had lost their lives, but they had fought bravely and held their own against the settlers.[45]

What were the motivations of the Aboriginal warriors fighting on the Port Phillip District frontier? Michael Christie argued in 1979 that the sole motivation was to defend their land from invasion and that an estimated 2000 Aborigines in the Port Phillip District died in the process. Richard Broome argues that Christie's estimate is too high and that the reasons every Aboriginal fought are simply 'unknowable'.[46] However, the motives of some Aboriginal warriors were recorded. As already mentioned, Critchett shows that the killings of Western District settlers were traditional revenge attacks. The Dantgurt group of the Wathaurong told

Francis Tuckfield, a Methodist missionary, that they took sheep simply as food gathering. However, on at least one occasion, warriors raided sheep in an attempt to push settlers off their land. Aborigines spoke to the shepherd, Joseph Ware, while they drove off his flock. Ware stated: 'I understood the language: they repeatedly told me to go or they would kill me'.[47]

Squatters bringing stock overland to the Port Phillip District from the Nineteen Counties of New South Wales crossed the Ovens and Goulburn rivers and trespassed on the lands of the Taungurong people. On 11 April 1838 one of these armed overlander parties, which was employed by William Pitt Faithfull, was attacked in an incident that became inaccurately known as the 'Faithfull massacre'. According to Diane Barwick, the Faithfull party came across a large group of Aborigines, including Waveroo and Kurnai elders and their families who had travelled into Taungurong country to attend male initiation ceremonies during April and May; on the other hand, GW Rusden, who many years later questioned British survivors, wrote that Faithfull's party was attacked because stockmen had refused to pay for sexual services provided by Aboriginal women.[48]

Faithfull's party, led by James Crossley and consisting of eighteen men, two drays, about 3400 sheep and 400 cattle, camped on the land of the Yeerun-Illam-Balluk clan on the Broken River, near what is now Benalla, from 7 to 11 April. Just after 10 o'clock on the morning of 11 April Crossley sent four shepherds and the slow-moving flocks off first, and was preparing the drays and the cattle to follow them when he heard the shepherds scream that they had been ambushed. Crossley's men went forward with their four muskets, but they were overwhelmed by a large number of Aboriginal warriors, who pursued them and killed seven of the British men. The drays were stripped of flour, tea and sugar, and Faithfull calculated that he lost 103 sheep and 150 cattle and £150 worth of goods in the attack.[49]

As in other parts of the Port Phillip District, settlers formed punitive parties following the Faithfull attack, and may have inflicted some revenge.[50] However, the Taungurong continued to attack and by late April all four pastoral runs on the Ovens River had been abandoned. Colonel HJ White (retired) buried his property in a hole in the ground before fleeing, Doctor George Mackay managed to herd together his stock before driving them to the Murray, but George Faithfull and William Bowman simply abandoned their sheep and cattle and fled. As Faithfull's stockman John Todd later said, everyone at the station simply 'ran away' to Yass.[51]

The Port Phillip District settlers knew they did not have enough weapons or men to fight back and demanded military assistance from Governor Gipps. They petitioned him to 'levy war against the blacks, or sanction the enrolment of a militia for that purpose, and allow them to be supplied with arms and munitions of war from Her Majesty's stores'. Gipps refused both requests, the New South Wales Colonial Secretary telling the settlers that, as the governor 'has the most positive directions from Her Majesty's government to treat the aboriginal natives as subjects of Her Majesty, it is entirely out of his power to authorize the levying of war against them'. Gipps accepted that, while the Crown had 'taken entire possession of the country, without reference to the rights of the aborigines', it was 'now too late for the Government to refuse protection to persons who have come hither'. However, the New South Wales garrison's ability to protect the settlers was limited. As Gipps confessed to Lord Glenelg, 'the resources of the Government would be quite insufficient to keep military parties always in advance of persons who are migrating in search of pasturage'.[52]

When settlers from the Port Phillip District had requested military assistance in 1837, acting governor Snodgrass had sent a Mounted Police sergeant and six other ranks to Melbourne, and had authorised soldiers stationed at Geelong to ride pack-horses if required. Gipps decided the best use of his limited resources was to send more Mounted Police to the Port Phillip District. Men with horses were of most use on the frontier. George Faithfull later wrote that the only way he was able to hold his station on the Ovens (once he had re-occupied it) was for him and another horseman 'to keep continually perambulating' around the pastoral run. However, horses in the Port Phillip District at this time were rare and expensive for settlers to purchase, costing between £60 and £80. Settlers were therefore relieved that the Mounted Police was to be deployed to the frontier 'to inspire confidence and to alarm the blacks'.[53]

Following the Faithfull attack, Gipps immediately ordered Mounted Police to the Ovens River and began investigating the creation of military outposts to protect overlanders travelling on the Melbourne Road. A Mounted Police detachment arrived at the Ovens River on 19 April to collect evidence and witnesses of the attack, which was described by Lieutenant William Waddy, the Goulburn Mounted Police commander, as 'a most daring outrage'.[54] This was followed by a more extensive expedition, in which Waddy and twelve men left Goulburn on 9 May with Police Magistrate George Stewart. To avoid a repeat of Nunn's behaviour during his Gwydir expedition, Gipps instructed that 'the police magistrate will bear in mind that the black natives of New South Wales are in every respect to be considered subjects of the Queen, and not as aliens against whom, the Queen's troops may exercise belligerent rights'. The Mounted Police party arrived at Colonel

White's station on 22 May and patrolled the Ovens for two days. The men found no Aborigines and returned to the Murray. On hearing rumours of a sighting of clothes taken from Faithfull's dray, Waddy's men rode out for a five-day patrol, which again found nothing. After resting their horses, the Mounted Police detachment left for Goulburn on 9 June.[55]

Gipps asked Stewart and Major Thomas Mitchell, the New South Wales surveyor-general, to recommend two or three sites for military outposts on the Yass–Melbourne road and decided on constructing Mounted Police barracks on the Murray, Ovens and Goulburn rivers (see map 7.1).[56]

The New South Wales Mounted Police was increased in size to man the new outposts, and on 26 September Nunn led an expedition south consisting of two sergeants, a corporal, ten privates, together with a cart of building materials. Nunn personally supervised the construction of the barracks. An anonymous correspondent told the *Australian* that Nunn's presence in the Port Phillip District had 'effectually restored security and general good order', but whether this was achieved merely by building the outposts or by punitive expeditions was not explained.[57]

The main problem in deploying Mounted Police to the Melbourne road was logistics. Waddy's detachment had been forced to withdraw to Goulburn in June because 'it was found to be exceedingly difficult to get supplies for so many men in that remote part of the country'. The new outposts had to be placed slightly away from the road as passing sheep and cattle would eat the grass and leave nothing for the Mounted Police's horses. Gipps presented the New South Wales Executive Council on 10 August with calculations that it would cost £1 a day to supply a member of the Mounted Police and his horse stationed on the Murray River. To transport a horse's daily ration of 8 pounds (3.6 kg) of corn from Sydney to Albury would cost 12 shillings (not including the cost of the corn). While local squatters like Dr Mackay on the Ovens contracted to provide the Mounted Police with some supplies, other items would still need to be transported long distances at great expense.[58]

Frontier warfare would continue in the Port Phillip District for many years beyond 1838. George Faithfull wrote that his station on the Ovens was 'in a perpetual state of alarm' for years on end. Aboriginal resistance prevented the British occupation of some parts of the Western Districts until 1843, and even longer in Gippsland and the Wimmera.[59]

How the British fought on the Australian frontier changed in several ways after 1838. The first change was in the status of the men in the Mounted Police. Until now they had continued to be paid by their regiment while they were on detachment. However, in 1838 the War Office, following Lieutenant-Colonel Breton's complaint that the Mounted Police ruined good soldiers, demanded that men in the Mounted Police would no longer receive military pay. In future, men serving in the Mounted Police would be taken off the active strength of the regiment and would be paid by colonial governments.[60]

The second change was the creation of a Border Police to operate permanently on the frontier beyond the Limits of Location. Liverpool Plains settlers presented a petition to Gipps on 18 September 1838 asking for the establishment of 'an Interior Police' funded by a land tax. Edward Mayne, the Crown Lands Commissioner for the Gwydir, proposed to Gipps that this force could be established cheaply by using soldiers who had been transported from South Africa to New South Wales as convicts. Gipps presented the Legislative Council with a bill to form the Border Police, and in December Mayne left for the Gwydir with six new recruits for the Border Police and six Mounted Police to train them.[61]

The third change was that the British Army ceased fighting on the Australian frontier after 1838. There were a few exceptions, such as the 96th Regiment's deployment to Port Lincoln in South Australia in 1842[62], but generally settlers and civilian police carried the fight on the frontier after this date. The withdrawal of the army from the Australian frontier was British government policy. As Lord Glenelg wrote in 1837 to Governor Stirling in Western Australia:

> The Settlers must not be led to depend on a Military Force for internal protection. It is the desire of H.M. Govt to encourage the establishment of local Corps in the different Colonies and to induce the Colonist to provide as much as possible for their own defence. In cases where it is unfortunately necessary to adopt active measures for restraining the aggressions of the Natives, military aid may be indispensible in support of the Civil Force, but the latter ought to be the principal means on wh[ich] reliance is habitually to be placed for internal security. [I cannot] too strongly deprecate the habitual employment of the Military on such a Service.[63]

The fourth change was that frontier warfare became more violent from the time the government expected settlers to fight for themselves and settlers became better equipped with guns and horses to do so. Broome points out how the cost of firearms dropped and the weapons themselves became more reliable as muskets were replaced with breech-loading rifles. Settlers taking the war into their own hands created vigilante parties to attack Aborigines. As George Faithfull wrote: 'People formed themselves into bands of alliance and allegiance to each other, and it was then the destruction of the natives really did take place.' Fighting continued on the Australian frontier until at least 1928 with the killing of at least thirty-one Warlpiri people by a police punitive expedition at Coniston in the Northern Territory.[64]

While the frontier was more violent after 1838, it was not universally so. Successful settlers followed Peter Cunningham's advice and employed local Aborigines to work around their stations, enabling better relations with the people whose land they had usurped. The benefits for settlers of taking a conciliatory approach was shown in Victoria after the gold rush began in 1851. Settlers needed Aborigines to work for them when their British stockmen flocked to the diggings. John G Robertson of Portland wrote in 1853 that those pastoralists who had been 'severe on the natives' were quitting their properties, presumably because Aborigines refused to work for them.[65]

Warfare on the Australian frontier was not inevitable. Ged Martin points out that, unlike the British colonies in Australia, South Africa and New Zealand, there were no frontier wars on the Canadian prairies. Here the Canadian Dominion government offered treaties to indigenous Canadians, which they were willing to sign because the government provided medical supplies to reservations and impartial law and order through the North-West Mounted Police.[66]

Peter Dennis wrote in 1995 that war 'has been one of the defining forces in Australian history'.[67] The frontier wars defined Australia in two ways. The wars swept away Aboriginal sovereignty and replaced it with British institutions and cultures and six colonies that would form the Commonwealth of Australia in 1901. The British victory was so overwhelming that it determines the relationship between the descendants of the victors and the descendants of the defeated even to this day.

By 1838 the British had established outposts around the coastlines of Australia and the invasion of the inland rivers and plains had commenced. On 20 January 1838, almost fifty years to the day since Captain Arthur Phillip established Sydney at the eastern end of the continent, the missionary James Backhouse walked along the Swan River, now part of a British colony in the west. Backhouse wrote in his diary:

> In our walk, several places were pointed out, as sites for the destruction of Blacks, either by their own tribes, according to their barbarous customs, or by the White Inhabitants; and others, where white men had been destroyed by the Blacks.[68]

In fifty years, sites of conflict like these had been created across Australia: from the meandering Swan to the broad river-flats of the

Hawkesbury, and from the sticky Arnhem Land mangroves to the soft green hills of Tasmania. Men with guns would fight men with spears far beyond 1838, and armed men on both sides would kill unnumbered unarmed men, women and children. The Australian frontier wars would continue until the conquest was complete.

NOTES

INTRODUCTION

1   John K Thornton, 'The Art of War in Angola, 1575–1680', in Douglas M Peers (ed.), *Warfare and Empires*, Ashgate Publishing, Aldershot and Brookfield, Vermont, 1997, pp 81–99; Joan B Townsend, 'Firearms against Native Arms: A Study in Comparative Efficiencies with an Alaskan Example', *Arctic Anthropology*, 20(2), 1983, pp 1–33.

2   See the author's entries on the Australian frontier wars in Joan Beaumont (ed.), *Australian Defence: Sources and Statistics*, Oxford University Press, Melbourne, 2001, pp 369–72; and in Charles Messenger (ed.), *Reader's Guide to Military History*, Fitzroy Dearborn, London, 2001, pp 40–41.

3   Richard Broome, 'The Struggle for Australia: Aboriginal-European Warfare, 1770–1930', in M McKernan & M Browne (eds), *Australia Two Centuries of War & Peace*, Australian War Memorial in association with Allen & Unwin, Canberra, 1988, pp 92–120; Jeffrey Grey, *A Military History of Australia*, Cambridge University Press, Melbourne (rev. edn) 1999 [1990], pp 25–37; John Coates, *An Atlas of Australia's Wars*, Oxford University Press, Melbourne, 2001, pp 6–12.

4   WEH Stanner, *After the Dreaming: Black and White Australians — An Anthropologist's View*, 1968 Boyer Lectures, ABC, Sydney, 1968, pp 18, 43; RHW Reece, 'The Aborigines in Australian Historiography', in John A Moses (ed.), *Historical Disciplines and Culture in Australasia: An Assessment*, University of Queensland Press, Brisbane, 1979, pp 253–81; Henry Reynolds, *The Other Side of the Frontier*, Penguin, Ringwood, Victoria, 1982 [1981]; for a critique of Reynolds's work, see Jonathan Fulcher, 'The *Wik* Judgement, Pastoral Leases and Colonial Office Policy and Intention in NSW in the 1840s', *Australian Journal of Legal History*, 4(1), 1998, pp 33–56. I am indebted to Associate Professor David Philips for this reference.

5   Beverley Nance, 'The Level of Violence: Europeans and Aborigines in Port Phillip, 1835–1850', [Australian] *Historical Studies*, 19, October 1981, pp 532–49; Graeme Davison, John Hirst & Stuart Macintyre (eds), *The Oxford Companion to Australian History*, Oxford University Press, Melbourne, 1998, pp 72–73; Keith Windschuttle, 'The Myths of Frontier Massacres in Australian

History', Pt II, *Quadrant*, November 2000, p 25; Richard Broome, *Aboriginal Australians: Black Responses to White Dominance*, Allen & Unwin, Sydney (2nd edn) 1994 [1982]; Richard Broome, 'Aboriginal Victims and Voyagers, Confronting Frontier Myths', *Journal of Australian Studies*, 42, 1994, pp 70–77; Heather Goodall, *Invasion to Embassy: Land in Aboriginal Politics in New South Wales 1770–1972*, Allen & Unwin in association with Black Books, Sydney, 1996.

6   Colin Tatz, *Genocide in Australia*, AIATSIS Research Discussion Paper No 8, Australian Institute of Aboriginal and Torres Strait Islander Studies, Canberra, 1999; Henry Reynolds, *An Indelible Stain? The Question of Genocide in Australia's History*, Penguin, Ringwood, Victoria, 2001, pp 16, 30, 50–51, 117; Alison Palmer, *Colonial Genocide*, Crawford Publishing House, Adelaide, 2000, p 19.

7   *New Zealand Herald*, 9 November 2000 <www.nzherald.co.nz> downloaded 27 August 2001. I am indebted to Damien Fenton for bringing this issue to my attention.

8   Book review of *The Oxford Companion to Australian Military History* in *The Australian National Review*, August 1996, p 48; Peter Stanley, 'While acting under orders': The Slaughterhouse Creek massacre of 1838, paper presented to the Australian War Memorial Bicentennial Military History Seminar, Canberra, 1981, p 3; Broome, 'Struggle for Australia', p 94; Grey, *Military History of Australia*, pp 25–26.

9   By contrast, Ken Fry uses the term 'koori' to describe the Wiradjuri in the 1820s. *Beyond the Barrier: Class Formation in a Pastoral Society Bathurst 1818–1848*, Crawford House Press, Bathurst, 1993, p 51. For the development of the 'Aboriginal' identity, see Bain Attwood, *The Making of the Aborigines*, Allen & Unwin, Sydney, 1989.

10 David Horton (ed.), *The Encyclopaedia of Aboriginal Australia: Aboriginal & Torres Strait Islander history, society and culture*, 2 vols, Aboriginal Studies Press in association with the Australian Institute of Aboriginal and Torres Strait Islander Studies, Canberra, 1994. For the use of 'Darug' rather than 'Dharug', see James Kohen, *The Darug and their Neighbours: the traditional Aboriginal owners of the Sydney Region*, Daruglink in association with Blacktown & District Historical Society, Blacktown, NSW, 1993.

11 Lyndall Ryan, having used the term 'European' in the first edition of *Aboriginal Tasmanians* in 1981, commented in the preface of the second edition in 1996 that if she was writing the book from scratch she would now use the term 'British' instead. *The Aboriginal Tasmanians*, Allen & Unwin, Sydney (2nd edn) 1996, p xx. Again this contrasts with Fry who uses the term 'European' because 'the early settlers were not "white" and they were not all British'. *Beyond the Barrier*, p 51.

12 Craig Wilcox, 'The Culture of Restrained Force in British Australia', in Carl Bridge (ed.), *Ranging Shots: New Directions in Australian Military History*, Sir Robert Menzies Centre for Australian Studies, University of London, London, 1998, p 11.

13 Henry Reynolds, *Why Weren't We Told? A Personal Search for the Truth about Our History*, Penguin, Ringwood, Victoria, 1999, p 166.

14 As Bill Thorpe points out, many settlers were ex-soldiers, and the part these men played in frontier warfare needs to be examined. *Colonial Queensland: Perspectives on a Frontier Society*, University of Queensland Press, Brisbane, 1996, pp 47–48.

15 John Keegan, *The Face of Battle*, Jonathan Cape, London, 1976; Broome, 'Struggle for Australia', pp 109–16.

16 A good summary of this debate is provided in Lyndall Ryan, 'The Aboriginal History Wars', *Australian Historical Association Bulletin*, 92, 2001, pp 31–37.

Windschuttle and many of the authors he had criticised attended the 'Frontier Conflict: the Australian Experience' conference at the National Museum of Australia, 13–14 December 2001. The papers from this conference will be published.

17 Micheal Clodfelter, *Warfare and Armed Conflicts: A Statistical Reference to Casualty and Other Figures, 1618–1991*, 2 vols, McFarland & Co, Jefferson, North Carolina, 1992, 1: xxi; 'Civil War deaths' discussion on H-Demog Discussion Network, January 2001 <www2.h-net.msu.edu/~demog/> downloaded 24 July 2001.
18 Beaumont (ed.), *Sources and Statistics*, p 11.

I   WARRIORS AND SOLDIERS

1   Peter Turbet, *The Aborigines of the Sydney District Before 1788*, Kangaroo Press, Sydney (rev. edn) 2001 [1989], pp 36–53; Michael Martin, *On Darug Land: An Aboriginal Perspective*, Greater Western Education Centre, St Marys, NSW, 1988, pp 11, 30.
2   Goodall, *Invasion to Embassy*, p 13; Henry Reynolds, *Fate of a Free People*, Penguin, Ringwood, Victoria, 1995, p 34; Broome, 'Struggle for Australia', pp 109–10.
3   Lawrence H Keeley, *War Before Civilization*, Oxford University Press, New York, 1996. I am indebted to Jean Bou for bringing this book to my attention.
4   John F Guilmartin Jr, 'Ideology and Conflict: The Wars of the Ottoman Empire, 1453–1606', in Peers (ed.), *Warfare and Empires*, pp 2, 5; TM Charles-Edwards, 'Irish Warfare Before 1100', in Thomas Bartlett & Keith Jeffrey (eds), *A Military History of Ireland*, Cambridge University Press, Cambridge, 1996, p 26; Leroy V Eid, '"National" War Among Indians of Northeastern North America', *The Canadian Review of American Studies*, 16(2), 1985, p 129.
5   Glynn Barratt, *The Russians at Port Jackson 1814–1822*, Australian Institute of Aboriginal Studies, Canberra, 1981, p 39.
6   David Collins (ed. Brian Fletcher), *An Account of the English Colony of New South Wales, with remarks on the dispositions, customs, manners, etc. of the native inhabitants of that country*, 2 vols [1798, 1802], Reed in association with the Royal Historical Society, Sydney, 1975, I: 456; Watkin Tench (ed. LF Fitzhardinge), *Sydney's First Four Years: being a reprint of A Narrative of the Expedition to Botany Bay and A Complete Account of the Settlement at Port Jackson* [1788, 1793], Royal Australian Historical Society in association with Angus & Robertson, Sydney, 1961, pp 230–31; Nance, 'Level of Violence', p 539.
7   Quoted in Tim Flannery, *The Future Eaters: An Ecological History of the Australasian Lands and People*, Reed Books, Melbourne, 1994, p 271.
8   Collins, *An Account*, I: 466, 485; diary — Ensign Francis Barrallier, NSW Corps, *Historical Records of New South Wales* (hereafter *HR NSW*) 7 vols, NSW Government Printer, Sydney, 1892–1901, V: 767; *Australian*, 14 October 1826; Alan EJ Andrews (ed.), *Hume and Hovell 1824*, Blubber Head Press, Hobart, 1981, p 234; John Bulmer (comp. Alastair Campbell, ed. Ron Vanderwal), *Victorian Aborigines: John Bulmer's Recollections 1855–1908*, Museum of Victoria Occasional Papers Anthropology & History No 1, Museum of Victoria, Melbourne, 1994, pp 1–2.
9   Horatio Hale, *United States Exploring Expedition During the Years 1838, 1839, 1840, 1841, 1842. Under the command of Charles Wilkes, U.S.N. Ethnography and Philology* [1846], The Gregg Press, Ridgewood, New Jersey, 1968, p 116.
10 Keeley, *War Before Civilization*, pp 90–91.
11 Daniel Paine (eds RJB Knight & Alan Frost), *The Journal of Daniel Paine 1794–1797 Together with Documents Illustrating the Beginning of Government*

boat-building and Timber-gathering in New South Wales, 1795–1805, Library of Australian History, Sydney, 1983, p 40.

12   Ensign Alexander Huey, 73rd Regiment, The Voyage of the 73rd Regiment of Foot, p 24, State Library of NSW (hereafter SLNSW) ML B1514; diary — Daniel Southwell, 7 September 1790, National Library of Australia (hereafter NLA) Australian Joint Copying Project (hereafter AJCP) Reel M1538; Collins, *An Account*, I: 486; Barratt, *Russians at Port Jackson*, p 23.

13   Broome, 'Struggle for Australia', p 94.

14   John Uniacke, 'Narrative of Mr Oxley's Expedition to survey Port Curtis and Moreton Bay, with a view to form Convict Establishments There in pursuance of the Recommendation of the Commissioner of Inquiry' [1823], in George Mackaness (ed.), *The Discovery and Exploration of Moreton Bay and the Brisbane River (1799–1823)*, 2 Pts, Review Publications, Dubbo, 1979 [1956], II: 35, 37.

15   Hale, *Exploring Expedition*, p 116; JO Balfour, *A Sketch of New South Wales*, Smith, Elder & Co, London, 1845, pp 16–17; James Backhouse, 'Account of a Journey from Parramatta, Across the Blue Mountains to Wellington', in George Mackaness (ed.), *Fourteen Journeys Over The Blue Mountains of New South Wales 1813–1841*, 3 Pts, Review Publications, Dubbo, 1978 [1950], III: 19.

16   Bulmer, *Victorian Aborigines*, pp 16, 62–63.

17   Broome, 'Struggle for Australia', pp 109–10; NG Butlin, *Economics and the Dreamtime: A Hypothetical History*, Cambridge University Press, Cambridge, 1993, p 82.

18   Bulmer, *Victorian Aborigines*, pp 8–9; Tench, *First Four Years*, pp 201–02; Nicolas Baudin (trans. Christine Cornell), *The Journal of Post Captain Nicolas Baudin Commander-in-Chief of the Corvettes* Géographe *and* Naturaliste *Assigned by Order of the Government to a Voyage of Discovery*, Libraries Board of South Australia, Adelaide, 1974, p 340; NJB Plomley, *The Baudin Expedition and the Tasmanian Aborigines*, Blubber Head Press, Hobart, 1983, p 127.

19   Collins, *An Account*, II: 47, I: 488; diary — Richard Atkins, 8 June 1792, NLA mfm G2198; Bulmer, *Victorian Aborigines*, p 25.

20   Henry Melville (ed. George Mackaness), *The History of Van Diemen's Land: From the Year 1824 to 1835, inclusive*, [1836], Horwitz Publications & The Grahame Book Co, Sydney, 1965, p 38; Edward Duyker (trans. & ed.), *The Discovery of Tasmania: Journal extracts from the expeditions of Abel Janszoon Tasman and Marc-Joseph Marion Dufresne 1642 and 1772*, St Davids Park Publishing, Hobart, 1992, pp 34, 42–43; George Mortimer, *Observations and Remarks made during a Voyage to the islands of Teneriffe, Amsterdam, Maria's Islands near Van Diemen's Lands, Otaheite, Sandwich islands, Owhyhee, The Fox Islands on the North West Coast of America, Tinian, and from thence to Canton, in the Brig* Mercury, *Commanded by John Henry Cox, Esq*, the author, London, 1791, p 20; Plomley, *Baudin Expedition*, pp 77, 79, 82, 129, 137, 185–86; diary — Barrallier, *HRNSW*, V: 775, 819; Gregory Blaxland, 'A Journal of a Tour of Discovery Across the Blue Mountains, New South Wales, in the Year 1813', in Mackaness (ed.), *Fourteen Journeys*, I: 19; Constance Campbell Petrie (ed.), *Tom Petrie's Reminiscences of Early Queensland* [1904], Currey O'Neil, Melbourne, 1980, p 101.

21   Helen Brayshaw, *Aborigines of the Hunter Valley: A Study of Colonial Records*, Scone & Upper Hunter Historical Society, Scone, 1986, p 65; memo — William Thomas, Port Phillip District Assistant Native Protector, [no date], in Thomas Francis Bride (ed.), *Letters from Victorian Pioneers: Being a series of papers on the early occupation of the colony, the Aborigines, etc* [1898], William Heinemann, Melbourne, 1969, p 403; Andrews (ed.), *Hume and Hovell*, pp 240–42.

22 Collet Barker (eds John Mulvaney & Neville Green), *Commandant of Solitude: The Journals of Captain Collet Barker 1828–1831*, Melbourne University Press, Melbourne, 1992, p 119; A Campbell, 'Geographical Memoir of Melville Island and Port Essington, on the Cobourg Peninsula, Northern Australia; with some Observations on the Settlements which have been established on the North Coast of New Holland', *The Journal of the Royal Geographical Society of London*, IV, 1834, pp 156, 170.

23 Collins, *An Account*, I: 487; letter — Lachlan Macquarie, NSW Governor, to Lord Bathurst, British Colonial Secretary, 30 June 1815, *Historical Records of Australia* Series 1 (hereafter *HRA*), Governors' Despatches to and from England, 1788–1848, 26 vols, Parliament of the Commonwealth of Australia, Melbourne, 1914–25, VIII: 610; Major Henry Colden Antill, 73rd Regiment, 'A Journal of an excursion over the Blue or Western Mountains of New South Wales to visit a tract of the new discovered country with his Excellency Governor and Mrs Macquarie, and a Party of Gentlemen', in Mackaness (ed.), *Fourteen Journeys*, I: 91; John Oxley, *Journals of Two Expeditions into the Interior of New South Wales, Undertaken by Order of the British Government in the Years 1817–18* [1820], Libraries Board of South Australia, Adelaide, 1964, p 19.

24 Jakelin Troy, 'The Sydney Language', in Nick Thieberger & William McGregor (eds), *Macquarie Aboriginal Words: a dictionary of words from Australian Aboriginal and Torres Strait Islander languages*, The Macquarie Library, Sydney, 1994, p 62; Broome, 'Struggle for Australia', p 430; letter — Macquarie to Sergeant Jeremiah Murphy, 46th Regiment, 22 April 1816, NLA mfm N257 Reel 6065 Archives Office of New South Wales Colonial Secretary's Office (hereafter AONSW CSO) 4/1798.

25 Robert J King, *The Secret History of the Convict Colony: Alexandro Malaspina's report on the British settlement of New South Wales*, Allen & Unwin, Sydney, 1990, p 161; *Sydney Gazette*, 22 December 1805. Te Pahi and his sons visited Sydney as guests of Samuel Marsden. James Belich, *Making Peoples: A History of the New Zealanders. From Polynesian Settlement to the End of the Nineteenth Century*, Penguin, Auckland, 1996, pp 141–42.

26 Jorgen Jorgenson (ed. NJB Plomley), *Jorgen Jorgenson and the Aborigines of Van Diemen's Land: being a reconstruction of his 'lost' book on their customs and habits, and on his role in the Roving Parties and the Black Line*, Blubber Head Press, Hobart, 1991, p 57; *Sydney Gazette*, 27 January 1805, 23 December 1804; John Rowley, 'Language of George's River, Cowpastures and Appin', in William Ridley, *Kamilaroi and other Australian Languages*, NSW Government Printer, Sydney (2nd edn) 1875, p 105.

27 Campbell, 'Geographical Memoir', p 156; letter — David Blackburn to Margaret Blackburn, 15 November 1788, NLA AJCP Reel M971; *Sydney Gazette*, 6 November 1808; King, *Secret History*, p 162.

28 *Sydney Gazette*, 2 September 1804, 27 January 1805; Plomley, *Baudin Expedition*, p 104; Duyker (trans. & ed.), *Discovery of Tasmania*, p 25; Robert Knopwood (ed. Mary Nicholls), *The Diary of the Reverend Robert Knopwood 1803–1838: First Chaplain of Van Diemen's Land*, Tasmanian Historical Research Association, Launceston, 1977, pp 128, 171.

29 *Sydney Gazette*, 2 September 1804, 27 January 1805; *Perth Gazette*, 13 July 1833; Petrie, *Tom Petrie's Reminiscences*, pp 103–04.

30 Collins, *An Account*, I: 275, 345, 486, II: 40.

31 William Bradley, *A Voyage to New South Wales: The Journal of Lieutenant William Bradley of HMS* Sirius *1786–1792*, Public Library of NSW in association with Ure Smith, Sydney, 1969, p 127; Collins, *An Account*, I: 460, II: 89.

32 Balfour, *Sketch*, p 7; letter — William Lawson Junior to Nelson Lawson, 14 June 1824, William Lawson (ed. William Beard), *Old Ironbark: Some*

unpublished Correspondence (1817–1824) from and to William Lawson Explorer and Pioneer of Veteran Hall, N.S.W., Wentworth Press, Sydney, 1967, p 38; Jorgenson, *Jorgen Jorgenson*, p 52; Bulmer, *Victorian Aborigines*, p 27; Baudin, *Journal*, p 324.

33 Anthony Pagden, 'The Struggle for Legitimacy and the Image of Empire in the Atlantic to c.1700', in Nicholas Canny (ed.), *The Oxford History of the British Empire*, I, Oxford University Press, Oxford, 1998, pp 34–54; Jeremy Black, *War and the World: Military Power and the Fate of Continents, 1450–2000*, Yale University Press, New Haven, Connecticut, 1998, p 146; Alan Frost, 'New South Wales as *terra nullius:* the British denial of Aboriginal Land rights', [Australian] *Historical Studies*, 19, 1981, pp 513–23. Merete Borch, 'Rethinking the Origins of *Terra Nullius*', *Australian Historical Studies*, 117, 2001, pp 222–39.

34 Letter — Post-Captain Nicolas Baudin to Philip Gidley King, NSW Governor, 23 February 1802, *HRNSW*, V: 830; Price quoted in Anthony Pagden, *Lords of all the World: Ideologies of Empire in Spain, Britain and France c1500–c1800*, Yale University Press, New Haven, Connecticut, 1995, p 82.

35 For British Army organisation in this period, see Richard Glover, *Peninsular Preparation: The Reform of the British Army 1795–1809* Cambridge University Press, Cambridge, 1963.

36 Sources: Michael Barthorp, *The British Army on Campaign 1816–1902*, 1, Osprey Publishing, London, 1987, pp 4–5; Michael Duffy, 'World-Wide War and British Expansion 1793–1815', in PJ Marshall (ed.), *The Oxford History of the British Empire*, II, Oxford University Press, Oxford, 1998, pp 184–207; Roger Norman Buckley, *The British Army in the West Indies: Society and the Military in the Revolutionary Age*, University of Florida Press, Gainesville, Florida, 1998, pp 248–68.

37 For this detachment, see John Moore, *The First Fleet Marines 1786–1792*, University of Queensland Press, Brisbane, 1987.

38 For more on the British Army in Australia, see M Austin, *The Army in Australia 1840–50: Prelude to the Golden Years*, Australian Government Publishing Service, Canberra, 1979; Peter Stanley, *The Remote Garrison: The British Army in Australia 1788–1870*, Kangaroo Press, Sydney, 1986.

39 Maurice Austin, 'The First Australian "Digger": John Cox of the New South Wales Corps', *Sabretache*, 27(1), 1986, p 13; letter — J Stewart, British Treasury, to George Arthur, Van Diemen's Land Lieutenant-Governor, 15 May 1829, Archives Office of Tasmania (hereafter AOT) GO17 1; John Clarke, 'A young soldier in the Antipodes, 1830 to 1836', in TH McGuffie (ed.), *Rank and File: The Common Soldier at Peace and War 1642–1914*, Hutchinson, London, 1964, p 174; Barker, *Commandant of Solitude*, p 56; Geoff Blackburn, *Conquest and Settlement: The 21st Regiment of Foot (North British Fusiliers) in Western Australia 1833–1840*, Perth, Hesperian Press, 1999, p 14; letter — Sir Thomas Brisbane, NSW Governor, to Bruce, 28 March 1822, NLA MS4036 Box 1.

40 The New South Wales Corps lacks a comprehensive history, but for recent research, see Pamela Statham, *Ins and Outs: The Composition and Disposal of the NSW Corps, 1790–1810*, Working Papers in Economic History No 105, Australian National University, Canberra, 1988; Pamela Statham (ed.), *A Colonial Regiment: New Sources Relating to the New South Wales Corps 1789–1810*, ANU Central Printery, Canberra, 1992.

41 Buckley, *British Army in West Indies*, p 103; Ian K Steele, 'The Anointed, the Appointed, and the Elected: Governance of the British Empire, 1689–1784', in Marshall (ed.), *Oxford History of the British Empire*, II: 111; Grey, *Military History of Australia*, pp 7, 11.

42 Robert Fraser, 'The New South Wales Corps and their Occupation of

Massachusetts during the Anglo-American War of 1812', *Sabretache*, 29(2), 1988, pp 4–9.

43 Peter Burroughs, 'An Unreformed Army?', in David Chandler (ed.), *The Oxford Illustrated History of the British Army*, Oxford University Press, Oxford, 1994, p 176; Stanley, *Remote Garrison*, pp 79–80.

44 Gerald Walsh, 'The military and the development of the Australian colonies, 1788–1888', in McKernan & Browne (eds), *Two Centuries of War & Peace*, pp 43–64.

45 *Sydney Gazette*, 4 December 1803; Alan Atkinson, *The Europeans in Australia: A History*, Vol 1, Oxford University Press, Melbourne, 1997, p 254; KS Inglis, *The Australian Colonists: An Exploration of Social History 1788–1870*, Melbourne University Press, Melbourne, 1974, p 215.

46 King, *Secret History*, pp 48–49, 53–54; Collins, *An Account*, II: 147.

47 Duffy, 'World-Wide War', pp 203–04.

48 Evidence — Major James Nunn, OC NSW Mounted Police, 4 April 1839, *HRA*, XX: 250–51; letter — Captain Alexander Maconochie, RN, Van Diemen's Land Governor's Private Secretary, to *Murray's Review*, 16 January 1838, quoted in George Augustus Robinson (ed. NJB Plomley), *Weep in Silence: A History of the Flinders Island Aboriginal Settlement with the Flinders Island Journal of George Augustus Robinson 1835–1839*, Blubber Head Press, Hobart, 1987, p 1004; letters — Edward Deas Thomson, NSW Colonial Secretary, to Captain William Lonsdale, Melbourne Police Magistrate, 4 September 1837, Lonsdale to Thomson, 14 December 1838, *Historical Records of Victoria* (hereafter *HRV*), 7 vols, Victorian Government Printing Office, Melbourne, 1982–98, 2A: 244, 341; Marie Fels, *Good Men and True: The Aboriginal Police of the Port Phillip District 1837–1853*, Melbourne University Press, Melbourne, 1988.

49 Quoted in Sir John Fortescue, *A History of the British Army*, Macmillan & Co, London, 1899, II: 410. The original reference is Francis Parkman, *Montcalm and Wolfe*, 2 vols [1884], Macmillan & Co, London, 1912, II: 395.

50 Matthew C Ward, '"The European Method of Warring Is Not Practiced Here": The Failure of British Military Policy in the Ohio Valley, 1755–1759', *War in History*, 4(3), 1997, pp 253–55; Lorenzo M Crowell, 'Logistics in the Madras Army *circa* 1830', *War & Society*, 10(2), 1992, pp 1–33.

51 John Connor, 'British Frontier Warfare Logistics and the "Black Line", Van Diemen's Land (Tasmania) 1830', *War in History*, 9(2), 2002, pp 142–57.

52 Peter E Russell, 'Redcoats in the Wilderness: British Officers and Irregular Warfare in Europe and America, 1740 to 1760', *William and Mary Quarterly*, 3rd Series, 35(4), 1978, p 630; Daniel J Beattie, 'The Adaption of the British Army to Wilderness Warfare', in Maarten Ultee (ed.), *Adapting to Conditions: War and Society in the Eighteenth Century*, University of Alabama Press, University, Alabama, 1986, pp 70, 77.

53 *Perth Gazette*, 18 May 1833.

54 Frank Ongley Darvall, *Popular Disturbances and Public Order in Regency England*, Oxford University Press, Oxford, 1969 [1934]; JR Ward, 'The British West Indies in the Age of Abolition, 1748–1815', in Marshall (ed.), *Oxford History of the British Empire*, II: 437.

55 Letter — Major George Johnston, NSW Corps, to William Paterson, NSW Lieutenant-Governor, 9 March 1804, *HRA*, IV: 570; Hobart General Orders, 10 May 1817, SLNSW ML A1352.

56 JA Houlding, *Fit for Service: The Training of the British Army 1715–1795*, Clarendon Press, Oxford, 1981, p 388.

57 80th Regiment Digest, I, NLA AJCP Reel M815.

58 Letter — Sir Richard Bourke, NSW Governor, to Lord Fitzroy Somerset, British Colonial Secretary, 18 June 1833, *HRA*, XVII: 148.

59 Hew Strachan, *From Waterloo to Balaclava: Tactics, Technology, and the British Army 1815–1854*, Cambridge University Press, Cambridge, 1985, pp 16, 19–20.

60 Melville, *History of Van Diemen's Land*, p 33; Wilcox, 'Culture of Restrained Force', p 9.

61 Militias known as 'Loyal Associations' were formed in New South Wales during the war with France but they never fought the Aborigines. Duncan MacCallum, 'The Early "Volunteer" Associations in New South Wales and the Proposals in the First Quarter of the Nineteenth Century', *Journal of the Royal Australian Historical Society*, 47(6), 1961, pp 352–67; letter — Sir George Gipps, NSW Governor, to Lord Glenelg, British Colonial Secretary, 21 July 1838, *HRA*, XIX: 509; Wilcox, 'Culture of Restrained Force', p 9.

62 Broome, 'Struggle for Australia', p 100; *Australian*, 28 June 1826; *Perth Gazette*, 2 March 1833; letter — Brisbane to Bathurst, 8 November 1825, *HRA*, XI: 898.

63 Letter — Western District settlers to Bourke, 8 June 1837, *HRV*, 1: 219; Matthew Higgins, '"Deservedly respected": a first look at the 11th Regiment in Australia', *Journal of the Australian War Memorial*, 6, 1985, p 7.

64 *Sydney Gazette*, 6 May, 27 December 1826; letter — Lonsdale to Thomson, 5 June 1838, *HRV*, 2A: p 224; Gunther Rothenburg, 'The Age of Napoleon', in Michael Howard, George J Andreopoulos, & Mark R Shulman (eds), *The Laws of War: Constraints on Warfare in the Western World*, Yale University Press, Hartford, Connecticut, 1994, p 96; Governor's Proclamation, 23 June 1824, *British Parliamentary Papers* Colonies, Australia (hereafter *BPP* Australia) 34 vols, Irish University Press, Shannon, Ireland, 1968–70, 5: 191.

65 Grey, *Military History*, pp 30–31; David Denholm, *The Colonial Australians*, Penguin, Ringwood, Victoria, 1979, pp 33–36; Reynolds, *Other Side of the Frontier*, p 99; Reynolds, *Fate of a Free People*, p 41.

66 Donald Porch, 'Imperial Wars from the Seven Years War to the First World War', in Charles Townshend (ed.), *The Oxford Illustrated History of Modern War*, Oxford University Press, Oxford, 1997, pp 96–97.

67 Daniel R Headrick, *The Tools of Empire: Technology and European Imperialism in the Nineteenth Century*, Oxford University Press, New York, 1981, pp 86–88; Broome, 'Struggle for Australia', pp 104–09.

68 Howard L Blackmore, *British Military Firearms 1650–1850*, Herbert Jenkins, London, 1961, p 45; Strachan, *Waterloo to Balaclava*, pp 31–33; Peter Dennis et al. (eds), *The Oxford Companion to Australian Military History*, Oxford University Press, Melbourne (reprint with corrections) 1999 [1995], p 547.

69 Collins, *An Account*, I: 111; Denholm, *Colonial Australians*, p 34.

70 Lieutenant John Mitchell, *United Services Journal*, II, 1834, p 323, quoted in Strachan, *Waterloo to Balaclava*, pp 32–33.

71 Ward, 'European Method of Warring', p 252; *Australian*, 1 July 1826; BP Hughes, *Firepower: Weapons effectiveness on the battlefield, 1630–1850*, Arms & Armour Press, London, 1974, p 164.

72 Evidence — Dr Stephen Geury Wilks, 29 May 1824, NLA mfm N257 Reel 6065 AONSW CSO 4/1799; Broome, 'Struggle for Australia', p 99; Strachan, *Waterloo to Balaclava*, p 31; Reginald Magee, 'Muskets, Musket Balls and the Wounds They Made', *The Australian and New Zealand Journal of Surgery*, 65(12), 1995, p 892; Robert G Richardson, *Larrey: Surgeon to Napoleon's Imperial Guard*, John Murray, London, 1974, p 161; Rutherford Alcock, *Notes on the Medical History and Statistics of the British Legion of Spain; Comprising the results of gun-shot wounds in relation to important questions in surgery*, John Churchill, London, 1838, p 55; Dennis et al (eds), *Oxford Companion to Australian Military History*, p 7.

73 Collins, *An Account*, I: 111, 117, 144; letter — John Harris, Surgeon NSW

Corps, 20 March 1791, SLNSW ML A1597; letter — Roderic O'Connor to WJ Parramore, Van Diemen's Land Lieutenant-Governor's Secretary, 11 December 1827, AOT CSO1 323/7578/8.

74 Belich, *Making Peoples*, pp 133, 149–51; JE Indikori, 'The Import of Firearms into West Africa, 1750–1807: A Qualitative Analysis', in Peers (ed.), *Warfare and Empires*, pp 245–74; Peter C Mancall, 'Native Americans and Europeans in English America, 1500–1700', in Canny (ed.), *Oxford History of the British Empire*, I: 346–47.

75 James Belich, *The New Zealand Wars and the Victorian Interpretation of Racial Conflict*, Penguin, Auckland (rev. edn) 1998 [1986], pp 293–98; for critiques of Belich, see Christopher Pugsley, 'Maori Did Not Invent Trench Warfare', *New Zealand Defence Quarterly*, Spring 1998, pp 33–37; John M Gates, 'James Belich and the Maori Pa: Revisionist History Revised', *War & Society*, 19(2), 2001, pp 47–68.

76 Dennis *et al* (eds), *Oxford Companion to Australian Military History*, p 5.

77 Evidence — Edward Wedge, 28 October 1836, *HRV*, 2A: 49; John Hunter (ed. John Bach), *An Historical Journal of Events at Sydney and at Sea 1787–1792* [1793], Royal Australian Historical Society in association with Angus & Robertson, Sydney, 1968, p 329; letter — Harris, 20 May 1791, SLNSW ML A1597; Plomley, *Baudin Expedition*, p 136; memo — Thomas, in Bride (ed.), *Letters*, p 403.

78 Dennis *et al* (eds), *Oxford Companion to Australian Military History*, p 5; Eid, '"National" War', pp 139, 146.

79 Duffy, 'World-Wide War', p 142; Black, *War and the World*, p 145; Armstrong Starkey, *European and Native American Warfare 1675–1815*, University of Oklahoma Press, Norman, Oklahoma, 1998, p 123.

80 George Raudzens, 'Military Revolution or Maritime Evolution? Military Superiorities or Transportation Advantages as Main Causes of European Colonial Conquests to 1788', *The Journal of Military History*, 63, 1999, pp 631–42; Jeremy Black, *War: Past, Present & Future*, St Martin's Press, New York, 2000, p 19.

2 SYDNEY, 1788–1791

1 Tench, *First Four Years*, p 51.

2 For more on the Eora and their neighbours, see Turbet, *Aborigines of the Sydney District*; JL Kohen & Ronald Lampert, 'Hunters and Fishers in the Sydney Region', in DJ Mulvaney & J Peter White (eds), *Australians to 1788*, Fairfax, Syme & Weldon Associates, Sydney, 1987, pp 343–65.

3 Tench, *First Four Years*, p 208.

4 Bradley, *Voyage to New South Wales*, p 133; Tench, *First Four Years*, p 287; John White (ed. Alec Chisholm), *Journal of a Voyage to New South Wales* [1790], Royal Australian Historical Society in association with Angus & Robertson, Sydney, 1962, p 137; diary — Arthur Bowes Smyth, 21 January 1788, NLA AJCP Reel M933.

5 Ged Martin (ed.), *The Founding of Australia: The Arguments about Australia's Origins*, Hale & Iremonger, Sydney, 1978.

6 For the wars with France, see Duffy, 'World-Wide War'; John B Hattendorf, 'The Struggle With France, 1690–1815', in JR Hill (ed.), *The Oxford Illustrated History of the Royal Navy*, Oxford University Press, Oxford, 1995, pp 80–119; David Gates, 'The Transformation of the Army 1783–1815', in Chandler (ed.), *Oxford Illustrated History of the British Army*, pp 133–59.

7 See Alan Frost's books: *Convicts and Empire: A Naval Question, 1776–1811*, Oxford University Press, Melbourne, 1980; *Arthur Phillip, 1738–1814: His Voyaging*, Oxford University Press, Melbourne, 1987; *Botany Bay Mirages:*

Illusions of Australia's Convict Beginnings, Melbourne University Press, Melbourne, 1994.

8   Black, *War and the World*, p 147.

9   Memo — Arthur Phillip, NSW Governor, [1787], *HRNSW*, I(2): 52; letter — Phillip to Lord Sydney, British Home Secretary, 12 February 1790, *HRA*, I: 143.

10 Hyacinthe de Bougainville (trans. & ed. Marc Serge Rivière), *The Governor's Noble Guest: Hyacinthe de Bougainville's account of Port Jackson, 1825*, Melbourne University Press, Melbourne, 1999, p 112; Bradley, *Voyage to New South Wales*, pp 81, 126, 99.

11 Moore, *First Fleet Marines*, pp 124–31.

12 Tench, *First Four Years*, pp 40, 292; Bradley, *Voyage to New South Wales*, p 126; White, *Journal of a Voyage*, p 111; letter — Lieutenant Ralph Clark to Dr B Hartwell, Plymouth, 1 October 1788, Ralph Clark (eds Paul G Fidlon & RJ Ryan), *The Journal and Letters of Lt. Ralph Clark 1787–1792*, Australian Documents Library in association with the Library of Australian History Pty Ltd, Sydney, 1981, p 271; letter — anonymous Marine officer to Sir Joseph Banks, 18 November 1788, *HRNSW*, I(2): 221.

13 Bradley, *Voyage to New South Wales*, p 118; Tench, *First Four Years*, pp 137–38.

14 AJ Gray, 'Peter Burn: The First Convict Officially Presumed Killed by Natives at Sydney Cove', *Journal of the Royal Australian Historical Society*, 45(2), 1959, pp 96–104; Bradley, *Voyage to New South Wales*, pp 93–94, 108.

15 British casualties are listed in: Bradley, *Voyage to New South Wales*; Clark, *Journal and Letters*; Collins, *An Account*; John Easty, *Memorandum of the transactions of a voyage from England to Botany Bay 1787–1793: A First Fleet Journal*, Public Library of NSW in association with Angus & Robertson, Sydney, 1965; Hunter, *Historical Journal*; James Scott, *Remarks on a Passage to Botany Bay 1787–1792 A First Fleet Journal*, Public Library of NSW in association with Angus & Robertson, Sydney, 1963; Tench, *First Four Years*; White, *Journal of a Voyage*.

16 JF Nagle, *Collins, the Courts & the Colony: Law and Society in Colonial New South Wales 1788–1796*, UNSW Press, Sydney, 1996, p 68; Moore, *First Fleet Marines*, pp 160–61.

17 Tench, *First Four Years*, pp 179–80.

18 Hunter, *Historical Journal*, pp 331–33; Tench, *First Four Years*, p 215; Bradley, *Voyage to New South Wales*, p 177; Collins, *An Account*, I: 67.

19 Hunter, *Historical Journal*, pp 326–27; Tench, *First Four Years*, p 206.

20 Memo — Phillip, [1787], *HRNSW*, I(2): 52; General Orders, 13 December 1790, *HRA*, I: 293; diary — Smyth, 18–22 February 1788, NLA AJCP Reel M933.

21 Bradley, *Voyage to New South Wales*, p 183; letter — Phillip to William Grenville, British Home Secretary, 7 November 1791, *HRA*, I: 294; Tench, *First Four Years*, pp 212, 209.

22 Collins, *An Account*, I: 107.

23 Tench, *First Four Years*, p 221; Collins, *An Account*, I: 148.

24 Tench, *First Four Years*, p 181; Collins, *An Account*, I: 122.

25 Goodall, *Invasion to Embassy*, p 27; *Sydney Gazette*, 20 January 1805.

26 Isabel McBryde, 'Exchange in southeastern Australia: an ethnohistorical perspective', in Valerie Chapman & Peter Read (eds), *Terrible Hard Biscuits: A Reader in Aboriginal History*, Allen & Unwin, Sydney, 1996, pp 42–68; Collins, *An Account*, I: 250; Clark, *Journal and Letters*, p 109.

27 White, *Journal of a Voyage*, p 112; Hunter, *Historical Journal*, p 329; Collins, *An Account*, I: 249, 464, 137, 461.

28 Letter — Philip to Grenville, 17 June 1790, *HRA*, I: 179.

29 Collins, *An Account*, I: 122, II: 9.

30   Isabel McBryde, '"… To establish a commerce of this sort" — Cross-Cultural Exchange at the Port Jackson Settlement', in John Hardy & Alan Frost (eds), *Studies from Terra Australis to Australia*, Australian Academy of the Humanities, Canberra, 1989, p 180; Tench, *First Four Years*, pp 160, 200, 209; Hunter, *Historical Journal*, pp 327, 332, 358; Atkinson, *Europeans in Australia*, p 157.

31   Bradley, *Voyage to New South Wales*, pp 161–62; Collins, *An Account*, I: 496; Tench, *First Four Years*, p 146.

32   David Day, *Claiming a Continent: A New History of Australia*, Harper Collins, Sydney (rev. edn) 2001 [1996], p 43.

33   Elizabeth A Fenn, 'Biological Warfare in Eighteenth-Century North America: Beyond Jeffery Amherst', *The Journal of American History*, 86(4), 2000, pp 1552–80; Douglas Pike (gen. ed.), *Australian Dictionary of Biography 1788–1850* (hereafter *ADB*), 2 vols, Melbourne University Press, Melbourne, 1966–67, 2: 397; Reynolds, *An Indelible Stain?*, p 47.

34   Letter — Major Robert Ross to Sir Philip Stephens, British Admiralty Secretary, 10 July 1788, *HRNSW*, I(2): 171; *ADB*, 2: 397; M Austin, 'The Early Defences of Australia', *Journal of the Royal Australian Historical Society*, 49(3), 1963, p 192; Moore, *First Fleet Marines*, p 134.

35   Fenn, 'Biological Warfare', pp 1553–54.

36   NG Butlin, *Our Original Aggression: Aboriginal Populations of Southeastern Australia 1788–1850*, George Allen & Unwin, Sydney, 1983, p 22.

37   James Watt, 'The Colony's Health', in Hardy & Frost (eds), *Studies from Terra Australis to Australia*, p 145. The ABC television documentary 'Frontier', broadcast in 1997, stated that an epidemic took place but did not attempt to identify the disease.

38   Letter — Phillip to Evan Nepean, British Admiralty Secretary, 9 July 1788, *HRNSW*, I(2): 148; Collins, *An Account*, I: 25, 35, 48; White, *Journal of a Voyage*, p 133; Tench, *First Four Years*, p 144.

39   Tench, *First Four Years*, p 181.

40   The description of the punitive expeditions in the following paragraphs is based on Tench's account. *First Four Years*, pp 207–14.

41   Henry Reynolds, 'From Armband to Blindfold', *Australian Review of Books*, April 2001, p 8; Douglas Hay, 'Property, Authority and the Criminal Law', in Douglas Hay *et al.*, *Albion's Fatal Tree: Crime and Society in Eighteenth-Century England*, Allen Lane, London, 1975, p 63; Inga Clendinnen, 'First Contact', *Australian Review of Books*, May 2001, p 7. I am indebted to Dr David Blaazer for the Hay reference.

42   Moore, *First Fleet Marines*, p 118.

43   Easty, *Memorandum*, p 121.

44   Letters — Lord Hobart, British Colonial Secretary, to King, 14 February 1803, King to Hobart, 16 April 1804, Macquarie to Bathurst, 19 July 1819, *HRA*, IV: 9, V: 612, X: 178; John Sweetman, 'The Military Establishment at King George Sound (Frederickstown) 1826–1831', *Sabretache*, 28(3), 1987, pp 22 24.

45   Black, *War: Past, Present & Future*, p 11.

46   Barker, *Commandant of Solitude*, p 244; James Backhouse, *A Narrative of a Visit to the Australian Colonies*, Hamilton, Adams & Co, London, 1843, p 526.

47   Evidence — Edward White, 16 March 1830, AOT CBE1 1; Knopwood, *Diary*, p 51; *Sydney Gazette*, 2 September 1804; *ADB*, 2: 124.

48   Bob Reece, 'Inventing Aborigines', in Chapman & Read (eds), *Terrible Hard Biscuits*, p 34; Alan Atkinson & Marian Aveling (eds), *Australians 1838*, Fairfax, Syme & Weldon Associates, Sydney, 1987, p 220; Nance, 'Level of Violence', p 533.

49   Letter — Lieutenant Charles Menzies, RM, Newcastle Commandant, to King,

5 October 1804, *HRA*, V: 420; *Sydney Gazette*, 22 December 1805; Clem Sargent, *The Colonial Garrison 1817–1824: The 48th Foot the Northamptonshire Regiment in the Colony of New South Wales*, TCS Publications, Canberra, 1996, p 125; Barker, *Commandant of Solitude*, pp 380–82.

50   Marie Fels, 'Culture Contact in the County of Buckinghamshire, Van Diemen's Land, 1803–1811', *Tasmanian Historical Research Association Papers and Proceedings*, 29(2), 1982, pp 55, 65.

51   Fels, 'Culture Contact', p 48; Hobart General Orders, 13 March 1819, SLNSW ML A1352.

3   THE HAWKESBURY-NEPEAN RIVER, 1795–1816

1   Collins, *An Account*, I: 323, 348; GP Walsh, 'The English Colony in New South Wales: A.D. 1803', *New Zealand Geographer*, XVIII(2), 1962, pp 149–69.

2   For more on the Darug, Darawal and Gandangara in this period, see Kohen & Lampert, 'Hunters and Fishers in the Sydney Region'; Kohen, *The Darug and their Neighbours*; Carol Liston, 'The Dharawal and Gandangera in Colonial Campbelltown, New South Wales, 1788–1830', *Aboriginal History*, 12(1), 1988, pp 49–62; Turbet, *Aborigines of the Sydney District*.

3   There had been limited conflict around these farms: three New South Wales Corps soldiers were sent to Prospect Hill in late 1791 to protect the settlers, and the Darug raided the corn harvest at Toongabbie in 1794. Hunter, *Historical Journal*, pp 355–56; Tench, *First Four Years*, p 251; Collins, *An Account*, I: 285, 304–05.

4   Government and General Orders, 29 September 1795, *HRA*, II: 678; Collins, *An Account*, I: 326–27, 329–30, 338; diary — Atkins, 26 September 1794, 12 February, 9 May 1795, NLA mfm G2198.

5   Collins, *An Account*, I: 346; Megan Martin, *Settlers & Convicts of the Bellona 1793: A Biographical Dictionary*, *Bellona* Muster Committee, Sydney, 1992, p 106.

6   Diary — Atkins, 7 June 1795, NLA mfm G2198; letter — Reverend Fyshe Palmer to Dr John Disney, May 1795, quoted in J Brook & JL Kohen, *The Parramatta Native Institution and the Black Town: A History*, UNSW Press, Sydney, 1991, p 15; Collins, *An Account*, I: 348–49, II: 7; letters — Lieutenant-Governor William Paterson to Henry Dundas, British Colonial Secretary, 15 June 1795, Duke of Portland, British Colonial Secretary, to John Hunter, NSW Governor, 8 June 1796, *HRA*, I: 499, 572.

7   Collins, *An Account*, I: 349; letters — Paterson to Dundas, 15 June 1795, Hunter to Portland, 25 October 1795, *HRA*, I: 509, 534–35; Return of public buildings erected in New South Wales since October 1796 ..., [September 1800], and evidence — William Goodall, 17 October 1799, *HRA*, II: 561, 417.

8   Collins, *An Account*, II: 209, 213.

9   State of His Majesty's Settlements in New South Wales, 31 December 1801, *HRA*, III: 420; *Sydney Gazette*, 3 June, 1 July 1804, 12 May 1805.

10   Collins, *An Account*, II: 20, 69; letters — King to Banks, 5 June 1802, Banks to King, 8 April 1803, *HR NSW*, IV: 784, V: 835. Banks told King that he presented Pemulwuy's head to the Hunterian Museum in London (now part of The Royal College of Surgeons of England). However, its location is unknown as it is not listed in the Museum's acquisitions in 1802 or 1803, and is not mentioned either in any later Museum records or when the bulk of the collection was transferred to the Natural History Museum after 1941. Email Simon Chaplin, Senior Curator, Museums of The Royal College of Surgeons of England, to author, 30 July 2001.

11   Letter — Hunter to Portland, 2 January 1800, *HRA*, I: 401–22.

12 The Hawkesbury was the focus of these attacks, but raids also took place at Parramatta, the George's River, and even a farm at the South Head of Sydney Harbour. *Sydney Gazette*, 12 & 26 May, 9 June 1805.

13 Charles-Edwards, 'Irish Warfare Before 1100', p 32; *Sydney Gazette*, 26 May 1805.

14 *Sydney Gazette*, 17 & 24 June 1804; Collins, *An Account*, I: 348, 349, II: 41. Other unsuccessful attacks on boats of unknown cargo are described in Collins, I: 346, 389; *Sydney Gazette*, 28 April, 5 May, 8 & 15 September, 22 December 1805.

15 *Sydney Gazette*, 19 May 1805.

16 *Sydney Gazette*, 29 September 1804, 21 April 1804, 23 June 1805, 24 September 1809.

17 *Sydney Gazette*, 19 August 1804, 23 June, 7 July 1805; Government and General Orders, 22 February 1796, *HRA*, II: 689.

18 Flannery suggests in *The Future Eaters* that the Sydney Aborigines used fire in their traditional warfare, but his assertion is based on a quotation from John White's diary in which White describes how, when setting up camp for the night, his party set fire to the grass around their campsite 'for fear the natives should surprise us in the night by doing the same, a custom in which they seem always happy to indulge themselves'. It is more likely, as suggested by Alec Chisholm, the editor of White's diary, that White meant he was afraid of being accidently caught up in a fire lit for hunting animals, rather than falling victim to a deliberate attack. Flannery, *Future Eaters*, pp 221–22; White, *Journal of a Voyage*, pp 151, 261.

19 Collins, *An Account*, II: 23; *Sydney Gazette*, 8 December 1805.

20 *Sydney Gazette*, 2 & 9 June 1805.

21 *Sydney Gazette*, 7 July 1805; Keith Willey, *When the Sky Fell Down: The Destruction of the Tribes of the Sydney Region 1788–1850s*, Collins, Sydney, 1979, pp 178–79.

22 *Sydney Gazette*, 6 December 1804.

23 Collins, *An Account*, II: 201.

24 Government Orders, 22 November 1801, *HRA*, III: 466.

25 Evidence — Robert Braithwaite, 14 October 1799, *HRA*, II: 411.

26 Lesley D Hall, 'The Physiography and Geography of the Hawkesbury River between Windsor and Wiseman's Ferry', *The Proceedings of the Linnean Society of New South Wales*, 51(4), 1926, p 576; TM Perry, *Australia's First Frontier: The Spread of Settlement in New South Wales 1788–1829*, Melbourne University Press in association with the Australian National University, Melbourne 1963, pp 14–15.

27 Collins, *An Account*, I: 371, II: 11.

28 Letters — King to Hobart, 14 August, 20 December 1804, *HRA*, V: 17, 166–67.

29 Brook & Kohen, *Parramatta Native Institution*, p 18. Heather Goodall is incorrect when she claims King offered the Darug land along the Nepean; King explicitly states he is referring to the lower Hawkesbury. Heather Goodall, 'New South Wales', in Ann McGrath (ed.), *Contested Ground: Australian Aborigines under the British Crown*, Allen & Unwin, Sydney, 1995, p 65.

30 Letter — King to Camden, 30 April 1805, *HRA*, V: 306–07; Lachlan Macquarie, *Journals of His Tours in New South Wales and Van Diemen's Land 1810–1822*, Public Library of NSW, Sydney, 1956, p 29.

31 *Sydney Gazette*, 15 December 1804, 24 & 31 March 1805.

32 Letter quoted in Brook & Kohen, *Parramatta Native Institution*, p 263.

33 *Sydney Gazette*, 16 November 1811, 2 June 1805, 5, 12 & 19 May 1805.

34 *Sydney Gazette*, 1 July 1804.

35 The men being pursued were: Talboon, Corriangee and Doollon, described as

'Mountain natives' (Gandangara?); Moonaning and Doongial, described as 'Branch Natives' (Kurrajong or Darkinung?); and Boon-du-dullock of Richmond Hill (Burraberongal). *Sydney Gazette*, 5, 12 & 19 May 1805.

36 Letter — King to Hobart, 9 May 1803, *HRA*, IV: 73; *Sydney Gazette*, 16 November 1806.

37 Brook & Kohen, *Parramatta Native Institution*, pp 23–24, 29.

38 Sir William Macarthur, A Few Memoranda reflecting the Aboriginal Natives, pp 1–2, SLNSW ML A4360.

39 Letter — King to Viscount Castlereagh, British Colonial Secretary, 27 July 1806, *HRA*, V: 753; *Sydney Gazette*, 30 January 1808, 20 August, 1 October 1809; James Finucane (ed. Anne-Maree Whitaker), *Distracted Settlement: New South Wales after Bligh. From the Journal of Lieutenant James Finucane 1808–1810*, Melbourne University Press, Melbourne, 1998, pp 87–88.

40 *Sydney Gazette*, 20 July 1811, 14 May 1814.

41 Goodall, *Invasion to Embassy*, pp 25–26.

42 Brook & Kohen, *Parramatta Native Institution*, pp 18–19; Perry, *First Frontier*, p 29.

43 *Sydney Gazette*, 9 & 30 March 1816; letter — Macquarie to Bathurst, 18 March 1816, *HRA*, IX: 53.

44 Jean Quoy, Charles Gaudichaud & Alphonse Pellion, 'Excursion to the Town of Bathurst, 1819', in Mackaness (ed.), *Fourteen Journeys*, II: 9–10; *Sydney Gazette*, 14 May, 4 June 1814.

45 Liston, 'The Dharawal and Gandangera in Colonial Campbelltown', p 54.

46 Letters — Hunter to Portland, 20 June 1797, King to Camden, 30 April 1805, *HRA*, II: 24, V: 306–07; George Caley to Banks, 25 August 1801, *HRNSW*, IV: 514; *Sydney Gazette*, 17 June 1804.

47 Letters — Macquarie to Castlereagh, 30 April 1810, Macquarie to Bathurst, 28 April 1814, *HRA*, VII: 258, VIII: 148; General Statement of the Inhabitants of His Majestys Territory of New South Wales ..., 12 December 1813, NLA AJCP Reel 1076 PRO WO57/35.

48 Letter — Macquarie to Bathurst, 18 March 1816, *HRA*, IX: 54.

49 Collins, *An Account*, I: 383.

50 Letter — Samuel Hassall to Thomas Hassall, 16 March 1816, SLNSW ML A1677/4.

51 *Sydney Gazette*, 14 May 1814.

52 Collins, *An Account*, II: 20; *Sydney Gazette*, 21 April, 23 June 1805, 15 October 1804.

53 *Sydney Gazette*, 19 August 1804; evidence — Jonas Archer, 17 October 1799, *HRA*, I: 412.

54 *Sydney Gazette*, 9 March 1816.

55 *Sydney Gazette*, 21 April, 12 May 1805.

56 The party was sent out with three weeks' rations and orders to capture certain Aborigines. Liston takes the amount of rations the expedition was issued with, and the blank record of their return, to state that the expedition returned empty-handed after three weeks. This is a reasonable assumption, but not based on any evidence. Letter — Macquarie to D Allen, Deputy Commissary-General, 21 July 1814; memo — William Sutton, Storekeeper, 15 August 1814, NLA mfm N257 Reel 6044 AONSW CSO 4/1730; Government & General Orders, 12 November 1814, NLA mfm N257 Reel 6038 AONSW CSO SZ758; Liston, 'The Dharawal and Gandangera in Colonial Campbelltown', p 51.

57 There are several incidents in which settlers travelling on the Parramatta and Hawkesbury Roads survived Aboriginal attacks because they were mounted. *Sydney Gazette*, 16 September, 15 October 1804, 12 May 1805.

58 Letter — Macquarie to Murphy, 22 April 1816, NLA mfm N257 Reel 6065 AONSW CSO 4/1798.

59 Diary — Macquarie, 10 April 1816, NLA mfm G27296 ML A773; letter — Macquarie to Bathurst, 18 March 1816, *HRA*, IX: 54.

60 The other ranks figure is calculated by taking the number of boots issued in 1817 for men involved in punitive expeditions (85 pairs) and subtracting the 17 men who served in a later expedition. Diary — Macquarie, 10 April 1816, NLA mfm G27296 ML A773; memo — Macquarie, 17 August 1817; letter — Macquarie to Sergeant Robert Broadfoot, 46th Regiment, 8 May 1816, NLA mfm N257 Reel 6046 AONSW CSO 4/1736; memo — Macquarie, 10 April 1816, NLA mfm N257 Reel 6065 AONSW CSO 4/1798; letter — Macquarie to Schaw, 9 April 1816, NLA mfm N257 Reel 6045 AONSW CSO 4/1735; letter — Captain James Wallis, 46th Regiment, to Macquarie, 9 May 1816, NLA mfm N257 Reel 6045 AONSW CSO 4/1733.

61 Letter — Macquarie to Schaw, 9 April 1816, NLA mfm N257 Reel 6045 AONSW CSO 4/1734; letters — Macquarie to Lieutenant Charles Dawe, 46th Regiment, 9 April 1816, and Wallis to Macquarie, 9 May 1816, NLA mfm N257 Reel 6045 AONSW CSO 4/1735; Anonymous, 'Old Memories: General Reminiscences of Early Colonists II, Mr William Byrne Snr', *Old Times* [Sydney], I(2), 1903, p 105.

62 Letter — Macquarie to Schaw, 9 April 1816, NLA mfm N257 Reel 6045 AONSW CSO 4/1734.

63 Letters — Schaw to Macquarie, 8 May 1816, Dawe to Macquarie, 4 May 1816, NLA mfm N257 Reel 6045 AONSW CSO 4/1735.

64 Letter — Wallis to Macquarie, 9 May 1816, NLA mfm N257 AONSW CSO Reel 6045 4/1735; Anonymous, 'Old Memories', p 105.

65 Letter — Macquarie to Schaw and Wallis, 30 April 1816, NLA mfm N257 AONSW CSO Reel 6045 4/1735; letter — Macquarie to Bathurst, 8 June 1816, *HRA*, IX: 139. For other accounts of the expedition, see Brook & Kohen, *Parramatta Native Institution*; Liston, 'The Dharawal and Gandangera in Colonial Campbelltown'.

66 Diary — Macquarie, 4 May, 4 June 1816, NLA mfm G27296 ML A773; The Trustees of the Police Fund in Account with D'arcy Wentworth Esq, Treasurer For the Quarter ending 31st March 1817, f 160, SLNSW ML D1; Government & General Orders, 1 November 1816, 30 April 1817, NLA mfm N257 AONSW CSO Reel 6038 SZ759; memo — Macquarie, 17 August 1817, NLA AONSW CSO Reel 6046 4/1736.

67 Letters — Schaw to Macquarie, 8 May 1816; Parker to Wallis, [May 1816], NLA mfm N257 AONSW CSO Reel 6045 4/1735.

68 Governor's Proclamation, 1 November 1816; letter — Macquarie to Bathurst, 4 April 1817, *HRA*, IX: 365, 342. For an analysis of Macquarie's Aboriginal policy, see Brook & Kohen, *Parramatta Native Institution*.

4   THE BATHURST AND HUNTER VALLEY DISTRICTS, 1822–1826

1 Baker's expedition did take place, but the description of Baker making camp on a wintry evening is an imaginative reconstruction. Letters — Major James Morisset, Bathurst Commandant, to Sergeant John Baker, 40th Regiment, 22 June 1824, to Major Frederick Goulburn, NSW Colonial Secretary, 25 June 1824, NLA mfm N257 Reel 6065 AONSW CSO 4/1800. I am indebted to Clem Sargent for the details of Baker's military career.

2 For more on the Wiradjuri around Bathurst, Mudgee and Wellington, see Michael Pearson, 'Bathurst Plains and Beyond: European Colonisation and Aboriginal Resistance', *Aboriginal History*, 8(1), 1984, pp 63–79.

3 Letter — Macquarie to Bathurst, 24 June 1815, *HRA*, VIII: 558; Antill, 'Journal of an excursion, 1815', in Mackaness (ed.), *Fourteen Journeys*, I: 96;

letter — Macquarie to Murphy 22 April 1816, NLA mfm N257 Reel 6065 AONSW CSO 4/1798; letter — Rowland Hassall to Macquarie, 16 June 1819, NLA mfm N257 Reel 6048 AONSW CSO 4/1742; Sargent, *Colonial Garrison*, p 42.

4   Perry, *First Frontier*, pp 28–35; Pearson, 'Bathurst Plains and Beyond', p 71; Barron Field, 'Journal of an Excursion Across the Blue Mountains of New South Wales'; 'XYZ' [Captain William Dumaresq], 'A Ride to Bathurst, 1827', in Mackaness (ed.), *Fourteen Journeys*, II: 44, 96.

5   Pearson, 'Bathurst Plains and Beyond', pp 72–73; letter — William Cox to Goulburn, 7 December 1823, NLA mfm N257 Reel 6017 AONSW CSO 4/5783; letters — Lieutenant William Lawson to Goulburn, 10 April 1822, 22 December 1823, NLA mfm N257 Reel 6065 AONSW CSO 4/1798.

6   Letter — John Maxwell, Government Stock Superintendent Bathurst, to Goulburn, 2 September 1823, NLA mfm N257 Reel 6031 AONSW 4/7029A; letter — John Wylde, NSW Judge-Advocate, to Goulburn, 22 January 1824, and evidence — Wilks, 1 June 1824, NLA mfm N257 Reel 6065 AONSW 4/1799; *Sydney Gazette*, 3 August 1824.

7   Letters — Maxwell to Goulburn, 26 November 1823, Lawson to Andrew Dunn, Wylde's overseer, 12 October 1823, NLA mfm N257 Reel 6065 AONSW 4/1798; letter — Wylde to Goulburn, 12 February 1824, NLA mfm N257 Reel 6065 AONSW CSO 4/1799; René Lesson, 'Journey Across the Blue Mountains, 1824', in Mackaness (ed.), *Fourteen Journeys*, II: 70.

8   Charles Darwin, 'Journey Across the Blue Mountains to Bathurst in January, 1836', in Mackaness (ed.), *Fourteen Journeys*, III: 38–39; Goodall, *Invasion to Embassy*, pp 14–15.

9   *Sydney Gazette*, 12 & 19 August 1824; WH Suttor, *Australian Stories Retold and Sketches of Country Life*, Glyndwr Whalan, Bathurst, 1887, p 44.

10   Letter — Morisset to Goulburn, 2 April 1824, and evidence — Privates Softly and Epslom, 3rd Regiment, Patrick Ryan, 22 March 1824, NLA mfm N257 Reel 6065 AONSW CSO 4/1800.

11   Memorial — Cox and others to Brisbane, 3 June 1824, NLA mfm N257 Reel 6065 AONSW CSO 4/1799; letter — William Lawson Junior to Nelson Lawson, 14 June 1824, Lawson, *Old Ironbark*, p 37; *Sydney Gazette*, 29 July, 12 August 1824.

12   Governor's Proclamation, 14 August 1824, *HRA*, XI: 410.

13   Port Regulations, 1 October 1810, *HRNSW*, VII: 418; Tony Hayter, *The Army and the Crowd in Mid-Georgian England*, Macmillan, London, 1978, pp 32–33; Roger Milliss, *Waterloo Creek: The Australia Day Massacre of 1838, George Gipps and the British Conquest of New South Wales*, McPhee Gribble, Ringwood, Victoria, 1992, p 66.

14   Atkinson, *Europeans in Australia*, p 164; Judge-Advocate Atkins's opinion on the treatment of Natives [1805], *HRA*, V: 503; evidence — Corporal Peter Farrell, NSW Corps, 17 October 1799, *HRA*, I: 418. Evidence by non-Christian Aborigines did not become readily admissible in New South Wales courts until 1876. Nancy E Wright, 'The Problem of Aboriginal evidence in early colonial New South Wales', in Diane Kirkby & Catharine Coleborne (eds), *Law, history, colonialism: The reach of Empire*, Manchester University Press, Manchester, 2001, pp 140–55.

15   Letters — Brisbane to Bathurst, 31 December 1824, 18 June 1824, *HRA*, XI: 431, 283; letters — Morisset to Goulburn, 25 June, 26 July 1824, NLA mfm N257 Reel 6065 AONSW CSO 4/1800; letter — Goulburn to Morisset, 22 July 1824, NLA mfm N257 Reel 6013 AONSW CSO 4/3512. There is no correspondence in the relevant file (AONSW CSO 4/3512) requesting Major John Ovens, Acting Chief Engineer, to fill the requisition for pack-horses and saddles.

16   *Sydney Gazette*, 16 September 1824; WB Ranken, *The Rankens of Bathurst*,
     Townsend, Sydney, 1916, pp 19–20; Peter Cunningham (ed. David
     S MacMillan), *Two Years in New South Wales* [1827], Angus & Robertson,
     Sydney, 1966, p 196; Stock Return, 26 June 1824, NLA mfm N257 Reel 6031
     AONSW CSO 4/7029A. I am indebted to Clem Sargent for his insights on the
     likely organisation of Morisset's expedition.
17   Letter — George Ranken to Janet Ranken, 28 September 1824, quoted in
     Ranken, *Rankens of Bathurst*, p 20; letter — Brisbane to Bathurst,
     31 December 1824, *HRA*, XI: 431.
18   *Sydney Gazette*, 14 October, 25 November, 30 December 1824; *Australian*,
     30 December 1824; letter — Brisbane to Bathurst, 31 December 1824,
     Governor's Proclamation, 11 December 1824, *HRA*, XI: 431–32.
19   Pearson, 'Bathurst Plains and Beyond', p 77.
20   T Salisbury & PT Gresser, *Windradyne of the Wiradjeri: Martial Law in
     Bathurst 1824*, Wentworth Books, Sydney, 1971, pp 31–32; Al Grassby &
     Marji Hill, *Six Australian Battlefields: The Black Resistance to Invasion and the
     White Struggle against Colonial Oppression*, Allen & Unwin, Sydney (rev. edn)
     1998 [1988], pp 160–61; Mary Coe, *Windradyne, a Wiradjuri Koorie*,
     Aboriginal Studies Press, Canberra, 1989, pp 57–58; Day, *Claiming a
     Continent*, p 66; Bruce Elder, *Blood on the Wattle: Massacres and Maltreatment
     of Australian Aborigines Since 1788*, Allen & Unwin, Sydney (rev. edn) 1998
     [1988], p 59; Fry, *Beyond the Barrier*, pp 32–33; David Roberts, 'Bells Falls
     Massacre and Bathurst's History of Violence: Local Tradition and Australian
     Historiography', *Australian Historical Studies*, 105, 1995, pp 615–33; Keith
     Windschuttle, 'How Not to Run a Museum', *Quadrant*, September 2001,
     p 19.
21   *Sydney Gazette*, 16 September 1824; letter — Brisbane to Bathurst,
     31 December 1824, *HRA*, XI: 431.
22   Letters — Brisbane to Bathurst, 8 November 1825, Bathurst to Ralph Darling,
     NSW Governor, 4 June 1826, Darling to Bathurst, 5 May 1827, *HRA*, XI:
     897, XII: 341, XIII: 275; Estimate of the Annual Expense of the several Public
     Departments and Estimates, which form a charge on the Colonial Revenue of
     New South Wales, [1827], *HRA*, XIII: 540.
23   Letters — George Arthur, Van Diemen's Land Lieutenant-Governor, to
     Bathurst, 11 April 1826, 24 March 1827, *Historical Records of Australia*
     Series 3 (hereafter *HRA* Series 3), Despatches and Papers Relating to the
     Settlement of the States, 6 vols, Parliament of the Commonwealth of
     Australia, Melbourne, 1921–23, V: 138–39, 693–94; letter — Colonel
     William Stewart, Acting NSW Governor, to Bathurst, 12 December 1825,
     HRA, XII: 85.
24   *Sydney Gazette*, 15 Sepember, 7 November 1825; *Australian*, 14 October
     1826; letter — Goulburn to Lieutenant Percy Simpson, Wellington
     Commandant, 11 November 1825, NLA mfm N257 Reel 6015 AONSW CSO
     4/3515.
25   Letters — Stewart to Bathurst, 12 December 1825, Captain Francis Allman,
     Newcastle Commandant, to Lieutenant Thomas de la Condamine, Acting
     Military Secretary, 27 June 1826, *HRA*, XII: 85, 621 22; W Allan Wood,
     Dawn in the Valley: The Story of Settlement in the Hunter River Valley to 1833,
     Wentworth Books, Sydney, 1972, p 103; Cunningham, *Two Years in New South
     Wales*, p 77. For the Hunter Valley Aborigines, see Brayshaw, *Aborigines of the
     Hunter Valley*.
26   Wood, *Dawn in the Valley*, pp 113–14, 117–18; Cunningham, *Two Years in
     New South Wales*, pp 118, 197; letter — Robert Scott & Alexander MacLeod,
     Magistrates, to Alexander McLeay, NSW Colonial Secretary, 3 October 1826,
     HRA, XII: 610–11.

27 Letters — Condamine to Allman, 21 June 1826, Allman to Condamine, 27 June 1826, *HRA*, XII: 620, 621; *Australian*, 24 June 1826; *Sydney Gazette*, 21 May 1827.

28 Letter — Scott & MacLeod to McLeay, 3 October 1826, *HRA*, XII: 611; *Australian*, 26 August 1826; Harold E Selesky, 'Colonial America', in Howard, Andreopoulos, & Shulman (eds), *Laws of War*, p 61.

29 *Australian*, 28 June 1826.

30 *Australian*, 5 & 26 August 1826; letters — Darling to Bathurst, 6 October 1826, Darling to Robert Hay, British Colonial Under-Secretary, 23 March 1827, *HRA*, XII: 623, XIII: 179; Wood, *Dawn in the Valley*, p 131.

31 Letters — Bathurst to Darling, 14 July 1825, Saxe Bannister, NSW Attorney-General, to Darling, 5 September 1826, Darling to Bathurst, 6 October 1826, *HRA*, XII: 21, 578, 609, 623; evidence — Bannister, 14 March 1837, *British Parliamentary Papers* Anthropology, Aborigines (hereafter *BPP* Aborigines), 3 vols, Irish University Press, Shannon, Ireland, 1968–69, 2: 21.

32 Letters — Allman to Condamine, 23 June 1826, and Scott & MacLeod to McLeay, 3 October 1826, *HRA*, XII: 622, 611–12; Wood, *Dawn in the Valley*, pp 121–25.

33 Wood, *Dawn in the Valley*, pp 128–30; evidence — John Woodbury, 29 August 1826, *HRA*, XII: pp 613–14; *Sydney Gazette*, 9 September 1826.

34 *Sydney Gazette*, 6 September 1826; letter — Captain John Foley, 3rd Regiment, to Condamine, 22 September 1826, *HRA*, XII: 618–19.

35 Letter — Foley to Condamine, 22 September 1826, *HRA*, XII: 617; Wood, *Dawn in the Valley*, p 130.

36 CE Callwell, *Small Wars: Their Principles and Practice*, His Majesty's Stationery Office, London (3rd edn) 1906 [1896], p 420; Malcolm J Kennedy, *Hauling the Loads: A History of Australia's Working Horses and Bullocks*, Melbourne University Press, Melbourne, 1992, pp 56, 72–73, 157; Strachan, *Waterloo to Balaclava*, p 63.

37 Letter — Reverend Lancelot Threlkeld to London Missionary Society, 11 September 1826, quoted in Wood, *Dawn in the Valley*, p 120; letters — Darling to Bathurst, 6 October 1826, to Hunter Valley Landholders, 5 September 1826, *HRA*, XII: 609, 577; *Australian*, 28 June, 16 September 1826; Wood, *Dawn in the Valley*, pp 133–34.

38 For an annotated report of this trial, see the Macquarie University Division of Law's Decisions of the Superior Courts of New South Wales, 1788–1899 web-site <www.law.mq.edu.au/scnsw/Cases1827-28/html/r_v_lowe__1827.htm> downloaded 22 August 2001.

39 *Sydney Gazette*, 21 May 1827; *Australian*, 23 May 1827; JE Calder, *Some Account of the Wars, Extirpation, Habits, &c., of the Native Tribes of Tasmania* [1875], Fullers Bookshop, Hobart, 1972, pp 46–47.

5 NORTHERN AND WESTERN AUSTRALIA, 1824–1834

1 Letter — Major John Campbell, Commandant Fort Dundas, to Macleay, 9 November 1827, and inquest evidence, [November 1827], *HRA*, Series 3, V: 823, VI: 702–04; letter — Lieutenant William Coke, 39th Regiment, to D'Ewes Coke, father, 10 February 1828, NLA AJCP Reel M793 f 278.

2 For more on the Tiwi and Iwaidja at this time, see JMR Cameron, 'The British Meet the Tiwi: Melville Island, 1824', in Tony Austin & Suzanne Parry (eds), *Connection and Disconnection: Encounters between settlers and Indigenous people in the Northern Territory*, NTU Press, Darwin, 1998, pp 27–48; Barker, *Commandant of Solitude*.

3 For a discussion of the trepang trade, see CC MacKnight, *The Voyage to Marege': Macassan trepangers in northern Australia*, Melbourne University Press, Melbourne, 1976.

4   Jules Dumont d'Urville (trans. & ed. Helen Rosenman), *Two Voyages to the South Seas*, 2 vols, Melbourne University Press, Melbourne, 1987, II: 390.

5   Andrew Griffin, 'London, Bengal, the China Trade and the Unfrequented Extremities of Asia: The East India Company's Settlement in New Guinea, 1793–95', *British Library Journal*, 16, 1990, pp 151–73; Cameron, 'British Meet the Tiwi', pp 28–29.

6   East India Trade Committee petition to Bathurst, 13 December 1823, *HRA*, Series 3, V: 742; Campbell, 'Geographical Memoir', p 177.

7   Letters — Captain James Bremer, RN, to John Croker, British Admiralty Secretary, [August 1824], 11 November 1824, *HRA*, Series 3, V: 766, 772; Wilcox, 'Culture of Restrained Force', p 9; Dumont d'Urville, *Two Voyages*, II: 399.

8   NAM Rodger, *The Wooden World: An Anatomy of the Georgian Navy*, Collins, London, 1986, p 55. I am indebted to Dr John Reeve for explaining this point.

9   Letter — Captain George Burn, 27 December 1824, *HRA*, Series 3, V: 791; Campbell, 'Geographical Memoir', p 130.

10 Cameron, 'British Meet the Tiwi', pp 45–46.

11 Campbell, 'Geographical Memoir', p 132; letters — Captain Maurice Barlow, Commandant Fort Dundas, to MacLeay, 28 February 1826, Campbell to MacLeay, 29 September 1827, 20 June 1828, Captain Humphrey Hartley, Commandant Fort Dundas, to MacLeay, 8 September 1828, *HRA*, Series 3, VI: 656, 700, 721, 760.

12 Letter — Campbell to MacLeay, 7 June 1827, *HRA*, Series 3, VI: 691; Barker, *Commandant of Solitude*, p 140.

13 Letter — Bathurst to Darling, 18 December 1826, *HRA*, XII: 224; Report — Captain James Stirling, RN, [June 1827], *HRA*, Series 3, VI, p 815; Barker, *Commandant of Solitude*, p 60.

14 British civilians erected small swivel guns at stations west of Geelong in the 1840s, but there is no record if they were used in anger. Jan Critchett, *A 'distant field of murder': Western District Frontiers 1834–1848*, Melbourne University Press, Melbourne, 1990, pp 91, 97.

15 Letter — Captain Henry Smyth, Commandant Fort Wellington, to Darling, 30 October 1829, *HRA*, Series 3, VI: 818; TB Wilson, *Narrative of a Voyage Round the World* [1835], Dawsons of Pall Mall, London, 1968, p 148. Smyth reported that the cannon fired round shot, while Braidwood's account refers to grape-shot, but both types are anti-personnel ammunition.

16 Letter — Smyth to Darling, 30 October 1827, and evidence — Smyth, 1 October 1827, *HRA*, Series 3, V: 816–20, VI: 777; letter — Coke to D'Ewes Coke, 10 February 1828, NLA AJCP Reel M793 f 278; Barker, *Commandant of Solitude*, pp 123, 151. Barker later traded these surplus muskets with Macassans for rice.

17 Letter — Smyth to MacLeay and attached sworn statements, 12 February 1828, *HRA*, Series 3, VI: 781–89.

18 Letter — Lieutenant George Sleeman, 39th Regiment, to MacLeay, 22 April 1828, *HRA*, Series 3, VI: 793; letter — Sir George Murray, British Colonial Secretary, to Darling, 3 September 1829, *HRA*, XV: 153–54.

19 Barker, *Commandant of Solitude*, pp 53, 79, 85, 89, 113.

20 Letter — Smyth to MacLeay, 20 March 1828, *HRA*, Series 3, VI: 789–90; letter — Murray to Darling, 1 November 1828, *HRA*, XIV: 411; Barker, *Commandant of Solitude*, pp 113, 141, 199, 224.

21 For the Fort Victoria settlement, see JMR Cameron (ed.), *Letters from Port Essington, 1838–1845*, Historical Society of the Northern Territory, Darwin, 1999.

22 For the Minang people at this time, see WC Ferguson, 'Mokaré's Domain', in Mulvaney & White (eds), *Australia to 1788*, pp 120–45.

23 Barker, *Commandant of Solitude*, pp 355–56, 23–26.
24 For more on the Nyungar peoples at this time, see Neville Green (ed.), *Nyungar – The People: Aboriginal customs in the southwest of Australia*, Creative Research Publishers in association with Mt Lawley College of Advanced Education, Perth, 1979.
25 Reece, 'Inventing Aborigines', pp 34–38; *Perth Gazette*, 13 April 1833.
26 Bob Reece, '"Laws of the White People": The Frontier of Authority in Perth in 1838', *The Push from the Bush*, 17, 1984, p 23. For a table listing instances of traditional Aboriginal warfare in southwest Western Australia 1830–50, see Neville Green, *Broken Spears: Aboriginals and Europeans in the southwest of Australia*, Focus Education Services, Perth, 1984, pp 226–34.
27 *Perth Gazette*, 7 September 1833, 18 October 1834.
28 *Perth Gazette*, 4 May, 1 June, 13 July, 10 August 1833.
29 *Perth Gazette*, 16 February, 6 & 27 April 1833, 1 March 1834.
30 *Perth Gazette*, 3 March, 23 March 1833, 26 April, 3 May, 24 June 1834; letter — Captain Frederick Irwin, Acting WA Governor, to Lord Goderich, British Colonial Secretary, 10 April 1833, House of Commons Select Committee on Aborigines (British Settlements) Report (hereafter Select Committee Report), Appendix No 4, *BPP* Aborigines, 2: 135.
31 Letter — Captain James Stirling, RN, WA Lieutenant-Governor, to Murray, 18 October 1830, Select Committee Report, Appendix No 4, *BPP* Aborigines, 2: 126; Blackburn, *Conquest and Settlement*, p 29; George Fletcher Moore, *Diary of Ten Years of Eventful Life of An Early Settler in Western Australia and also a Descriptive Vocabulary of the Language of the Aborigines* [1884], University of Western Australia Press, Perth, 1978, p 123.
32 *Perth Gazette*, 3 May, 14 June 1834.
33 *Perth Gazette*, 24 July, 2 August 1834; evidence — Edward Barron, 23 July 1834, Select Committee Report, Appendix No 4, *BPP* Aborigines, 2: 137.
34 *Perth Gazette*, 27 September 1834.
35 Supplementary List of Persons actually in the Colony … 15 January 1830, *BPP* Australia, 3: 453; minutes, WA Executive Council, 30 July 1832, Select Committee Report, Appendix No 4, *BPP* Aborigines, 2: 133; Blackburn, *Conquest and Settlement*, pp 230–31.
36 *Perth Gazette*, 18 October 1834.
37 Windschuttle, 'Myths of Frontier Massacres' Pt I, *Quadrant*, October 2000, p 18; letter — Thomas Peel to Stirling, 1 April 1835, quoted in Alexandra Hasluck, *Thomas Peel of Swan River*, Oxford University Press, Melbourne, 1965, p 161; Blackburn, *Conquest and Settlement*, p 56.
38 *Perth Gazette*, 1 November 1834.
39 'Battle' is used in: Moore, *Diary*, p 236; Dennis *et al.* (eds), *Oxford Companion to Australian Military History*, p 123; Grey, *Military History of Australia*, p 31; Horton (ed.), *Encyclopaedia of Aboriginal Australia*, 2: 890. 'Massacre' is used in: Tom Austen, *A Cry in the Wind: Conflict in Western Australia 1829–1929*, Darlington Publishing Group, Perth, 1998, p 21; Atkinson & Aveling (eds), *Australians 1838*, p 30; Christine Fletcher, 'The Battle of Pinjarra: A Revisionist View', in Bob Reece & Tom Stannage (eds), *European-Aboriginal Relations in Western Australian History* Studies in Western Australian History VIII, University of Western Australia Press, Perth, 1984, p 1; Sandy Toussaint, 'Western Australia', in McGrath (ed.), *Contested Ground*, p 245. Broome avoids using either term in 'Struggle for Australia'.
40 The following narrative is based on Blackburn, *Conquest and Settlement*, pp 56–58; with details from *Perth Gazette*, 1 November 1834, and Moore, *Diary*, p 236. I am indebted to Brad Manera for bringing Blackburn's book to my attention.
41 Moore, *Diary*, p 236; Green, *Broken Spears*, pp 102–03.

42 Leroy V Eid, '"A Kind of Running Fight": Indian Battlefield Tactics in the Late Eighteenth Century', *The Western Pennsylvania Historical Magazine*, 71(2), 1988, pp 153–54.

43 Letter — Stirling to Edward Stanley, British Colonial Secretary, 1 November 1834, Select Committee Report, Appendix No 4, *BPP* Aborigines, 2: 136; Blackburn, *Conquest and Settlement*, p 60.

44 Green, *Broken Spears*, p 208; Austen, *Cry in the Wind*, p 21.

45 Bill Thorpe, 'Frontiers of Discourse: Assessing Revisionist Australian Colonial Contact Historiography', *Journal of Australian Studies*, 46, 1995, pp 38–39.

46 Ian Knight & Ian Castle, *Zulu War 1879*, Osprey Publishing, London, 1992, pp 21, 32, 36–57; Dennis *et al.* (eds), *Oxford Companion to Australian Military History*, pp 114–16; CEW Bean, *The Story of Anzac. From 4 May, 1915 to the Evacuation of the Gallipoli Peninsula*, Angus & Robertson, Sydney (13th edn) 1944 [1924], pp 623–24.

47 Raymond Evans & Bill Thorpe, 'Indigenocide and the Massacre of Aboriginal History', *Overland*, 163, 2001, p 24; Davison *et al.* (eds), *Oxford Companion to Australian History*, p 415; Dennis *et al.* (eds), *Oxford Companion to Australian Military History*, p 489.

48 Grassby & Hill, *Six Australian Battlefields*, p 195; Mark Johnston, *Fighting the Enemy: Australian Soldiers and their Adversaries in World War II*, Cambridge University Press, Melbourne, 2000, p 49.

49 *Perth Gazette*, 28 March 1835; letter — Lieutenant Henry Bunbury, 21st Regiment, to Sir Henry Edward Bunbury, father, 10 July 1836, HW Bunbury (eds W St Pierre Bunbury & WP Morrell), *Early Days in Western Australia: Being the Letters and Journal of Lieut. H.W. Bunbury 21st Fusiliers*, Oxford University Press, London, 1930, p 27; Blackburn, *Conquest and Settlement*, pp 23, 29; Moore, *Diary*, p 302.

50 Green, *Broken Spears*, p 215; Broome, 'Struggle for Australia', p 108.

6 VAN DIEMEN'S LAND, 1826–1831

1 Evidence — John Sherwin, 23 February 1830, AOT CSO1 316/7578/1; Reynolds, *Fate of a Free People*, p 61. Reynolds and Sharon Morgan correctly name the owner of the farm as John Sherwin, however both Lloyd Robson and Lyndall Ryan refer to the man as Isaac Sherwin. Isaac Sherwin (1804–69) was the son of John Sherwin (1780?–1853). *ADB*, II: 441; Reynolds, *Fate of a Free People*, pp 60–61; Sharon Morgan, *Land Settlement in Early Tasmania: Creating an Antipodean England*, Cambridge University Press, Cambridge, 1992, p 157; Lloyd Robson, *A History of Tasmania. Volume I: Van Diemen's Land from the Earliest Times to 1855*, Oxford University Press, Melbourne, 1983, p 212; Ryan, *Aboriginal Tasmanians*, p 106.

2 Arthur was styled lieutenant-governor because, although Van Diemen's Land was a separate colony from 1825, the governorship remained subordinate to New South Wales.

3 Marie Fels, 'Culture Contact'; Maria Moneypenny, '"Going out and Coming in": Cooperation and Collaboration between Aborigines and Europeans in Early Tasmania', *Tasmanian Historical Studies*, 5(1), 1995–96, pp 64–75.

4 Jorgenson, *Jorgen Jorgenson*, p 113; Dumont d'Urville, *Two Voyages*, I: 192.

5 Source: NJB Plomley, The *Aboriginal/Settler Clash in Van Diemen's Land 1803–1831*, Occasional Paper No 6, Queen Victoria Museum and Art Gallery in association with the Centre for Tasmanian Historical Studies, Launceston, 1992, p 26.

6 Ryan, *Aboriginal Tasmanians*, pp 122, 174; Henry Reynolds, *The Law of the Land*, Penguin, Ringwood, Victoria, 1987, p 89; Reynolds, *Fate of a Free People*, pp 81–82; Windschuttle, 'Myths of Frontier Massacres' Pt II, p 18.

7 Plomley, *Aboriginal/Settler Clash*, p 27; minutes, Committee for the Care of

Captured Aborigines (hereafter Aborigines Committee), 17 March 1830, AOT CBE1 1; Melville, *History of Van Diemen's Land*, p 71.

8   George Augustus Robinson (ed. NJB Plomley), *Friendly Mission: The Tasmanian Journal and Papers of George Augustus Robinson 1829–1834*, Tasmanian Historical Research Association, Hobart, 1966, pp 219, 196.

9   Minutes, Aborigines Committee, 2 March 1830, AOT CBE1 1.

10 Calder, *Some Account of the Wars*, pp 46–47; Robinson, *Friendly Mission*, pp 192, 196.

11 Reynolds, *Fate of a Free People*, pp 49–50.

12 Minutes, Aborigines Committee, 17 March 1830, AOT CBE1 1; Robinson, *Weep in Silence*, p 88. For references to continued traditional warfare in Van Diemen's Land, see Calder, *Some Account of the Wars*, p 8; Robinson, *Friendly Mission*, pp 186, 257; Ernest Westlake Notebook No 3, NLA AJCP Reel M2413.

13 Ryan, *Aboriginal Tasmanians*, p 115; Robinson, *Friendly Mission*, pp 87, 257; minutes, Aborigines Committee, 17 March 1830, AOT CBE1 1.

14 James Bonwick, *The Last of the Tasmanians, or, The Black War of Van Diemen's Land* [1870], Libraries Board of South Australia, Adelaide, 1969, pp 107–08.

15 Robinson, *Friendly Mission*, p 215; letter — Lieutenant William Williams, Police Magistrate Bothwell, to John Burnett, Van Diemen's Land Colonial Secretary, 5 January 1829, AOT CSO1 320/7578/5.

16 Plomley, *Aboriginal/Settler Clash*, p 20.

17 Robinson, *Friendly Mission*, p 553; Jorgenson, *Jorgen Jorgenson*, p 57; Westlake Notebook No 5, pp 24–25, NLA AJCP Reel M2413.

18 Plomley, *Aboriginal/Settler Clash*, p 20; Robson, *History of Tasmania*, p 213.

19 Jorgenson, *Jorgen Jorgenson*, p 50; Robinson, *Friendly Mission*, pp 243, 363; Plomley, *Aboriginal/Settler Clash*, p 18.

20 Robinson, *Friendly Mission*, pp 510–11; Reynolds, *Fate of a Free People*, p 41.

21 Reynolds, *Fate of a Free People*, p 42.

22 Robinson, *Friendly Mission*, pp 517, 855.

23 Plomley, *Aboriginal/Settler Clash*, p 66; John West (ed. AGL Shaw), *The History of Tasmania* [1852], Angus & Robertson in association with the Royal Australian Historical Society, 1971, p 292; Robinson, *Friendly Mission*, pp 552, 579–80.

24 Letter — Browne to Mulgrave, 28 February 1828, AOT CSO1 323/7578/8; Reynolds, *Fate of a Free People*, p 47; Plomley, *Aboriginal/Settler Clash*, p 23.

25 Plomley, *Aboriginal/Settler Clash*, p 21.

26 Anne McKay (ed.), *Journals of the Land Commissioners for Van Diemen's Land 1826–1828*, University of Tasmania in conjunction with the Tasmanian Historical Research Association, Hobart, 1962, p 46.

27 Reynolds, *Fate of a Free People*, p 60. Sherwin later asked for £1000 compensation from the Van Diemen's Land government to cover the damage he had received from Aboriginal raids. His request was unsuccessful. Morgan, *Land Settlement*, p 157.

28 Morgan, *Land Settlement*, p158; letter — Lieutenant Henry Boden Torlesse, RN, to Michael Vicary, Police Magistrate Bothwell, 15 February 1830, AOT CSO1 316/7578/1.

29 Evidence — Sherwin, 23 February 1830, and letter — James Simpson, Police Magistrate Campbell Town, to Burnett, 4 September 1830, AOT CSO1 316/7578/1; minutes, Aborigines Committee, 12, 17 & 23 March 1830, AOT CBE1 1; Reynolds, *Fate of a Free People*, p 49; Plomley, *Aboriginal/Settler Clash*, p 16; Morgan, *Land Settlement*, pp 147, 156.

30 Source: Report, Aborigines Committee, 12 March 1830, AOT CBE1 1.

31 Robinson, *Friendly Mission*, p 508.

32 Jorgenson, *Jorgen Jorgenson*, p 113.

33 For Arthur's campaign against the bushrangers, see Robson, *History of Tasmania*.

34 Government Notice, 29 November 1826, *BPP* Australia, 4: 192–93; John F McMahon, The British army and the counter-insurgency campaign in Van Diemen's Land with particular reference to the Black Line, Master of Humanities thesis, University of Tasmania, Hobart, 1995, p 22. See also his article, JF McMahon, 'The British Army: Its Role in Counter-Insurgency in the Black War in Van Diemen's Land', *Tasmanian Historical Studies*, 5(1), 1995–96, pp 56–63. While excellent pieces of research, McMahon's attempt to compare the 'Black Line' to twentieth century counter-insurgency warfare is unsustainable.

35 Letter — Arthur to Goderich, 10 January 1828, and Governor's Proclamations, 15 April, 1 November 1828, *BPP* Australia, 4: 175, 179, 184. The British government approved the imposition of martial law. Letter — Murray to Arthur, 25 August 1830, *BPP* Australia, 4: 186.

36 Garrison Orders, 12 December 1828, *BPP* Australia, 4: 198; letter — Browne to Mulgrave, 28 February 1828, AOT CSO1 323/7578/8.

37 Garrison Orders, 4 & 15 September 1829, *BPP* Australia, 4: 204–05.

38 Bonwick, *Last of the Tasmanians*, p 107; minutes, Aborigines Committee, 23 March 1830, AOT CBE1 1.

39 Letter — Arthur to Murray, 15 April 1830, *BPP* Australia, 4: 187.

40 Governor's Proclamation, 1 November 1828, *BPP* Australia, 4: 184; letter — Thomas Anstey, Police Magistrate Oatlands, to Burnett, 8 December 1828, AOT CSO1 320/7578/5.

41 Garrison Order, 12 December 1828, *BPP* Australia, 4: 198.

42 Melville, *History of Van Diemen's Land*, p 79.

43 Letter — Simpson to Burnett, 16 December 1828, AOT CSO1 320/7578/5; Reynolds, *Fate of a Free People*, p 35.

44 Letter — Malcolm Laing Smith, Police Magistrate Norfolk Plains, to Burnett, 12 November 1827, AOT CSO1 316/7578/1.

45 Letter — Browne to Mulgrave, 28 February 1828, AOT CSO1 323/7578/8.

46 Letter — Williams to Burnett, 23 February 1829, AOT CSO1 320/7578/5; evidence — Private Charles Westwood, 40th Regiment, 17 January 1829, AOT CSO1 316/7578/1.

47 Letter — Browne to Mulgrave, 28 February 1828, AOT CSO1 323/7578/8; minutes, Aborigines Committee, 3 March 1830, AOT CBE1 1. Carbines were in short supply in Van Diemen's Land. Letter — Captain William Neilley, Ordnance Office Hobart, to Burnett, 20 May 1831, AOT CSO1 322/7578/7.

48 The Roving Parties also killed about sixty Aborigines. Ryan, *Aboriginal Tasmanians*, p 102.

49 Report, Aborigines Committee, *BPP* Australia, 4: 217.

50 Letter draft — Arthur to Anstey, 19 December 1829, AOT CSO1 320/7578/5; Government Order, 25 February 1830, *BPP* Australia, 4: 207; letter — 'Philohistoricus' to Archdeacon WG Broughton, Chairman Aborigines Committee, 20 March 1830, AOT CSO1 320/7578/5.

51 Murray was reacting to news that an Aboriginal woman had been killed by Van Diemen's Land Company employees on company land west of Launceston. Letter — Murray to Arthur, 23 April 1830, NLA AJCP Reel 290 PRO CO408/7.

52 Plomley, *Aboriginal/Settler Clash*, pp 26, 85–90.

53 Extract from Van Diemen's Land Executive Council Minutes, 27 August 1830, and letter — Arthur to Murray, 20 November 1830, NLA AJCP Reel 245 PRO CO280/25; letter — Arthur to Robert Hay, Colonial Under-Secretary, 24 September 1832, NLA AJCP Reel 251 PRO CO280/35; AGL Shaw, *Sir*

George Arthur, Bart., 1784–1854. Superintendent of British Honduras, Lieutenant-Governor of Van Diemen's Land and of Upper Canada, Governor of the Bombay Presidency, Melbourne University Press, Melbourne, 1980, pp 50–60.

54　Extract from Van Diemen's Land Executive Council Minutes, 27 August 1830, NLA AJCP Reel 245 PRO CO280/25 ff 403–04.

55　Letter draft — Arthur to Anstey, 21 November 1828, AOT CSO1 321/7578/6.

56　McMahon, British army and counter-insurgency, pp 47–50. McMahon also points out that Ryan's claim that it was Major Donaldson who planned 'the spring offensive' against the Aborigines is based on a misreading of a document. McMahon, British army and counter-insurgency, p 52; Ryan, *The Aboriginal Tasmanians*, p 110.

57　Government Order, 9 September 1830, memo — Arthur, 20 November 1830, *BPP* Australia, 4: 236, 244; letters — Arthur to Murray, 21 August, 20 November 1830, NLA AJCP reel 245 PRO CO280/25.

58　Anthony James Joes, *Guerilla Warfare: A Historical, Biographical, and Bibliographical Sourcebook*, Greenwood Press, Westport, Connecticut, 1996, pp 45–46, 170; C Van Dijk, *Rebellion Under the Banner of Islam: The Darul Islam in Indonesia*, Martinus Nijhoff, The Hague, 1981, pp 124–25. I am indebted to Gerry Walsh for this reference.

59　Government Order, 9 September 1830, *BPP* Australia, 4: 236–37; Major Edward Abbott, Launceston Civil Commandant, General Directions for the Gentlemen who have enrolled themselves to Guard the Town serving in the absence of the Military, 2 October 1830, AOT CSO1 324/7578/9 Pt E; Melville, *History of Van Diemen's Land*, p 94.

60　Letter — GTWB Boyes to Mary Boyes, 31 October 1830, Peter Chapman (ed.), *The Diaries and Letters of G.T.W.B. Boyes. Volume 1 1820–1832*, Oxford University Press, Melbourne, 1985, p 380.

61　Melville, *History of Van Diemen's Land*, p 92.

62　Memo — Arthur, 20 November 1830, *BPP* Australia, 4: 244; McMahon, British army and counter-insurgency, p 58; Van Diemen's Land Blue Book 1830, p 114, NLA AJCP reel 1155, PRO CO284/53.

63　An expanded discussion of Arthur's use of Van Diemen's Land's infrastructure to supply the 'Black Line' is found in the author's 'British Frontier Warfare Logistics and the "Black Line", Van Diemen's Land (Tasmania) 1830', *War in History*, 9(2), 2002, pp 142–57.

64　Although its officers accompanied the British Army into battle, the Commissariat was at this time a civilian organisation controlled by the Treasury. Glover, *Peninsular Preparation*, p 256; Hew Strachan, *Wellington's Legacy: The Reform of the British Army 1830–54*, Manchester University Press, Manchester, 1984, p 230.

65　Scott's annotation, on letter — Gilbert Robertson, Chief Constable Richmond, to Thomas Scott, Van Diemen's Land Assistant Surveyor, 19 October 1830, and letters — William Parramore, Arthur's private secretary, to Scott, 10 September 1830, George Frankland, Van Diemen's Land Chief Surveyor, to Assistant Surveyors, 10 September 1830, SLNSW ML A1055. Thomas Scott's incomplete map of Van Diemen's Land printed in September 1830 was widely used during the 'Black Line' operation. McMahon, British army and counter-insurgency, p 62.

66　Memo — Burnett, 25 September 1830, AOT CSO1 317/7578/2; *Hobart Town Courier*, 2 October 1830. At least some of the shoes would have been made in Van Diemen's Land. Letter — Hay to Arthur, 18 May 1830, NLA AJCP Reel 290 PRO CO408/7.

67　Government Order, 22 September 1830, *BPP* Australia, 4: 242.

68 Memo — Burnett, 25 September 1830; letter — W Armitage, Police Constable Bagdad, to Burnett, 30 October 1830, AOT CSO1 317/7578/2.

69 McMahon, British army and counter-insurgency, p 60.

70 Government Order, 22 September 1830, Governor's Proclamation, 1 October 1830, letter — Arthur to Murray, 20 November 1830, memo — Arthur, 20 November 1830, BPP Australia, 4: 239, 243, 231, 245, 244; letter — Arthur to Major Sholto Douglas, 63rd Regiment, 8 October 1830, AOT CSO1 324/7578/9 Pt A.

71 Government Order, 22 September 1830, BPP Australia, 4: 242.

72 Letter —Thomas Lemprière, Commissary Officer Oatlands, to Scott, 7 October 1830, SLNSW ML A1055; Hobart Town Courier, 28 August 1830; Government Order, 22 September 1830, memo — Arthur, 20 November 1830, BPP Australia, 4: 242, 244.

73 Letters — Arthur to Burnett, 12 October 1830, Arthur to Lemprière, 17 October 1830, AOT CSO1 324/7578/9 Pt A; Hobart Town Courier, 16 October 1830; George Hill, Commissary Officer Launceston, to Arthur, 20 & 21 October 1830, AOT CSO1 324/7578/9 Pt C. Hill's price was reasonable; men's walking shoes sold in Hobart Town in October for between 8 and 10 shillings, Hobart Town Courier, 1 October 1830.

74 Letter — Edward Walpole to Arthur, 29 October 1830, AOT CSO1 324/7578/9 Pt E; Robinson, Friendly Mission, p 318. Walpole incorrectly stated that the skirmish took place on 26 October. McMahon points out that it took place the previous day. McMahon, British army and counter-insurgency, p 68. Walpole received a land grant for the capture of the two men, Robinson, Friendly Mission, p 1045.

75 Memo — Arthur, 20 November 1830, BPP Australia, 4: 245; McMahon, British army and counter-insurgency, pp 67–71. Mark Cocker, in the most recent book on the 'Black Line', repeats Arthur's line, and refers to Walpole (even in the index) as a 'buffoon'. Rivers of Blood, Rivers of Gold: Europe's Conflict with Tribal Peoples, Pimlico, London, 1999, pp 151, 415.

76 Letters — Arthur to Douglas, and Wentworth, 24 October 1830, to Douglas 25 October 1830, AOT CSO1 324/7578/9 Pt A; letter — Douglas to Arthur, 26 October 1830, AOT CSO1 324/7578/9 Pt B; Hobart Town Courier, 30 October 1830.

77 Letter — R Neill to Scott, 30 October 1830, SLNSW ML A1055.

78 Four ounces (110 g) of tobacco was issued weekly, half an ounce (14 g) of salt issued daily. Letter — Arthur to Burnett, 12 October 1830, and memo — Arthur, 10 November 1830, AOT CSO1 324/7578/9 Pt A.

79 Letters — Joseph Browne, Deputy Assistant Commissary-General Van Diemen's Land, to Charles Arthur, 2 & 4 November 1830, AOT CSO1 324/7578/9 Pt C.

80 Letters — Arthur to Douglas, 10 November 1830, to Burnett, 3 November 1830, AOT CSO1 324/7578/9 Pt A; Nominal Return of Civilians in the Division under the Command of Lieut. Murray 17th Regiment, 20 November 1830, AOT CSO1 324/7578/9 Pt C.

81 Hobart Town Courier, 23 October 1830; [Hobart] Colonial Times, 26 November 1830.

82 Memo — Arthur, 20 November 1830, BPP Australia, 4: 244; letter — Charles Arthur to Browne, 24 November 1830, AOT CSO1 324/7578/9 Pt A.

83 Robinson, Friendly Mission, p 315.

84 Van Diemen's Land Blue Book 1830, pp 8, 10–11, NLA AJCP reel 1155 PRO CO284/53; Shaw, George Arthur, p 129.

85 Shaw, George Arthur, pp 130–31.

86 Jorgenson, Jorgen Jorgenson, p 69; Ryan, Aboriginal Tasmanians, p 110.

87 Letter — Arthur to Douglas, Captains Wentworth & Moriarty, 19 November

1830, AOT CSO1 324/7578/9 Pt A; Melville, *History of Van Diemen's Land*, p 104.

88   [Hobart] *Colonial Times*, 1 October 1830.

89   Letters — Arthur to Douglas and Wentworth, 24 October 1830; to Douglas, 25 October 1830, AOT CSO1 324/7578/9 Pt A; Robinson, *Friendly Mission*, p 315.

90   Callwell, *Small Wars*, p 143.

91   Letters — George Fordyce Story, Commissary Officer Waterloo Point, to Arthur, 25 October 1831, Lieutenant Francis Aubin, OC Waterloo Point, to Burnett, 27 October 1831, George Meredith to Arthur, 27 October 1831, AOT CSO1 316/7578/1.

92   Melville, *History of Van Diemen's Land*, p 104; Cocker, *Rivers of Blood*, p 151.

93   Jorgenson, *Jorgen Jorgenson*, p 109; Robinson, *Friendly Mission*, p 283.

94   For Robinson's expeditions, see Robinson, *Friendly Mission*. For two different interpretations of the negotiations between the Aborigines and Robinson, see Reynolds, *Fate of a Free People*, p 156; Ryan, *Aboriginal Tasmanians*, p xxviii.

95   Morgan, *Land Settlement*, p 71; letter — Michael Steel to Joseph Steel, 21 February 1827, quoted in Gwyneth & Hume Dow, *Landfall in Van Diemen's Land: The Steels' Quest for Greener Pastures*, Press of the Footscray Institute of Technology, Melbourne, 1990, p 45.

96   Robinson saw the dance performed on at least two different occasions. Robinson, *Friendly Mission*, pp 263, 278.

97   Reynolds, *Fate of a Free People*, p 71; letter — Sorell to Arthur, 22 May 1824, *HRA*, Series 3, IV: 149; *Launceston Examiner*, 22 November 1860, quoted in DM Wyatt, *A Lion in the Colony: An Historical Outline of the Tasmanian Colonial Volunteer Military Forces, 1859–1901*, 6th Military District Museum, Hobart, 1990, pp 4–5. I am indebted to Jean Bou for bringing this reference to my attention.

98   Letters — Arthur to Bathurst, 11 April 1826, 24 March 1827, *HRA*, Series 3, V: 138–39, 693–94.

99   Report, Aborigines Committee, 19 March 1830, and letter — Murray to Arthur, 5 November 1830, *BPP* Australia, 4: 216, 229.

100 John S Galbraith, *Reluctant Empire: British Policy on the South African Frontier 1834–1854*, Berkeley and Los Angeles, University of California Press, 1963, pp 35–36; Strachan, *Waterloo to Balaclava*, p 88; AJ Smithers, *The Kaffir Wars: 1779–1877*, Leo Cooper, London, 1973, p 162.

7   THE LIVERPOOL PLAINS AND PORT PHILLIP DISTRICTS, 1838

1   These people have been variously identified as Ngarabal, Weraerai (Wolaroi) or Kwiambal. Horton (ed.), *Encylopaedia of Aboriginal Australia*, 2: 746; Milliss, *Waterloo Creek*, p 279; Atkinson & Aveling (eds), *Australians 1838*, p 56.

2   Letters — Gipps to Glenelg, 19 December 1838, Henry Keck, Sydney Gaol, to Gipps, 21 December 1838, and evidence — Thomas Foster, William Hobbs, George Anderson, 15 November 1838, *BPP*, Australia, 5: 403–05, 426, 407, 408, 410–11. For other accounts of the Myall Creek massacre and trials, see Atkinson & Aveling (eds), *Australians 1838*, pp 54–61, 389–94; Milliss, *Waterloo Creek*, pp 274–321, 504–39; John N Molony, *An Architect of Freedom: John Hubert Plunkett in New South Wales 1832–1869*, Australian National University Press, Canberra, 1973, pp 140–47; RHW Reece, *Aborigines and Colonists: Aborigines and Colonial Society in New South Wales in the 1830s and 1840s*, Sydney University Press, Sydney, 1974, pp 145–66.

3   Perry, *Australia's First Frontier*, pp 43–46; Cunningham, *Two Years in New South Wales*, p 83.

4   For more on the Kamilaroi and their neighbours, see MJ O'Rourke, *Raw Possum and Salted Pork: Major Mitchell and the Kamilaroi Aborigines*, Plowpress, Canberra, 1995; Horton (ed.), *Encylopaedia of Aboriginal Australia*, 2: 782; Milliss, *Waterloo Creek*, pp 21–43.

5   O'Rourke, *Raw Possum and Salted Pork*, pp 86, 12; Milliss, *Waterloo Creek*, pp 76–78; TL Mitchell, *Three Expeditions into the interior of Eastern Australia, with descriptions of the recently explored region of Australia Felix, and of the present Colony of New South Wales*, 2 vols, 2nd edn, 1839, Libraries Board of South Australia, Adelaide, 1965, II: 44.

6   LE Threlkeld (ed. Niel Gunson), *Australian Reminiscences of L.E. Threlkeld, Missionary to the Aborigines 1824–1859*, 2 vols, Australian Aboriginal Studies No 40, Australian Institute of Aboriginal Studies, Canberra, 1974, I: 138; Reece, *Aborigines and Colonists*, p 45; Milliss, *Waterloo Creek*, pp 101–02.

7   Ridley, *Kamilaroi and other Australian Languages*, p 169; Milliss, *Waterloo Creek*, p 284.

8   Atkinson & Aveling (eds), *Australians 1838*, pp 40–41; Milliss, *Waterloo Creek*, pp 145–49; letter — Alexander Paterson, Crown Lands Commissioner, to Edward Deas Thomson, NSW Colonial Secretary, 6 December 1837, *HRA*, XX: 252–53

9   Letter — James Glennie to Robert Scott, 21 November 1837, quoted in Milliss, *Waterloo Creek*, p 160.

10 Milliss, *Waterloo Creek*, p 16; letters — Bourke to J Steward, British Treasury, 2 May 1833, to Earl of Aberdeen, British Colonial Secretary, 2 August 1835, *HRA*, XVII: 101, XVIII: 72.

11 Evidence — Lieutenant-Colonel Henry Breton, 4th Regiment, House of Commons Select Committee on Transportation, 12 May 1837, *British Parliamentary Papers*, Crime and Punishment, Transportation (hereafter *BPP* Transportation) 16 vols, Irish University Press, Shannon, 1968–71, 2: 136, 142.

12 Letter — Darling to Hay, 23 March 1827, *HRA*, XIII: 184; NSW Mounted Police Troop Orders, 19 November 1834, 6 January 1831, NLA MSS3221 3, 1.

13 NSW Mounted Police Troop Orders, 12 February, 12 March 1831, NLA MSS3221 1; memo — Captain James Williams, OC NSW Mounted Police, 8 May 1835, NLA MSS3221 3.

14 Evidence — Breton, 12 May 1837, *BPP* Transportation, 2: 137; letter — Captain John Forbes, Acting Brigade Major, to Lieutenant Browne, OC Bathurst Mounted Police Detachment, 28 November 1828; Lieutenant-Colonel Kenneth Snodgrass, OC NSW Mounted Police, to Officers Commanding NSW Mounted Police outposts, 19 July 1830, NSW Mounted Police Troop Orders, 2 December 1831, 29 February 1832, NLA MSS3221 1.

15 Troop order, 12 January 1832, NLA MSS3221 1.

16 Letters — Williams to Snodgrass, NSW Brigade Major, 1 December 1832, 21 January 1833, NSW Mounted Police Troop Order, 13 August 1836, NLA MSS3221 2; Mitchell, *Three Expeditions*, I: 140; Wood, *Dawn in the Valley*, p 228.

17 Letter — Lieutenant Zouch, 4th Regiment, to Williams, 7 December 1835, in Mitchell, *Three Expeditions*, I: 353–54.

18 Milliss, *Waterloo Creek*, pp 150–51; letter — Williams to Lieutenant Steele, OC Hunter River Mounted Police Detachment, 28 March 1833, NLA MSS3221 2.

19 Letter — Thomson to Major James Nunn, OC Mounted Police, 18 December 1837, quoted in Milliss, *Waterloo Creek*, p 164; evidence — Nunn, 4 April 1839, *HRA*, XX: 250.

20 Milliss, *Waterloo Creek*, pp 167–68; Windschuttle, 'Myths of Frontier Massacres' Pt I, p 15; evidence — Nunn, 4 April 1839, *HRA*, XX: 250.

21 Milliss, *Waterloo Creek*, p 169; evidence — Nunn, 4 April 1839, Lieutenant George Cobban, 50th Regiment, 17 May 1839, *HRA*, XX: 250, 254.
22 Milliss, *Waterloo Creek*, pp 170–71; evidence — Nunn, 4 April 1839, Sergeant John Lee, 4 April 1839, Cobban, 17 May 1839, *HRA*, XX: 250, 251, 254.
23 Milliss, *Waterloo Creek*, p 172; evidence — Nunn, 4 April 1839, Cobban, 17 May 1839, *HRA*, XX: 250, 254.
24 Milliss, *Waterloo Creek*, p 174; letter — Nunn to Thomson, 5 March 1838, *BPP* Australia, 5: 393; evidence — Nunn, 4 April 1839, *HRA*, XX: 250.
25 Milliss, *Waterloo Creek*, pp 175–76, 180; evidence — Nunn, 4 April 1839, *HRA*, XX: 251.
26 Evidence — Lee, 4 April 1839, Corporal Patrick Hannan, 4 April 1839, Cobban, 17 May 1839, *HRA*, XX: 251–52, 255.
27 Letter — Nunn to Thomson, 5 March 1838, *BPP* Australia, 5: 393; Milliss, *Waterloo Creek*, p 189; evidence — Lee, 4 April 1839, *HRA*, XX: 252.
28 Milliss, *Waterloo Creek*, p 192; letter — Nunn to Thomson, 5 March 1838, *BPP* Australia, 5: 393; *Sydney Gazette*, 21 April 1838; O'Rourke, *Raw Possum and Salted Pork*, p 48.
29 Milliss, *Waterloo Creek*, p 215; Select Committee Report, 26 June 1837, *BPP* Aborigines, 2: 81.
30 Select Committee Report, 26 June 1837, *BPP* Aborigines, 2: 5; Reynolds, *Law of the Land*, p 85; David Philips, Evangelicals, Aborigines and 'Land Rights': a critique of Henry Reynolds' understanding and use of the *Select Committee on Aborigines (British Possessions)* 1835–37, paper presented to the 11th Australasian Modern British History Association Conference, Canberra, 3 February 1999.
31 Select Committee Report, 26 June 1837, *BPP* Aborigines, 2: 82–83.
32 Select Committee Report, 26 June 1837, *BPP* Aborigines, 2: 83.
33 Letter — Glenelg to Bourke, 26 July 1837, *HRA*, XIX: 48.
34 Letter — Glenelg to Gipps, 16 November 1838, *HRA*, XIX: 678.
35 Letters — Gipps to Glenelg, 27 April, 21 July 1838, 22 July 1839, *HRA*, XIX: 399, 509, XX: 244.
36 Rex Harcourt, *Southern Invasion, Northern Conquest: The Story of the Founding of Melbourne*, Golden Port Press, Melbourne, 2001, pp 88–89; letter — Arthur to Glenelg, 22 July 1837, *HRV*, 2A: 26; letter — Glenelg to Gipps, 31 January 1838, *HRA*, XIX: 253.
37 For more on the Wathaurong and their neighbours, see Harry Lourandos, 'Swamp Managers of Southwestern Victoria', in Mulvaney & White (eds), *Australians to 1788*, pp 293–307.
38 Nance, 'Level of Violence', p 539; Critchett, *'distant field of murder'*, pp 91–92, 237–38; George Langhorne's reminiscences of William Buckley … [1837], *HRV*, 2A: 190.
39 Letters — Thomas Learmonth Junior, Hugh Murray, to La Trobe, 11 August, 18 August 1853, Bride (ed.), *Letters*, pp 94, 102; Critchett, *'distant field of murder'*, p 95; evidence — John Aitken, 15 May 1838, William Bowman, 21 April 1838, Samuel Fallon, 28 May 1838, *HRV*, 2A: 291–92, 335, 336.
40 Letter — John Hepburn to La Trobe, 10 August 1853, Bride (ed.), *Letters*, p 77; letter — Lonsdale to Thomson, 8 May 1838, and evidence — Aitken, 15 May 1838, and letter — Captain Foster Fyans, Geelong Police Magistrate, to Thomson, 24 May 1838, *HRV*, 2A: 220, 291–92, 306.
41 Letter — Lonsdale to Thomson, 23 April 1838, *HRV*, 2A: 324; letters — Gipps to Russell, 1 January 1841, Russell to Gipps, 26 August 1841, *HRA*, XXI: 148, 485.
42 Letter — Lonsdale to Thomson, 11 May 1838, *HRV*, 2A: 297–98; letters — Hepburn, Thomas Learmonth Junior, Hugh Murray to La Trobe, 10, 11, 18 August 1853, Bride (ed.), *Letters*, pp 63, 93–94, 102.

43 Letters — Hepburn, Murray to La Trobe, 10, 18 August 1853, Bride (ed.), *Letters*, pp 76, 102; evidence — Samuel Jackson, 20 April 1838, John Green, 27 April 1838, Henry Grinham, 27 April 1838, Dr Jonathan Clerke, 8 May 1838, David Fisher, 20 May 1838, William Bowman, 21 April 1838, *HRV*, 2A: 293–94, 294–95, 295, 297, 306, 335.

44 The Darug of Sydney and the Kurnai of Gippsland both used circular formations to hunt kangaroo. Diary, Barrallier, *HRNSW*, V: 751; Bulmer, *Victorian Aborigines*, p 50.

45 Evidence — John Coppock, 29 June 1838, Samuel Fuller, 7 July 1838, John Pittman, 7 July 1838, and letter — Lonsdale to Thomson, 2 July 1838, *HRV*, 2A: 336–38, 338, 340, 340.

46 MF Christie, *Aborigines in Colonial Victoria 1835–86*, Sydney University Press, Sydney, 1979, p 78; Richard Broome, 'Victoria', in McGrath (ed.), *Contested Ground*, p 127.

47 Diary, Reverend Francis Tuckfield, 15 December 1839, and evidence — Joseph Ware, 27 July 1838, *HRV*, 2A: 142, 308.

48 Diane E Barwick, 'Mapping the past: An atlas of Victorian clans 1835–1904', *Aboriginal History*, 8(2), 1984, pp 120, 126; Milliss, *Waterloo Creek*, p 253.

49 Evidence — James Crossley, 14 April 1838, George Faithfull, 22 April 1838, and letters — William Pitt Faithfull to Thomson, 8 May 1838, George Stewart, Goulburn Police Magistrate, to Thomson, 20 June 1838, *HRV*, 2A: 314, 318, 328, 333.

50 Evidence — Thomas Learmonth Senior, 9 April 1838, and letters — Fyans to Thomson 21 April 1838, Lieutenant George Smyth, 80th Regiment, to Lonsdale, 22 April 1838, *HRV*, 2A: 238, 288, 321; letter — Murray to La Trobe, 18 August 1853, Bride (ed.), *Letters*, pp 103–04; Barwick, 'Mapping the past', p 124.

51 Letter — George Edward MacKay to La Trobe, 30 August 1853, Bride (ed.), *Letters*, p 211; letter — Mackay to W Broughton, 15 May 1838, and evidence — Patrick Drain, 1 June 1838, *HRV*, 2A: 330, 331.

52 Letter — Gipps to Glenelg, 21 July 1838, *HRA*, XIX: 509; letter — Thomson to Port Phillip settlers, 23 June 1838, *BPP* Australia, 5: 400.

53 NSW General Order, 25 January 1838, NLA MSS3221 3; letter — Snodgrass to Glenelg 23 February 1838, *HRA*, XIX: 290–91; letters — Thomson to Fyans, 5 January 1838, Lonsdale to Thomson, 3 June 1838, *HRV*, 6: 205, 2A: 336; letter — George Faithfull to La Trobe, 8 September 1853, Bride (ed.), *Letters*, p 219; Critchett, *'distant field of murder'*, p 97.

54 Milliss, *Waterloo Creek*, p 250; letters — Smyth to Lonsdale, 22 April 1838, Lieutenant William Waddy, OC Goulburn Mounted Police Detachment, to Nunn, 25 April 1838, *HRV*, 2A: 321, 325.

55 Letter — Thomson to Port Phillip settlers, 23 June 1838, *BPP* Australia, 5: 400; letter — Gipps to Glenelg, 21 July 1838, *HRA*, XIX: 510; letter — George Stewart, Goulburn Police Magistrate, to Thomson, 20 June 1838, and memo — Gipps to Thomson, 28 April 1838, *HRV*, 2A: 322, 328.

56 Memo — Gipps, 23 June 1838, and letter — Thomson to Major Thomas Mitchell, NSW Surveyor-General, 12 June 1838, *HRV*, 2A: 333, 6: 208; letter — Gipps to Glenelg, 21 July 1838, *HRA*, XIX: 510.

57 Milliss, *Waterloo Creek*, pp 437–38; NSW General Order, 14 August 1838, NLA MSS3221 3; letter — Thomson to Port Phillip settlers, 23 June 1838, *BPP* Australia, 5: 400; letters — Joseph Docker, Ovens River settler, to La Trobe, Port Phillip District Superintendent, 20 November 1839, Nunn to Acting NSW Brigade Major, 1 August 1838, *HRV*, 1: 272, 6: 212; *Australian*, 24 November 1838.

58 Letters — Docker to La Trobe, 20 November 1839, George Stewart to Thomson, 20 June 1838, Waddy to Nunn, 27 June 1838, *HRV*, 1: 272,

2A: 322, 6: 209; *Australian*, 14 August 1838.

59 Letter — George Faithfull to La Trobe, 8 September 1853, Bride (ed.), *Letters*, p 219; Critchett, *'distant field of murder'*, p 187; Broome, 'Struggle for Australia', p 103.

60 Letter — Glenelg to Gipps, 15 September 1838, *HRA*, XIX: 584.

61 *Sydney Gazette*, 20 September 1838; letter — Gipps to Glenelg, 20 February 1839, *HRA*, XX: 6; Milliss, *Waterloo Creek*, pp 480–81, 569.

62 Chris Coulthard-Clark, *Where Australians Fought: The Encyclopaedia of Australia's Battles*, Allen & Unwin, Sydney, 1998, pp 20–21.

63 Letter — Glenelg to Stirling, 7 March 1837 [note that this letter is located in the 1835 correspondence file], NLA AJCP Reel 300 PRO CO18/15 ff 372–73.

64 Broome, 'Struggle for Australia', pp 105, 109; letter — George Faithfull to La Trobe, 8 September 1853, Bride (ed.), *Letters*, p 221.

65 Cunningham, *Two Years in New South Wales*, p 264; Critchett, *'distant field of murder'*, p 99; Christie, *Aborigines in Colonial Victoria*, p 146; letter — John G Robertson to La Trobe, 26 September 1853, Bride (ed.), *Letters*, p 167.

66 Ged Martin, 'Canada from 1815', in Andrew Porter (ed.), *The Oxford History of the British Empire*, Oxford University Press, Oxford, 1999, III: 533.

67 Dennis *et al.* (eds), *Oxford Companion to Australian Military History*, p xi.

68 Backhouse, *Narrative*, p 539.

SELECT BIBLIOGRAPHY

NOTE

For reasons of space, only material cited in the endnotes has been listed in the bibliography.

PRIMARY SOURCES

Archival material

ARCHIVES OFFICE OF TASMANIA, HOBART
Chief Secretary's Office [Van Diemen's Land], Correspondence, CSO1.
Committee for the Care of Captured Aborigines, Minutes of Meetings, 1830–33, CBE1.
Despatches, principally from Treasury, to the Officer-in-Command of His Majesty's Forces in the Colony, GO17.

AUSTRALIAN JOINT COPYING PROJECT
Blackburn, David, Correspondence, 1788, Reel M971.
Coke, William, Correspondence, 1825–28, Reel M793.
Colonial Secretary [United Kingdom]
    Despatches from New South Wales, September–October 1826, PRO CO201/173, Reel 147.
    Despatches from Van Diemen's Land, June–December 1830, PRO CO280/25, Reel 245.
    Despatches from Van Diemen's Land, September 1835, PRO CO280/35, Reel 251.
    Despatches to Van Diemen's Land, 1830–32, PRO CO408/7, Reel 290.
    Despatches to and from Western Australia, 1835, PRO CO18/15, Reel 300.
    Van Diemen's Land Blue Book, 1830, PRO CO284/53, Reel 1155.
80th (South Staffordshire) Regiment, Digest, Reel M815.
Smyth, Arthur Bowes, Diary, 1788, Reel M933.

Southwell, Daniel, Papers, 1788–90, Reel M1538.
War Office, Commissariat in-Letters New South Wales, 1810–15, PRO WO57/35, Reel 1076.
Westlake, Ernest, Notebooks, 1908–10, Reel M2413.

NATIONAL LIBRARY OF AUSTRALIA, CANBERRA
Atkins, Richard, Diary, 1792–99, mfm G2198.
Brisbane, Sir Thomas, Papers, 1815–58, MS4036.
Chief Secretary's Office [New South Wales], Papers, 1788–1825, mfm N257 AONSW CSO.
Macquarie, Lachlan, Diary, 1816–18, mfm G27296 ML A773.
New South Wales Mounted Police, Order Books, 1828–38, MSS3221

STATE LIBRARY OF NEW SOUTH WALES (THE MITCHELL LIBRARY), SYDNEY
Harris, John, Papers, 1790, ML A1597.
Hassall, Samuel, Correspondence, 1816, ML MSS1174/4.
Huey, Alexander, The Voyage of the 73rd Regiment of Foot, ML B1514.
Macarthur Family, Papers - Miscellaneous Papers, 1823–97, ML A4360.
Scott, Thomas, Papers, 1830, ML A1055.
Sorell, William, Orders, Notices & Proclamations, 1817–22, ML A1352.
Wentworth, D'arcy, Police reports and accounts, 1810–27, ML D1.

Published official documents

A List of the Officers of the Army and Royal Marines on Full, Retired and Half Pay [various years], His Majesty's Stationery Office, London.
British Parliamentary Papers
(1968–69) Anthropology, Aborigines, 3 vols, Irish University Press, Shannon, Ireland.
(1968–70) Colonies, Australia, 34 vols, Irish University Press, Shannon, Ireland.
(1968–71) Crime and Punishment, Transportation, 16 vols, Irish University Press, Shannon, Ireland.
Historical Records of Australia
(1914–25) Series 1, Governors' Despatches to and from England, 1788–1848, 26 vols, Parliament of the Commonwealth of Australia, Melbourne.
(1921–23) Series 3, Despatches and Papers Relating to the Settlement of the States, 6 vols, Parliament of the Commonwealth of Australia, Melbourne.
Historical Records of New South Wales
(1892–1901) 7 vols, New South Wales Government Printer, Sydney.
Historical Records of Victoria
(1982–98) 7 vols, Victorian Government Printing Office, Melbourne.

Contemporary books, published diaries and letters

Andrews, Alan EJ (ed.) (1981) *Hume and Hovell 1824*, Blubber Head Press, Hobart.
Backhouse, James (1843) *A Narrative of a Visit to the Australian Colonies*, Hamilton, Adams & Co, London.
Balfour, JO (1845) *A Sketch of New South Wales*, Smith, Elder & Co, London.
Barker, Collet (eds John Mulvaney & Neville Green) (1992) *Commandant of Solitude: The Journals of Captain Collet Barker 1828–1831*, Melbourne University Press, Melbourne.
Baudin, Nicolas (trans. Christine Cornell) (1974) *The Journal of Post Captain*

Nicolas Baudin Commander-in-Chief of the Corvettes Géographe *and* Naturaliste *Assigned by Order of the Government to a Voyage of Discovery*, Libraries Board of South Australia, Adelaide.

Bougainville, Hyacinthe de (trans. & ed. Marc Serge Rivière) (1999) *The Governor's Noble Guest: Hyacinthe de Bougainville's account of Port Jackson, 1825*, Melbourne University Press, Melbourne.

Boyes, GTWB (ed. Peter Chapman) (1985) *The Diaries and Letters of G.T.W.B. Boyes. Volume 1 1820–1832*, Oxford University Press, Melbourne.

Bradley, William (1969) *A Voyage to New South Wales: The Journal of Lieutenant William Bradley of HMS* Sirius *1786–1792*, Public Library of New South Wales in association with Ure Smith, Sydney.

Bride, Thomas Francis (ed.) (1969) *Letters from Victorian Pioneers: Being a series of papers on the early occupation of the colony, the Aborigines, etc* [1898], William Heinemann, Melbourne.

Bulmer, John (comp. Alastair Campbell, ed. Ron Vanderwal) (1994) *Victorian Aborigines: John Bulmer's Recollections 1855–1908*, Museum of Victoria Occasional Papers Anthropology & History No 1, Museum of Victoria, Melbourne.

Bunbury, HW (eds W St Pierre Bunbury & WP Morrell) (1930) *Early Days in Western Australia: Being the Letters and Journal of Lieut. H.W. Bunbury 21st Fusiliers*, Oxford University Press, London.

Cameron, JMR (ed.) (1999) *Letters from Port Essington, 1838–1845*, Historical Society of the Northern Territory, Darwin.

Campbell, A (1834) 'Geographical Memoir of Melville Island and Port Essington, on the Cobourg Peninsula, Northern Australia; with some Observations on the Settlements which have been established on the North Coast of New Holland', *The Journal of the Royal Geographical Society of London*, IV: 129–81.

Clark, Ralph (eds Paul G Fidlon & RJ Ryan) (1981) *The Journal and Letters of Lt. Ralph Clark 1787–1792*, Australian Documents Library in association with the Library of Australian History Pty Ltd, Sydney.

Clarke, John (1964) 'A Young Soldier in the Antipodes, 1830 to 1836'. In TH McGuffie (ed.), *Rank and File: The Common Soldier at Peace and War 1642–1914*, Hutchinson, London, pp 174–76.

Collins, David (ed. Brian Fletcher) (1975) *An Account of the English Colony of New South Wales, with remarks on the dispositions, customs, manners, etc. of the native inhabitants of that country*, 2 vols [1798, 1802], Reed in association with the Royal Historical Society, Sydney.

Cunningham, Peter (ed. David S Macmillan) (1966) *Two Years in New South Wales* [1827], Angus & Robertson in association with the Royal Australian Historical Society, Sydney.

Dumont d'Urville, Jules (trans. & ed. Helen Rosenman) (1987) *Two Voyages to the South Seas*, 2 vols, Melbourne University Press, Melbourne.

Duyker, Edward (trans. & ed.) (1992) *The Discovery of Tasmania: Journal extracts from the expeditions of Abel Janszoon Tasman and Marc-Joseph Marion Dufresne 1642 and 1772*, St Davids Park Publishing, Hobart.

Easty, John (1965) *Memorandum of the transactions of a voyage from England to Botany Bay 1787–1793: A First Fleet Journal*, Public Library of New South Wales in association with Angus & Robertson, Sydney.

Finucane, James (ed. Anne-Maree Whitaker) (1998) *Distracted Settlement: New South Wales after Bligh. From the Journal of Lieutenant James Finucane 1808–1810*, Melbourne University Press, Melbourne.

Hale, Horatio (1968) *United States Exploring Expedition During the Years 1838, 1839, 1840, 1841, 1842. Under the command of Charles Wilkes, U.S.N. Ethnography and Philology* [1846], The Gregg Press, Ridgewood, New Jersey.

Hunter, John (ed. John Bach) (1968) *An Historical Journal of Events at Sydney and at Sea 1787–1792* [1793], Royal Australian Historical Society in association with Angus & Robertson, Sydney.

Jorgenson, Jorgen (ed. NJB Plomley) (1991) *Jorgen Jorgenson and the Aborigines of Van Diemen's Land: being a reconstruction of his 'lost' book on their customs and habits, and on his role in the Roving Parties and the Black Line,* Blubber Head Press, Hobart.

Knopwood, Robert (ed. Mary Nicholls) (1977) *The Diary of the Reverend Robert Knopwood 1803–1838: First Chaplain of Van Diemen's Land,* Tasmanian Historical Research Association, Launceston.

Lawson, William (ed. William Beard) (1967) *Old Ironbark: Some Unpublished Correspondence (1817–1824) from and to William Lawson Explorer and Pioneer of Veteran Hall, N.S.W.,* Wentworth Press, Sydney.

Mackaness, George (ed.) (1978) *Fourteen Journeys Over The Blue Mountains of New South Wales 1813–1841,* 3 pts [1950], Review Publications, Dubbo.

— (1979) *The Discovery and Exploration of Moreton Bay and the Brisbane River (1799–1823),* 2 pts [1956], Review Publications, Dubbo.

McKay, Anne (ed.) (1962) *Journals of the Land Commissioners for Van Diemen's Land 1826–1828,* University of Tasmania in conjunction with the Tasmanian Historical Research Association, Hobart.

Macquarie, Lachlan (1956) *Journals of his tours in New South Wales and Van Diemen's Land 1810–1822,* Public Library of New South Wales, Sydney.

Melville, Henry (ed. George Mackaness) (1965) *The History of Van Diemen's Land: From the Year 1824 to 1835, inclusive* [1836], Horwitz Publications & The Grahame Book Co, Sydney.

Mitchell, TL (1965) *Three Expeditions into the interior of Eastern Australia, with descriptions of the recently explored region of Australia Felix, and of the present Colony of New South Wales,* 2 vols, 2nd edn, 1839, Libraries Board of South Australia, Adelaide.

Moore, George Fletcher (1978) *Diary of Ten Years of Eventful Life of An Early Settler in Western Australia and also a Descriptive Vocabulary of the Language of the Aborigines* [1884], University of Western Australia Press, Perth.

Mortimer, George (1791) *Observations and Remarks made during a Voyage to the islands of Teneriffe, Amsterdam, Maria's Islands near Van Diemen's Lands, Otaheite, Sandwich islands, Owhyhee, The Fox Islands on the North West Coast of America, Tinian, and from thence to Canton, in the Brig* Mercury, *Commanded by John Henry Cox, Esq,* the author, London.

Oxley, John (1964) *Journals of Two Expeditions into the Interior of New South Wales, Undertaken by Order of the British Government in the Years 1817–18* [1820], Libraries Board of South Australia, Adelaide.

Paine, Daniel (eds RJB Knight & Alan Frost) (1983) *The Journal of Daniel Paine 1794–1797 Together with Documents Illustrating the Beginning of Government Boat-building and Timber-gathering in New South Wales, 1795–1805,* Library of Australian History, Sydney.

Robinson, George Augustus (ed. NJB Plomley) (1966) *Friendly Mission: The Tasmanian Journal and Papers of George Augustus Robinson 1829–1834,* Tasmanian Historical Research Association, Hobart.

— (1987) *Weep in Silence: A History of the Flinders Island Aboriginal Settlement with the Flinders Island Journal of George Augustus Robinson 1835–1839,* Blubber Head Press, Hobart.

Scott, James (1963) *Remarks on a Passage to Botany Bay 1787–1792 A First Fleet Journal,* Public Library of New South Wales in association with Angus & Robertson, Sydney.

Tench, Watkin (ed. LF Fitzhardinge) (1961) *Sydney's First Four Years: being a reprint of A Narrative of the Expedition to Botany Bay and A Complete Account of the Settlement at Port Jackson* [1788, 1793], Royal Australian Historical Society in association with Angus & Robertson, Sydney.

Threlkeld, LE (ed. Niel Gunson) (1974) *Australian Reminiscences of L.E. Threlkeld, Missionary to the Aborigines 1824–1859*, 2 vols, Australian Aboriginal Studies No. 40, Australian Institute of Aboriginal Studies, Canberra.

White, John (ed. Alec Chisholm) (1962) *Journal of a Voyage to New South Wales* [1790], Royal Australian Historical Society in association with Angus & Robertson, Sydney.

Wilson, TB (1968) *Narrative of a Voyage Round the World* [1835], Dawsons of Pall Mall, London.

Newspapers

Australian [Sydney].
Colonial Times [Hobart].
Hobart Town Courier.
Perth Gazette.
Sydney Gazette and New South Wales Advertiser.

SECONDARY SOURCES

Articles and books

Alcock, Rutherford (1838) *Notes on the Medical History and Statistics of the British Legion of Spain; Comprising the results of gun-shot wounds in relation to important questions in surgery*, John Churchill, London.

Anonymous (1903) 'Old Memories: General Reminiscences of Early Colonists II, Mr William Byrne Snr', *Old Times* [Sydney], I(2): 105.

Atkinson, Alan (1997) *The Europeans in Australia: A History*, Vol 1, Oxford University Press, Melbourne.

Atkinson, Alan & Marian Aveling (eds) (1987) *Australian*Aboriginal frontier warfare *1838*, Fairfax, Syme & Weldon Associates, Sydney.

Attwood, Bain (1989) *The Making of the Aborigines*, Allen & Unwin, Sydney.

Austen, Tom (1998) *A Cry in the Wind: Conflict in Western Australia 1829–1929*, Darlington Publishing Group, Perth.

Austin, M (1963) 'The Early Defences of Australia', *Journal of the Royal Australian Historical Society*, 49(3): 189–204.

—— (1979) *The Army in Australia 1840–50: Prelude to the Golden Years*, Australian Government Publishing Service, Canberra.

—— (1986) 'The First Australian "Digger": John Cox of the New South Wales Corps', *Sabretache*, 27(1): 13–15.

Barratt, Glynn (1981) *The Russians at Port Jackson 1814–1822*, Australian Institute of Aboriginal Studies, Canberra.

Barthorp, Michael (1987) *The British Army on Campaign 1816–1902*, Vol 1, Osprey Publishing, London.

Barwick, Diane E (1984) 'Mapping the past: An atlas of Victorian clans 1835–1904', *Aboriginal History*, 8(2): 100–31.

Bean, CEW (1944) *The Story of Anzac. From 4 May, 1915 to the Evacuation of the Gallipoli Peninsula*, 13th edn [1924], Angus & Robertson, Sydney.

Beattie, Daniel J (1986) 'The Adaption of the British Army to Wilderness Warfare'. In Maarten Ultee (ed.), *Adapting to Conditions: War and Society in the Eighteenth Century*, University of Alabama Press, University, Alabama, pp 56–83.

Beaumont, Joan (ed.) (2001) *Australian Defence: Sources and Statistics*, Oxford University Press, Melbourne.

Belich, James (1996) *Making Peoples: A History of the New Zealanders. From Polynesian Settlement to the End of the Nineteenth Century*, Penguin, Auckland.

—— (1998) *The New Zealand Wars and the Victorian Interpretation of Racial Conflict*, rev. edn [1986], Penguin, Auckland.

Black, Jeremy (1998) *War and the World: Military Power and the Fate of Continents, 1450–2000*, Yale University Press, New Haven, Connecticut.

—— (2000) *War: Past, Present & Future*, St Martin's Press, New York.

Blackburn, Geoff (1999) *Conquest and Settlement: The 21st Regiment of Foot (North British Fusiliers) in Western Australia 1833–1840*, Perth, Hesperian Press.

Blackmore, Howard L (1961) *British Military Firearms 1650–1850*, Herbert Jenkins, London.

Bonwick, James (1969) *The Last of the Tasmanians; or, The Black War of Van Diemen's Land* [1870], Libraries Board of South Australia, Adelaide.

Borch, Merete (2001) 'Rethinking the Origins of *Terra Nullius*', *Australian Historical Studies*, 117: 222–39.

Brayshaw, Helen (1986) *Aborigines of the Hunter Valley: A Study of Colonial Records*, Scone & Upper Hunter Historical Society, Scone, New South Wales.

Brook, J & JL Kohen (1991) *The Parramatta Native Institution and the Black Town: A History*, UNSW Press, Sydney.

Broome, Richard (1994a) *Aboriginal Australians: Black Responses to White Dominance*, 2nd edn [1982] Allen & Unwin, Sydney.

—— (1994b) 'Aboriginal Victims and Voyagers, Confronting Frontier Myths', *Journal of Australian Studies*, 42: 70–77.

Buckley, Roger Norman (1998) *The British Army in the West Indies: Society and the Military in the Revolutionary Age*, University of Florida Press, Gainesville, Florida.

Butlin, NG (1983) *Our Original Aggression: Aboriginal Populations of Southeastern Australia 1788–1850*, George Allen & Unwin, Sydney.

—— (1993) *Economics and the Dreamtime: A Hypothetical History*, Cambridge University Press, Cambridge.

Calder, JE (1972) *Some Account of the Wars, Extirpation, Habits, &c., of the Native Tribes of Tasmania* [1875], Fullers Bookshop, Hobart.

Callwell, CE (1906) *Small Wars: Their Principles and Practice*, 3rd edn [1896], His Majesty's Stationery Office, London.

Cameron, JMR (1998) 'The British Meet the Tiwi: Melville Island, 1824'. In Tony Austin & Suzanne Parry (eds), *Connection and Disconnection: Encounters between settlers and Indigenous people in the Northern Territory*, NTU Press, Darwin, pp 27–48.

Canny, Nicholas (ed.) (1998) *The Oxford History of the British Empire*, I, Oxford University Press, Oxford.

Chandler, David (ed.) (1994) *The Oxford Illustrated History of the British Army*, Oxford University Press, Oxford.

Chapman, Valerie & Peter Read (eds) (1996) *Terrible Hard Biscuits: A Reader in Aboriginal History*, Allen & Unwin, Sydney.

Charles-Edwards, TM (1996) 'Irish Warfare Before 1100'. In Thomas Bartlett & Keith Jeffrey (eds), *A Military History of Ireland*, Cambridge University Press, Cambridge, pp 26–51.

Christie, MF (1979) *Aborigines in Colonial Victoria 1835–86*, Sydney University Press, Sydney.

Clendinnen, Inga (2001) 'First Contact', *Australian Review of Books*, May: 6–7, 26.

Clodfelter, Micheal (1992) *Warfare and Armed Conflicts: A Statistical Reference to Casualty and Other Figures, 1618–1991*, 2 vols, McFarland & Co, Jefferson, North Carolina.

Coates, John (2001) *An Atlas of Australia's Wars*, Oxford University Press, Melbourne.

Cocker, Mark (1999) *Rivers of Blood, Rivers of Gold: Europe's Conflict with Tribal Peoples*, Pimlico, London.

Coe, Mary (1989) *Windradyne, a Wiradjuri Koorie*, Aboriginal Studies Press, Canberra.

Connor, John (2001) 'Australia: Frontier Wars, 1788–1928'. In Charles Messenger (ed.), *Reader's Guide to Military History*, Fitzroy Dearborn, London, pp 40–41.

—— (2002) 'British Frontier Warfare Logistics and the "Black Line", Van Diemen's Land (Tasmania) 1830', *War in History*, 9(2): 142–57.

Coulthard-Clark, Chris (1998) *Where Australians Fought: The Encyclopaedia of Australia's Battles*, Allen & Unwin, Sydney.

Critchett, Jan (1990) *A 'distant field of murder': Western District Frontiers 1834–1848*, Melbourne University Press, Melbourne.

Crowell, Lorenzo M (1992) 'Logistics in the Madras Army *circa* 1830', *War & Society*, 10(2): 1–33.

Darvall, Frank Ongley (1969) *Popular Disturbances and Public Order in Regency England* [1934], Oxford University Press, Oxford.

Davison, Graeme, John Hirst & Stuart Macintyre (eds) (1998) *The Oxford Companion to Australian History*, Oxford University Press, Melbourne.

Day, David (2001) *Claiming a Continent: A New History of Australia*, rev. edn [1996], Harper Collins, Sydney.

Denholm, David (1979) *The Colonial Australians*, Penguin, Ringwood, Victoria.

Dennis, Peter, Jeffrey Grey, Ewan Morris, Robin Prior with John Connor (eds) (1999) *The Oxford Companion to Australian Military History*, reprint with corrections [1995], Oxford University Press, Melbourne.

Dow, Gwyneth & Hume (1990) *Landfall in Van Diemen's Land: The Steels' Quest for Greener Pastures*, Press of the Footscray Institute of Technology, Melbourne.

Eid, Leroy V (1985) '"National" War Among Indians of Northeastern North America', *The Canadian Review of American Studies*, 16(2): 125–54.

—— (1988) '"A Kind of Running Fight": Indian Battlefield Tactics in the Late Eighteenth Century', *The Western Pennsylvania Historical Magazine*, 71(2): 147–71.

Elder, Bruce (1998) *Blood on the Wattle: Massacres and Maltreatment of Australian Aborigines Since 1788*, rev. edn [1988], Allen & Unwin, Sydney.

Erikson, Rica (comp.) (1988) *The Bicentennial Dictionary of Western Australians pre-1829–1888*, 4 vols, University of Western Australia Press, Perth.

Evans, Raymond & Bill Thorpe (2001) 'Indigenocide and the Massacre of Aboriginal History', *Overland*, 163: 21–39.

Fels, Marie (1982) 'Culture Contact in the County of Buckinghamshire, Van Diemen's Land 1803–1811', *Tasmanian Historical Research Association, Papers and Proceedings*, 29(2): 47–79.

—— (1988) *Good Men and True: The Aboriginal Police of the Port Phillip District 1837–1853*, Melbourne University Press, Melbourne.

Fenn, Elizabeth A (2000) 'Biological Warfare in Eighteenth-Century North America: Beyond Jeffery Amherst', *The Journal of American History*, 86(4): 1552–80.

Flannery, Tim (1994) *The Future Eaters: An Ecological History of the Australasian Lands and People*, Reed Books, Melbourne.

Fletcher, Christine (1984) 'The Battle of Pinjarra: A Revisionist View'. In Bob Reece & Tom Stannage (eds), *European-Aboriginal Relations in Western Australian History*, Studies in Western Australian History VIII, University of Western Australia Press, Perth, pp 1–6.

Fortescue, John (1899) *A History of the British Army*, II, Macmillan & Co, London.

Fraser, Robert (1988) 'The New South Wales Corps and their Occupation of Massachusetts during the Anglo-American War of 1812', *Sabretache*, 29(2): 4–9.

Frost, Alan (1980) *Convicts and Empire: A Naval Question, 1776–1811*, Oxford University Press, Melbourne.

—— (1981) 'New South Wales as *terra nullius:* the British denial of Aboriginal Land rights', [Australian] *Historical Studies*, 19: 513–23.

—— (1987) *Arthur Phillip, 1738–1814: His Voyaging*, Oxford University Press, Melbourne.

—— (1994) *Botany Bay Mirages: Illusions of Australia's Convict Beginnings*, Melbourne University Press, Melbourne.

Fry, Ken (1993) *Beyond the Barrier: Class Formation in a Pastoral Society Bathurst 1818–1848*, Crawford House Press, Bathurst.

Fulcher, Jonathan (1998) 'The *Wik* Judgement, Pastoral Leases and Colonial Office Policy and Intention in NSW in the 1840s', *Australian Journal of Legal History*, 4(1): 33–56.

Galbraith, John S (1963) *Reluctant Empire: British Policy on the South African Frontier 1834–1854*, University of California Press, Berkeley & Los Angeles.

Gates, John M (2001) 'James Belich and the Maori Pa: Revisionist History Revised', *War & Society*, 19(2): 47–68.

Glover, Richard (1963) *Peninsular Preparation: The Reform of the British Army 1795–1809*, Cambridge University Press, Cambridge.

Goodall, Heather (1996) *Invasion to Embassy: Land in Aboriginal Politics in New South Wales 1770–1972*, Allen & Unwin in association with Black Books, Sydney.

Grassby, Al & Marji Hill (1998) *Six Australian Battlefields: The Black Resistance to Invasion and the White Struggle against Colonial Oppression*, rev. edn [1988], Allen & Unwin, Sydney.

Gray, AJ (1959) 'Peter Burn: The First Convict Officially Presumed Killed by Natives at Sydney Cove', *Journal of the Royal Australian Historical Society*, 45(2): 96–104.

Green, Neville (1984) *Broken Spears: Aboriginals and Europeans in the southwest of Australia*, Focus Education Services, Perth.

Green, Neville (ed.) (1979) *Nyungar – The People: Aboriginal customs in the south-west of Australia*, Creative Research Publishers in association with Mt Lawley College of Advanced Education, Perth.

Grey, Jeffrey (1999) *A Military History of Australia*, rev. edn [1990], Cambridge University Press, Melbourne.

Griffin, Andrew (1990) 'London, Bengal, the China Trade and the Unfrequented Extremities of Asia: The East India Company's Settlement in New Guinea, 1793–95', *British Library Journal*, 16: 151–73.

Hall, Lesley D (1926) 'The Physiography and Geography of the Hawkesbury River between Windsor and Wiseman's Ferry', *The Proceedings of the Linnean Society of New South Wales*, 51(4): 545–54.

Harcourt, Rex (2001) *Southern Invasion, Northern Conquest: The Story of the Founding of Melbourne*, Golden Port Press, Melbourne.

Hardy, John & Alan Frost (eds) (1989) *Studies from Terra Australis to Australia*, Australian Academy of the Humanities, Canberra.

Hasluck, Alexandra (1965) *Thomas Peel of Swan River*, Oxford University Press, Melbourne.

Hattendorf, John B (1995) 'The Struggle With France, 1690–1815'. In JR Hill (ed.) *The Oxford Illustrated History of the Royal Navy*, Oxford University Press, Oxford, pp 80–119.

Hay, Douglas (1975) 'Property, Authority and the Criminal Law'. In Douglas Hay et al., *Albion's Fatal Tree: Crime and Society in Eighteenth-Century England*, Allen Lane, London, pp 17–63.

Hayter, Tony (1978) *The Army and the Crowd in Mid-Georgian England*, Macmillan, London.

Headrick, Daniel R (1981) *The Tools of Empire: Technology and European Imperialism in the Nineteenth Century*, Oxford University Press, New York.

Higgins, Matthew (1985) '"Deservedly respected": a first look at the 11th Regiment in Australia', *Journal of the Australian War Memorial*, 6: 3–12.

Horton, David (ed.) (1994) *The Encyclopaedia of Aboriginal Australia: Aboriginal & Torres Strait Islander history, society and culture*, 2 vols, Aboriginal Studies Press in association with the Australian Institute of Aboriginal and Torres Strait Islander Studies, Canberra.

Houlding, JA (1981) *Fit for Service: The Training of the British Army 1715–1795*, Clarendon Press, Oxford.

Howard, Michael, George J Andreopoulos, & Mark R Shulman (eds) (1994) *The Laws of War: Constraints on Warfare in the Western World*, Yale University Press, Hartford, Connecticut.

Hughes, BP (1974) *Firepower: Weapons effectiveness on the battlefield, 1630–1850*, Arms & Armour Press, London.

Inglis, KS (1974) *The Australian Colonists: An exploration of social history 1788–1870*, Melbourne University Press, Melbourne.

Joes, Anthony James (1996) *Guerilla Warfare: A Historical, Biographical, and Bibliographical Sourcebook*, Greenwood Press, Westport, Connecticut.

Johnston, Mark (2000) *Fighting the Enemy: Australian Soldiers and their Adversaries in World War II*, Cambridge University Press, Melbourne.

Keegan, John (1976) *The Face of Battle*, Jonathan Cape, London.

Keeley, Lawrence H (1996) *War Before Civilization*, Oxford University Press, New York.

Kennedy, Malcolm J (1992) *Hauling the Loads: A History of Australia's Working Horses and Bullocks*, Melbourne University Press, Melbourne.

King, Robert J (1990) *The Secret History of the Convict Colony: Alexandro Malaspina's report on the British settlement of New South Wales*, Allen & Unwin, Sydney.

Knight, Ian, & Ian Castle (1992) *Zulu War 1879*, Osprey Publishing, London.

Kohen, James (1993) *The Darug and their Neighbours: the traditional Aboriginal owners of the Sydney Region*, Daruglink in association with Blacktown & District Historical Society, Blacktown, New South Wales.

Liston, Carol (1988) 'The Dharawal and Gandangera in Colonial Campbelltown, New South Wales, 1788–1830', *Aboriginal History*, 12(1): 49–62.

MacCallum, Duncan (1961) 'The Early "Volunteer" Associations in New South Wales and the Proposals in the First Quarter of the Nineteenth Century', *Journal of the Royal Australian Historical Society*, 47(6): 352–67.

McGrath, Ann (ed.) (1995) *Contested Ground: Australian Aborigines under the British Crown*, Allen & Unwin, Sydney.

McKernan, M & M Browne (eds) (1988) *Australia: Two Centuries of War & Peace*, Australian War Memorial in association with Allen & Unwin, Canberra.

MacKnight, CC (1976) *The Voyage to Marege': Macassan trepangers in northern Australia*, Melbourne University Press, Melbourne.

McMahon, JF (1995–96) 'The British Army: Its Role in Counter-Insurgency in the Black War in Van Diemen's Land', *Tasmanian Historical Studies*, 5(1): 56–63.

Magee, Reginald (1995) 'Muskets, Musket Balls and the Wounds They Made', *Australian and New Zealand Journal of Surgery*, 65(12): 890–95.

Marshall, PJ (ed.) (1998) *The Oxford History of the British Empire*, II, Oxford University Press, Oxford.

Martin, Ged (1999) 'Canada from 1815'. In Andrew Porter (ed.), *The Oxford History of the British Empire*, Vol III, Oxford University Press, Oxford, pp 522–45.

Martin, Ged (ed.) (1978) *The Founding of Australia: The argument about Australia's origins*, Hale & Iremonger, Sydney.

Martin, Megan (1992) *Settlers & Convicts of the* Bellona *1793: A Biographical Dictionary, Bellona* Muster Committee, Sydney.

Martin, Michael (1988) *On Darug Land: An Aboriginal Perspective*, Greater Western Education Centre, St Marys, New South Wales.

Milliss, Roger (1992) *Waterloo Creek: The Australia Day Massacre of 1838, George Gipps and the British Conquest of New South Wales*, McPhee Gribble, Ringwood, Victoria.

Molony, John N (1973) *An Architect of Freedom: John Hubert Plunkett in New South Wales 1832–1869*, Australian National University Press, Canberra.

Moneypenny, Maria (1995–96) '"Going out and Coming in": Cooperation and Collaboration between Aborigines and Europeans in Early Tasmania', *Tasmanian Historical Studies*, 5(1): 64–75.

Moore, John (1987) *The First Fleet Marines 1786–1792*, University of Queensland Press, Brisbane.

Morgan, Sharon (1992) *Land Settlement in Early Tasmania: Creating an Antipodean England*, Cambridge University Press, Cambridge.

Mulvaney, DJ & J Peter White (eds) (1987) *Australians to 1788*, Fairfax, Syme & Weldon Associates, Sydney.

Nagle, JF (1996) *Collins, the Courts & the Colony: Law and Society in Colonial New South Wales 1788–1796*, UNSW Press, Sydney.

Nance, Beverley (1981) 'The Level of Violence: Europeans and Aborigines in Port Phillip, 1835–1850', [Australian] *Historical Studies*, 19: 532–49.

O'Rourke, MJ (1995) *Raw Possum and Salted Pork: Major Mitchell and the Kamilaroi Aborigines*, Plowpress, Canberra.

Pagden, Anthony (1995) *Lords of all the World: Ideologies of Empire in Spain, Britain and France c1500–c1800*, Yale University Press, New Haven, Connecticut.

Palmer, Alison (2000) *Colonial Genocide*, Crawford Publishing House, Adelaide.

Parkman, Francis (1912) *Montcalm and Wolfe*, 2 vols [1884], Macmillan & Co, London.

Pearson, Michael (1984) 'Bathurst Plains and Beyond: European Colonisation and Aboriginal Resistance', *Aboriginal History*, 8(1): 63–79.

Peers, Douglas M (ed.) (1997) *Warfare and Empires*, Ashgate Publishing, Aldershot and Brookfield, Vermont.

Perry, TM (1963) *Australia's First Frontier: The Spread of Settlement in New South Wales 1788–1829*, Melbourne University Press in association with the Australian National University, Melbourne.

Petrie, Constance Campbell (ed.) (1980) *Tom Petrie's Reminiscences of Early Queensland* [1904], Currey O'Neil, Melbourne.

Pike, Douglas (gen. ed.) (1966–67) *Australian Dictionary of Biography 1788–1850*, 2 vols, Melbourne University Press, Melbourne.

Plomley, NJB (1983) *The Baudin Expedition and the Tasmanian Aborigines*, Blubber Head Press, Hobart.

—— (1992) *The Aboriginal/Settler Clash in Van Diemen's Land 1803–1831*, Occasional Paper No 6, Queen Victoria Museum and Art Gallery in association with the Centre for Tasmanian Historical Studies, Launceston.

Porch, Donald (1997) 'Imperial Wars from the Seven Years War to the First World War'. In Charles Townshend (ed.), *The Oxford Illustrated History of Modern War*, Oxford University Press, Oxford, pp 81–99.

Pugsley, Christopher (1998) 'Maori Did Not Invent Trench Warfare', *New Zealand Defence Quarterly*, Spring: 33–37.

Ranken, WB (1916) *The Rankens of Bathurst*, Townsend, Sydney.

Raudzens, George (1999) 'Military Revolution or Maritime Evolution? Military Superiorities or Transportation Advantages as Main Causes of European Colonial Conquests to 1788', *The Journal of Military History*, 63: 631–42.

Reece, RHW (1974) *Aborigines and Colonists: Aborigines and Colonial Society in New South Wales in the 1830s and 1840s*, Sydney University Press, Sydney.

—— (1979) 'The Aborigines in Australian Historiography'. In John A Moses (ed.), *Historical Disciplines and Culture in Australasia: An Assessment*, University of Queensland Press, Brisbane, pp 253–81.

—— (1984) '"Laws of the White People": The Frontier of Authority in Perth in 1838', *The Push from the Bush*, 17: 2–28.

Reynolds, Henry (1982) *The Other Side of the Frontier* [1981], Penguin, Ringwood, Victoria.

—— (1987) *The Law of the Land*, Penguin, Ringwood, Victoria.

—— (1995) *Fate of a Free People*, Penguin, Ringwood, Victoria.

—— (1999) *Why Weren't We Told? A Personal Search for the Truth about Our History*, Penguin, Ringwood, Victoria.

—— (2001a) *An Indelible Stain? The Question of Genocide in Australia's History*, Penguin, Ringwood, Victoria.

—— (2001b) 'From Armband to Blindfold', *Australian Review of Books*, April: 8–9, 26.

Richardson, Robert G (1974) *Larrey: Surgeon to Napoleon's Imperial Guard*, John Murray, London.

Ridley, William (1875) *Kamilaroi and other Australian Languages*, 2nd edn, New South Wales Government Printer, Sydney.

Roberts, David (1995) 'Bells Falls Massacre and Bathurst's History of Violence: Local Tradition and Australian Historiography', *Australian Historical Studies*, 105: 615–33.

Robson, Lloyd (1983) *A History of Tasmania. Volume I: Van Diemen's Land from the Earliest Times to 1855*, Oxford University Press, Melbourne.

Rodger, NAM (1986) *The Wooden World: An Anatomy of the Georgian Navy*, Collins, London.

Russell, Peter E (1978) 'Redcoats in the Wilderness: British Officers and Irregular Warfare in Europe and America, 1740 to 1760', *William and Mary Quarterly*, 3rd Series, 35(4): 629–52.

Ryan, Lyndall (1996) *The Aboriginal Tasmanians*, 2nd edn [1981], Allen & Unwin, Sydney.

—— (2001) 'The Aboriginal History Wars', *Australian Historical Association Bulletin*, 92: 31–37.

Salisbury, T & PT Gresser (1971) *Windradyne of the Wiradjeri: Martial Law in Bathurst 1824*, Wentworth Books, Sydney.

Sargent, Clem (1996) *The Colonial Garrison 1817–1824: The 48th Foot the Northamptonshire Regiment in the Colony of New South Wales*, TCS Publications, Canberra.

Shaw, AGL (1980) *Sir George Arthur, Bart., 1784–1854. Superintendent of British Honduras, Lieutenant-Governor of Van Diemen's Land and of Upper Canada, Governor of the Bombay Presidency*, Melbourne University Press, Melbourne.

Smithers, AJ (1973) *The Kaffir Wars 1779–1877*, Leo Cooper, London.

Stanley, Peter (1986) *The Remote Garrison: The British Army in Australia 1788–1870*, Kangaroo Press, Sydney.

Stanner, WEH (1968) *After the Dreaming: Black and White Australians – An Anthropologist's View*, The 1968 Boyer Lectures, ABC, Sydney.

Starkey, Armstrong (1998) *European and Native American Warfare 1675–1815*, University of Oklahoma Press, Norman, Oklahoma.

Statham, Pamela (1988) *Ins and Outs: The Composition and Disposal of the NSW Corps, 1790–1810*, Working Papers in Economic History No 105, Australian National University, Canberra.

Statham, Pamela (ed.) (1992) *A Colonial Regiment: New Sources Relating to the New South Wales Corps 1789–1810*, ANU Central Printery, Canberra.

Strachan, Hew (1984) *Wellington's Legacy: The Reform of the British Army 1830–54*, Manchester University Press, Manchester.

—— (1985) *From Waterloo to Balaclava: Tactics, Technology, and the British Army 1815–1854*, Cambridge University Press, Cambridge.

Suttor, WH (1887) *Australian Stories Retold and Sketches of Country Life*, Glyndwr Whalan, Bathurst.

Sweetman, John (1987) 'The Military Establishment at King George Sound (Frederickstown) 1826–1831', *Sabretache*, 28(3): 22–24.

Tatz, Colin (1999) *Genocide in Australia*, AIATSIS Research Discussion Papers No 8, Australian Institute of Aboriginal and Torres Strait Islander Studies, Canberra.

Thorpe, Bill (1995) 'Frontiers of Discourse: Assessing Revisionist Australian Colonial Contact Historiography', *Journal of Australian Studies*, 46: 34–45.

—— (1996) *Colonial Queensland: Perspectives on a Frontier Society*, University of Queensland Press, Brisbane.

Townsend, Joan B (1983) 'Firearms against Native Arms: A Study in Comparative Efficiencies with an Alaskan Example', *Arctic Anthropology*, 20(2): 1–33.

Troy, Jakelin (1994) 'The Sydney Language'. In Nick Thieberger & William McGregor (eds), *Macquarie Aboriginal Words: a dictionary of words from Australian Aboriginal and Torres Strait Islander languages*, The Macquarie Library, Sydney, pp 61–78.

Turbet, Peter (2001) *The Aborigines of the Sydney District before 1788*, rev. edn [1989], Kangaroo Press, Sydney.

Van Dijk, C (1981) *Rebellion Under the Banner of Islam: The Darul Islam in Indonesia*, Martinus Nijhoff, The Hague.

Walsh, GP (1962) 'The English Colony in New South Wales: A.D. 1803', *New Zealand Geographer*, XVIII(2): 149–69.

Ward, Matthew C (1997) '"The European Method of Warring Is Not Practiced Here": The Failure of British Military Policy in the Ohio Valley, 1755–1759', *War in History*, 4(3): 247–63.

West, John (ed. AGL Shaw) (1971) *The History of Tasmania* [1852], Angus & Robertson in association with the Royal Australian Historical Society, Sydney.

Wilcox, Craig (1998) 'The Culture of Restrained Force in British Australia'. In Carl Bridge (ed.), *Ranging Shots: New Directions in Australian Military History*, Sir Robert Menzies Centre for Australian Studies, University of London, London, pp 7–18.

Willey, Keith (1979) *When the Sky Fell Down: The Destruction of the Tribes of the Sydney Region 1788–1850s*, Collins, Sydney.

Windschuttle, Keith (2000) 'The Myths of Frontier Massacres in Australian History', 3 pts, *Quadrant*, October: 8–21, November: 17–25, December: 6–20.

—— (2001) 'How Not to Run a Museum', *Quadrant*, September: 11–19.

Wood, W Allan (1972) *Dawn in the Valley: The Story of Settlement in the Hunter River Valley to 1833*, Wentworth Books, Sydney.

Wright, Nancy E (2001) 'The problem of Aboriginal evidence in early colonial New South Wales'. In Diane Kirkby & Catharine Coleborne (eds), *Law, history, colonialism: The reach of Empire*, Manchester University Press, Manchester, pp 140–56.

Wyatt, DM (1990) *A Lion in the Colony: An Historical Outline of the Tasmanian Colonial Volunteer Military Forces, 1859–1901*, 6th Military District Museum, Hobart.

Theses and unpublished material

Connor, John (1999) Armed Conflict between Aborigines and British Armed Forces in Southeast Australia, 1788–1831, Master of Arts thesis, University of New South Wales at the Australian Defence Force Academy, Canberra.

McMahon, John F (1995) The British army and the counter-insurgency campaign in Van Diemen's Land with particular reference to the Black Line, Master of Humanities thesis, University of Tasmania, Hobart.

Philips, David (1999) Evangelicals, Aborigines and 'Land Rights': a critique of Henry Reynolds' understanding and use of the *Select Committee on Aborigines (British Possessions)* 1835–7, paper presented to the 11th Australasian Modern British History Association Conference, Canberra.

Stanley, Peter (1981) 'While acting under orders': The Slaughterhouse Creek massacre of 1838, paper presented to the Bicentennial Military History Seminar, Australian War Memorial, Canberra.

INDEX